thenewitaly

a complete guide to contemporary Italian wine

The New Italy

by Marco Sabellico and Daniele Cernilli

Published in North America, 2001 by The Wine Appreciation Guild, 360 Swift Avenue, South San Francisco 94080; 800 231-9463; wineappreciation.com

ISBN 1-891267-32-9

A CIP catalogue record for this book is available from the British Library.

Commissioning Editor: Rebecca Spry
Design: Colin Goody
Managing Editor: Lucy Bridgers
Editor: Adrian Tempany
Cartography: Hardlines, Colin Goody
Picture Research: Sandra Assersohn, Carla Bertini, Kali Dhillon,
                    Clare Gouldstone, Helen Stallion
Production: Jessame Emms
Index: Hilary Bird

Typeset in Helvetica Neue and Versailles
Printed and bound by Toppan Printing Company in China

Daniele Cernilli & Marco Sabellico

thenewitaly

a complete guide to contemporary Italian wine

The Wine Appreciation Guild, San Francisco

Contents

Preface

The description "fascinating chaos" may be an unusual way to describe the world of wine in Italy, but it is nonetheless an appropriate one. There are over 300 DOCs (*Denominazioni di Origine Controllata*) and DOCGs (*Denominazioni di Origine Controllata e Garantita*), and the number of classifications exceeds 500 when the IGT (*Indicazioni Geografica Tipica*) are added. Some 50,000 wineries are producing an enormous number of different wines, a complicated situation that confuses even the most competent consumers and risks discouraging wine lovers who might otherwise be attracted to Italian wine.

It is extremely difficult to fully get to grips with Italian wines and their production zones. A knowledge of geography, the history of popular traditions, botany, organic chemistry and biology would all be required. One would have to be an expert taster; in other words, to have experience as well as knowledge.

We do not expect to solve all these problems in this book, but we hope to provide the basis for further discoveries. Whilst avoiding complicated wine terms, we have sought to present detailed information in the form of a journey through places and names, enabling the reader to discover an Italy which in many respects is still a country divided into separate communities. Often the types of grapes cultivated and the wines produced still reflect ancient boundaries, and preserve traditions which would otherwise have fallen into oblivion.

But this book is not only about wine. Behind each wine there is the story of communities large and small, the story of an Italy only recently united, and the story of an historical and venerable culture. Many people still feel a sense of belonging to a particular locality, to a particular region, and the winemaking reflects this.

Most importantly, Italy is a country where the grape

left *Inspirational landscapes, unique winemaking talent and several millennia of history turn a tour of Italy into a wine odyssey.*

harvest involves almost one million people and where, between September and October, many provincial roads are almost impossible to use because of the incessant coming and going of tractors, their trailers overflowing with grapes. Probably more than anywhere else in the world, the harvest demonstrates how much winegrowing is part of the country's oldest traditions.

With greater knowledge comes greater under-standing, and the progress that has been made in recent years by thousands of wineries in most of the important viticultural areas across the Italian peninsula is little short of breathtaking. Many of the advances have been in the methods used to cultivate vines, and in the techniques of vinification and maturation of the wines themselves. This movement towards greater innovation has largely been encouraged by the development of Italy's international and domestic markets.

So what of the future? The trend is clearly towards increased improvements in mid-range wines selling at reasonable prices, and world-class quality among the top-of-the-range offerings in the higher price brackets. This is very much the French recipe for success: image plus exclusivity. Today, a leading producer such as Angelo Gaja in Piedmont has shown that there is an international market for great Italian wines at high prices that didn't truly exist in the past.

The quality revolution has also been built on the renovation of many vineyards, and the ambition even among many of the large, bulk-producing wineries to occupy the higher-quality, more interesting sectors of the market. These are all sound reasons for optimism. At this rate, Italy might soon find itself listed among the senior members of the *Who's Who* of international viticulture. It wouldn't be a day too soon for this ancient wine culture.

The Story of Italian Wine

taly may not have been the first European country to make wine, but its vineyards have been a cause for celebration since the pre-historic era. Fossil records show that some wild strains of *Vitis vinifera* were native to the peninsula, and the tribes which first inhabited Italy were known to be aspiring winegrowers and makers. This tribal culture was recorded by the Phoenicians; the ancient traders who dominated the Mediterranean for centuries, and who found crude winemaking practices in place when they arrived in Puglia, in the south, around 2000BC.

Early Italian winemaking was influenced by the Greeks, who settled in the south and in Sicily. Their vine-growing techniques were adapted by indigenous peoples as far north as Piedmont and Valtellina, in the Alps, while in the centre of the country the Etruscans developed their own trade, which stretched as far as Gaul. Given the success of these early winemakers, and the country's benevolent climate and soil, it is hardly surprising that the Italian peninsula quickly became known as Oenotria – the "Land of Wine".

The Romans took the best of both Greek and Etruscan methods and improved them, developing vine-training and pruning methods that remained until the 17th and 18th centuries. Soon, Roman vineyards were producing as much as 1,500 kilos of grapes per hectare, a figure that compares favourably with the production of today's intensively cultivated vineyards. A collapse in the Greek winemaking industry enhanced ancient Italy's standing, and during the Republic and Empire periods (509BC to 27BC and 27BC to AD395 respectively) vine-growing became increasingly popular in Roman lands. According to poets and historians, such as Horace and Pliny, the most prestigious wines were Falernum and Massican (from Northern Campania), the Caecuban of Southern Latium, Sicily's Mamertine, the Venetian Raethic and wines from Albalonga, south of Rome.

The Romans exported their winemaking practices to the new territories, including Provence, the Narbonnais, and the area round Vienne – the modern Côtes du Rhône – and established enormous vineyards around Tarragona and Valencia, exporting vast quantities of wine. From the 2nd century AD, vines were grown to the north of the Cevennes – now the Côte d'Or, the home of great burgundy – in the neighbourhood of Lutetia (imperial Paris), along the Rhine and Moselle rivers, and even in England.

Transporting and ageing wine

One of the casualties of this Roman winemaking was the amphora, the favoured wine vessel. Invented by the Canaanites before 1500BC, these two-handled terracotta vessels, closed with plugs of cork oak or wood and sealed with pitch, had capacities ranging from 26-40 litres, and delivered wine to every corner of the Empire.

With its tapered shape the amphora could be secured in the ground or in a layer of sand in a ship's hold. Its hermetic seal enabled wine to age and mature in an environment effectively free of oxygen – much like modern wine bottles – and explains the enthusiastic contemporary accounts of tasting wines more than 40 years old; or in the great vintages, such as the Opimian vintage of 121BC (during the time of consul Opimius), over 100 years old. However, the amphorae proved to be brittle and were gradually replaced by wooden vessels made by the Celts, renowned carpenters.

The style of wine was also vulnerable to fashion. Originally, most Roman wine resembled a thick, alcoholic syrup: strong and sweet, it was usually diluted with water. This tradition eventually disappeared during the Middle Ages, but even in Roman times some people already drank merum: pure, undiluted wine – but then they were often

right *Wine has always been integral to the Italian lifestyle and it is no coincidence that Italy was dubbed Oenotria (the "Land of Wine"). This painting by Giorgio Morandi, from 1938, reveals the enduring strength of the image of wine.*

accused of being alcoholics. Towards the end of the Empire, in the fifth century, wine began to more closely resemble its modern incarnation: it became "thinner", less sweet and usually contained a lower alcoholic strength.

The Decline of Oenotria

With the fall of the Roman Empire, Italy and Italian winemaking entered its own Dark Ages. Viniculture survived, but largely in the monasteries, and quality wine was consigned to memory. Production plummeted and as wines did not travel well they were used only for local, religious or medicinal consumption. With the amphorae obsolete and bottles yet to evolve, barrels took over. But they did not foster ageing of even the best vintages for long, so wine was usually drunk within its first five years.

Italy at this stage consisted of numerous independent states. Little information exists about Italian wines of the Middle Ages, as there was no national industry – only during the Risorgimento were records reintroduced. Still, we know that for centuries the Republic of Venice ruled over the Mediterranean, monopolising the export of sweet wines from Sicily, Cyprus, Crete and Greece to the markets of northern Europe. And in Italy itself, certain legendary Tuscan red wines were made, including Montepulciano (later known as Vino Nobile), the white Vernaccia from San Gimignano, and the sweet white of Orvieto.

The early 18th century was to prove decisive in the history of modern European wine. Until 1709, vineyards existed as far north as Wales and Scotland, but the severe frost of that year completely destroyed every vineyard in those regions, and seriously affected vines in a large part of France, Germany and northern Italy. Only the southernmost areas were spared, and in the following year the price of wine increased fivefold. This dramatic sequence of events encouraged Italian growers to plant new vineyards with the most resistant and productive grape varieties – hence the proliferation of Pagadebit (Bombino Bianco), the Trebbiano varieties and Verduzzo. In just a few years, winemaking had been transformed.

In 1716, spurred on by these developments Cosimo III, grand duke of Tuscany, drew up the first wine laws. These pertained only to Chianti and its neighbouring regions, as Chianti was so prized that it needed protection. But it was difficult to develop high-quality wines throughout Italy, due largely to the country's political instability. Wine was produced and consumed by rural people, and was not the aristocrat's pleasure – as it so often was in France. In contrast to French wines, which were expensive yet highly favoured at almost every European court, Italian wines tended to be consumed where they were produced.

The 19th and 20th centuries

French wines dominated Europe throughout the 19th and much of the 20th centuries. But since the early 1960s, with the introduction of the *Denominazione di Origine Controllata* (DOC) quality regime, Italian wines have greatly improved and now enjoy international recognition.

One of the most prestigious is Brunello di Montalcino. Brunello was first produced in 1888 by Biondi Santi, but it wasn't until 1964 and from its next "stable" – the Fattoria Barbi Colombini – that Brunello received a commercial profile worthy of the name. Another great Italian red, Barolo, developed mainly during the second half of the 19th century. Chianti, Vino Nobile di Montepulciano and Vernaccia from San Gimignano have an older lineage, but they were not widely exported until a few years ago.

The low foreign profile is an even more acute concern for spumante, or sparkling wine. Although Carlo Gancia, Giuseppe Contratto and Antonio Carpenè attempted to produce quality spumante at the end of the 19th century, today only Asti enjoys great international success: most Italian sparkling wine is confined to the domestic market.

below *By Roman times, viticulture and winemaking were already well established in Italy, having originally been "imported" from Greece and the Middle East. This vase from the house of Fabius Rufus in Pompeii depicts Dionysos, the god of wine, with Ariadne on the Greek island of Naxos.*

Nonetheless, Italian winemakers are now aware of the great potential of their wines. But they also realise that whereas French consumers are familiar with their nation's key wine regions and premier wines and winemakers, in Italy few can locate Montalcino on a map, or know where to find Collio Goriziano, or even the best districts in Chianti. Indeed, in many restaurants wine is still listed as either "red" or "white", an oversimplified approach reflected abroad, where Italian wine is often placed on a par with Spanish wines – yet to attract the sustained acclaim bestowed upon French, German, American and even Portuguese wines.

One reason for the popularity of French varieties in Italy is phylloxera, which attacks the roots of vines to suck the sap. It invaded Italy from America at the end of the 19th century with devastating effects. In the Veneto, Friuli and Trentino regions (parts of which were still within the Austro-Hungarian Empire), the only way to replace damaged vines was to import French vines that had already been grafted onto American rootstocks, which are resistant to phylloxera. Thus, today, you will find "classic French" varieties such as Cabernet, Chardonnay and Pinot growing next to Tocai, Refosco, Marzemino, Nosiola, Ribolla, Verduzzo and Malvasia Istriana – the varieties traditional to these regions.

Revival of classical winemaking

Wines that could be considered direct descendants of the ancient Greco-Roman tradition are still traceable in Italy, but they are rare. Whereas in Greece the tradition of resinated wine has survived in the form of the popular Retsina, in Italy direct heirs are found mainly among the raisin wines of the south: the likes of Greco di Bianco, a sweet wine also known as Greco di Gerace, produced in Reggio Calabria. However, an increasing number of vineyards are now planted with ancient grape varieties. This has fuelled the revival of white wines such as Fiano di Avellino and Timorasso in Allessandrino, and reds such as Ruchè or Pelaverga in Piedmont, and Tazzelenghe and Schioppettino in Friuli, wines that might otherwise have been threatened by extinction.

In Italy in recent decades, as part of a programme of fast, almost frantic improvement in quality, attempts to produce fine wines in classical regions such as Falernum and Caecubo have produced some excellent results. If authoritative wine writers can now herald a "renaissance"

in Italian wines, it is due to the – often intrepid – efforts of winemakers who have sought to improve quality, and the skill of oenologists brave enough to adopt new techniques of vinification and ageing. Such is their impact that the success of an Italian wine in an international tasting, or the mention of a world-class Italian wine no longer makes headline news. Regions such as Chianti Classico, Langhe and Collio have given us wines that can stand alongside the world's finest.

No other country enjoys such a variety of soil and microclimates, or such abundant "native" vineyards as the Italian peninsula. In a world where wine is following the global trend for standardised tastes, and "international varieties" such as Chardonnay and Cabernet Sauvignon prevail, Italy can point to a unique and idiosyncratic line-up of producers, modern and traditional, and a fascinating range of ancient and contemporary wines.

above *During the Renaissance, wine was frequently celebrated in art. One of the most famous images is Caravaggio's painting of the young Bacchus (c.1593-4), which hangs in the Uffizi Gallery in Florence.*

Winemaking in Italy

Italian wine production may have fallen below the threshold of 50 million hectolitres in 1997, but this figure was offset by a net increase in the average price of the wines and an increase in their overall quality – the result of notable progress in vinification and maturation techniques. This has ensured more reliable wines and led to the substitution of chemical stabilising agents with filtration, low-temperature fermentation and specially selected yeasts.

There is still considerable room for improvement: there is a widespread need for research into clonal selection, the choice of rootstocks and methods of cultivation, while different regions need to be "zoned" by analysing their soil compositions and climatic exposures.

Italian producers have now to compete with countries vying for European, American and Asian consumers increasingly on the lookout for quality wines. It might be a quick fix to join the great flood of "international" wines – Cabernet Sauvignon, Merlot and Chardonnay – but to some producers this would mean sacrificing the ancient, varied traditions of Italian viticulture. It would mean standardisation, albeit of good-quality wines, and the forfeit of a quintessentially Italian style, which remains the nation's trump card at international level.

below *Harvest-time just outside Barolo. The pickers carefully cut each bunch from the vine and place them into plastic boxes.*

Yet Italy must demonstrate a capacity to produce its best wines consistently and reliably, and an enormous effort is required on the part of the public agencies responsible for Italian agricultural policy. Decisive measures are now taking place within the main vine-growing and wine-producing areas.

Northwestern Italy

In Piedmont, the search is underway for a more modern vinification style for premium wines. Increasingly, Barolo and Barbaresco producers are trying to create wines that demand less ageing and are easier to drink. This has upset traditionalists, but the worldwide success achieved by the best of these innovative winemakers partly vindicates their eschewal of the old methods – at least for the immediate future. Shorter maceration times and the widespread use of barrels have appeased consumers in many countries, and this spirit of innovation has spread to regions such as Asti, albeit with varied results.

Substantial developments are also taking place in the most progressive regions of Lombardy, such as Franciacorta. Yet the modernist movement is not gaining ground everywhere: regions such as Oltrepò and Valtellina remain closely connected to local tradition and rely very much on local markets.

Northeastern Italy

That productive giant, the Veneto, is also in the midst of a substantial overhaul, with the Valpolicella absorbing the greatest changes: numerous winemakers have made dramatic leaps of quality in recent years – a case in point is Amarone, which enjoys international adulation.

The Alto Adige has witnessed extraordinary technical and qualitative advances on a similarly large scale, assisted by the best vine-growing and wine-producing cooperatives in Italy. In neighbouring Trentino, a high-profile sparkling sector is being developed alongside normal still-wine production; an initiative fostered by the major cooperatives, which control 90 per cent of the region's production. Meanwhile, the region of Friuli-Venezia Giulia has stood firm for white wine during the last few years, against the global trend for reds.

In recent years, consumers have discovered that the wines of Emilia-Romagna go far beyond Lambrusco. Today this region is home to a fascinating range of wines,

from the Colli Piacentini to the Colli Bolognesi and the Romagnola sub-region.

Despite this new international "edge", some producers continue to make limited quantities of traditional wine, selling virtually their entire production within their "home" regions, most notably in the Valle d'Aosta and Liguria.

Western and Central Italy

Tuscany remains the barometer of Italy's oenological renaissance. Modern methods, an array of distinguished producers and some of the most capable and famous oenologists in Italy have netted results which would have been unthinkable even two decades ago. Chianti Classico, Vino Nobile di Montepulciano, Brunello di Montalcino

above *Once the grapes have been harvested they are taken to the winery. These Sangiovese, at Castello di Volpaia in Tuscany, will be sorted to root out leaves, twigs and inferior grapes.*

above *Once the fermentation has taken place (most often in stainless steel tanks) the winemaker has the option of ageing the wine in barrels. The larger barrels are called* botti.

Quality is rising slowly too in Latium: this region may have lost more than any other by discarding ancient, distinguished traditions and typicity in favour of more standardised wines. However, with new developments taking shape at Montefiascone, Frascati and Marino, the region's best oenologists are developing an attractive selection of wines.

Abruzzo, where the quality-to-price ratio of wines is remarkable, seems to have the best prospects of all the central regions. Montepulciano and Trebbiano are firmly among the region's most interesting wines, and the area's production structure – dominated by the great cooperatives – is already first-class.

South of here, Molise, Basilicata and Calabria, on the other hand, present mountainous terrain that demands contrasting approaches at the viti- and vinicultural levels. Aglianico del Vulture and Cirò are interesting wines, but they are still the preserve of a select few.

Towards the South

The situation is altogether different in Campania, where indigenous grape varieties such as Aglianico, Greco, Fiano and Falanghina, together with a division of high-profile wineries, have revamped the image of the region's wines. Here, the future looks decidedly bright, and production and commercial decisions currently being made should drive this region to the heights of Italian winemaking in the near future.

Puglia and Sicily may represent the new frontier, the "California" of Italy. Production here is immense, and the basic quality level is better than most: consequently, high-quality wines offer incredible value, but are still largely unknown. Admittedly, only around 20 state-of-the-art establishments yield exceptional styles amid an ocean of blending wines, but even this bulk wine should soon equal that of its overseas competitors. The indigenous grapes here are Negroamaro, Primitivo, Nero d'Avola and Inzolia, while the up-and-coming areas are Salento, Gravina, and Pachino. All that is required now is a little investment and long-term confidence.

Finally, Sardinia's potential has already been glimpsed in regions such as Sulcis, Gallura and Alghero; from grapes such as Cannonau, Carignano, Vermentino, Torbato, Vernaccia di Oristano and Nasco. Vermentino di Gallura was awarded a DOCG in 1997, and conveys the tough but generous character of Sardinia's people.

and all the "Super-Tuscans" (some from regions such as Bolgheri, which have achieved the DOC) have marked the revival of the region and its keynote vine – Sangiovese. Today, Tuscany belongs among wine's international elite, and Sangiovese is deservedly up there alongside.

On a similar note, the impressive relaunch of Verdicchio has galvanised quality production in the Marches. Whether at Matelica or in the much larger region of Castelli di Jesi, Verdicchio – one of Italy's best indigenous white grape varieties – is enjoying a revival.

In Umbria, too, great progress is being made in viticulture and winemaking, particularly in the areas served by the two DOCG wines, Torgiano Rosso Riserva and Sagrantino di Montefalco. The fate of white wines is admittedly less dramatic, with the classic Orvieto grape and the emerging area of Colli Amerini firmly ensconced in the driving seat.

left *Here, Gianfranco Repellino of Giordano is checking the progress of his Chardonnay in temperature-controlled stainless steel tanks.*

Classifications: Laws and Labels

There have been laws governing Italian wine for almost as long as there have been Italian winemakers, but many of these were ignored well into the 20th century. The present classification system of *denominazione di origine controllata* (DOC) and *denominazione di origine controllata e garantita* (DOCG) was introduced in Italy in 1963, as Law 930 of the Italian parliament. Modelled loosely on the *appellation contrôlée* laws of France, these regulations provided the modern framework for quality control in Italian wine.

Vernaccia di San Gimignano, a famous Tuscan white, was the first wine (and region) to be regulated and was followed over the next few years by a huge swathe of DOCs, embracing wines from every point on the country's oenological spectrum – from Chianti to Barolo, from Amarone to Brunello di Montalcino.

About 30 years later it became apparent that new regulations were required, and in 1992 Law 164 updated and completed the previous system of appellation. In Italy today there is a four-tier hierarchy, including some 300 DOCs and DOCGs, with each tier promoting several different types of wine and 18,000 varieties in total.

Vini da tavola

This table wine is the basic level, and a generic term. Besides carrying the name and trademark of the bottling establishment, the label on these wines usually only identifies the colour (bianco, rosso, rosato – white, red, rosé). The wines are fairly simple in style, and may consist of a fruity, harmonious blend of grapes from various geographical zones, of assorted varieties and even from various vintages. That, at least, is the theory.

IGT

Indicazione Geografica Tipica The second-level designation, roughly equivalent to the French *vin de pays*. IGT wines may list the geographical region from which they hail (eg Tuscany), the main grape variety (eg Sangiovese) and the year of the vintage.

DOC

Denominazione di Origine Controllata The third level, incorporating wines of greater quality, made in a clearly defined region under regulations known as *disciplinari*. These define the permissible styles of wine – such as *vendemmia tardiva* or *rosso riserva* – the quantity of grapes grown and varieties used, the yields and the type and length of subsequent ageing. The entire production cycle is controlled by the relevant state organisations and before going on the market these wines are analysed by tasting commissions set up by each chamber of commerce, which checks that production requirements are observed.

The DOC designation always appears on the label. Unlike IGT wines, DOC and DOCG wines may also indicate a sub-region – Valtellina Superiore Sassella, for instance – as well as the serial number of the bottle. There is also a range of specific descriptions: the most important are *riserva*, for high-quality wines sufficiently aged; and *superiore* or *auslese*, for wines with a higher alcoholic content and greater sophistication than the ordinary wines of the same DOC. For example, Frascati wines must have a minimum alcohol content of 11 per cent alcohol by volume (abv), but when classed as Frascati Superiore it must be 11.5 per cent abv. The term *classico* is applied to wines produced in the smaller, more traditional or "classic" area within a region. These tend to be more expensive, as in the case of Valpolicella and Valpolicella Classico.

DOCG

Denominazione di Origine Controllata e Garantita This designation sits at the apex of the pyramid. There are currently about 20 DOCGs, ranging from Piedmont's Asti to the Vermentino di Gallura of Sardinia. According to the

below *This label explains that the wine is DOC Verdicchio dei Castelli di Jesi (from the Marches region). It is also "classico superiore", which indicates that it comes from the smaller, "classic" part of Castelli di Jesi and has a higher alcohol content than the regular DOC Castelli di Jesi wines (in this case 13% volume).*

1998

Casal di Serra

VERDICCHIO
DEI CASTELLI DI JESI
DENOMINAZIONE DI ORIGINE CONTROLLATA
CLASSICO SUPERIORE

IMBOTTIGLIATO DA UMANI RONCHI SPA - OSIMO - ITALIA

750 ml e   Umani Ronchi   ITALIA 13% vol

law, the largest-sized bottle that may be sold is five litres and each must be supplied with the emblem of its respective region, in the form of a band issued by the government. The DOCG designation is reserved especially for prestigious wines that have served an "apprenticeship" of at least five years as DOC wines. They must pass two stages of analysis to progress to this higher bracket: initially at the time they are made (like DOC wines), and then before they are bottled.

According to EU regulations, the first two categories – *vini da tavola* and IGT – fall under the broader category of *vini da tavola*. But the third and fourth levels – DOC and DOCG – are combined by European law into a single group, known as *vini di qualità prodotti in una regione determinata*, or VQPRD. These standards are very similar to those of France and Germany. The first category, for example, includes the French *vins de table* and *vins de pays* and the German *Tafelwein* and *Landwein*, while the second group incorporates the French ACs and the German *Qualitätswein*.

From "cru" to "vigna"

In the last few years, Italian winemakers have responded to the need for a more accurate definition of wines from vineyards of distinction. Many wines may boast superior geological characteristics or have traditionally enjoyed higher quality status – or a different character – from those of surrounding vineyards. This distinction has led to the use of the term "vigna" on some bottles, which is similar in meaning to the French "cru". Its usage is controlled by law and is relevant only to DOC and DOCG wines. These must always be accompanied strictly by the vineyard – and not a geographical – name. The law provides very precise controls for wines employing the vineyard name: the boundaries of the plot are accurately marked on maps and any grapes grown in this area must be vinified separately.

The label

Such a complicated system of classification and naming naturally reaches its artistic peak on the wine label. This is vital, because of its inevitable powers of persuasion over the consumer and because it communicates a range of important facts about the wine. Obviously it must present clear, complete and verifiable information and, conscious of the need for a certain uniformity, the EU stipulates exacting labelling standards throughout Europe.

Every label carries the name of the wine (eg Barolo, Chianti, Frascati, Soave), the category (*vini da tavola*, DOC etc), followed by the name of the producer and the business name and address of the bottler. The alcohol content is expressed in abv terms (eg 12 per cent abv). In the case of semi-sweet and sweet wines, which contain residual sugar, the stated alcohol content is supplemented by a 'plus' sign, followed by the potential alcohol content, such as 10 + 2%. All these elements are required by law to appear on all Italian wine labels.

As the quality of the nation's wine rises, so do the options for displaying an increasing barrage of vinous information. The level of dryness or sweetness is usually included, using the terms *secco* (dry), *asciutto* (bone-dry), *abboccato* (lightly sweet), *amabile* (semi-sweet), and *dolce* (sweet). Many labels include suggestions of food dishes that will best accompany the wine – where one wine is better suited to fish dishes, another might be perfect with roast meat or game. Other labels include the ideal temperature for serving the wine and the way in which it should be served – the latter is usually reserved for red wines with bottle age. Sometimes the labels may even carry a potted history of the wine, or of the estate at which it was made.

The vini da tavola paradox

In the last 20 years, a peculiar phenomenon has brought glamour and controversy to the Italian wine scene. Wines of high value using innovative methods of production have been sold simply as *vini da tavola*, yet at prices as high as those of the best DOC wines. These are "new concept" wines, from producers sufficiently brave or headstrong to eschew the route prescribed by DOC regulations and search for alternative solutions – with regard to grape content, maturation techniques, the length of ageing and so on.

The most famous are the "Super-Tuscans" and the great *vini da tavola* of Piedmont. Recognised all over the world, the only thing they share in common with the poor *vini da tavola* is the designation. In the last few years, many new-concept wines have become classics and have subsequently obtained the official DOC designation, among them the celebrated Sassicaia , now known as the Bolgheri Sassicaia DOC. It will be worth keeping an eye on the progress of other "pretenders".

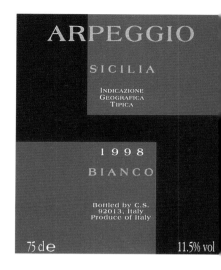

above *This label is for a fairly straightforward wine from Sicily. The name of the wine is Arpeggio and it is made from a blend of grapes that are not mentioned on the label; the label simply says "bianco" (white). Its quality level is Indicazione Geografica Tipica and the only geographical reference is to Sicily.*

Climate, Soil & Viticultural Techniques

Italy has myriad climates, soils and systems for cultivating vines, as befits such a geographically and politically diverse country. There are over 2,000 kilometres between the island of Pantelleria and the vines of the Abbey of Novacella near Bressanone, in the Valle Isarco of the Upper Adige, respectively the southernmost and northernmost wine areas. These stretch from 36° 42' to 46° 45' degrees north, from the volcanic hills of Pantelleria roasted by the Mediterranean sun, to the lush green heights of the South Tyrol at the foot of the Alps. In between lies an extraordinary range of climates, often varying significantly even among relatively close regions.

The last five or six years have witnessed a substantial renovation of vineyards, which kicked off with serious research into clonal selection of the main traditional vines. This encouraged a shift towards more densely planted vineyards, in an attempt to increase the number of quality wines by lowering the grape yield of individual rootstocks. Certain production requirements for important DOC and DOCG wines even specify the minimum number of vines permitted per hectare, which represents a mini-revolution in a country that has often tolerated a loosely quantitative approach. Now, the official momentum is behind careful cultivation and research.

Our journey begins in the northwest of Italy. The Valle d'Aosta is gateway to this region, a small mountainous melting pot of Italian and French cultures. Viticulture is confined to the valley of the Dora Baltea river, which runs longitudinally throughout the region. Vines are planted inland, on terraces on the lowest slopes of the mountains, or in the rare level areas beside the river. Soils are mostly calcareous and the climate continental, with fairly cool summers and harsh winters. Vineyards are planted mostly with low rows of vines, usually to the traditional Guyot system that is also evident in Valtellina, the most northern region of Lombardy. In both cases, vinegrowing methods are dictated by the mountains and climate.

In Piedmont and Lombardy climatic conditions are fairly continental, with hot, dry summers and cold, wet winters. Piedmont's famously reliable humidity gives its name to the region's trademark Nebbiolo grape. In Piedmont and central-southern Lombardy the soils are predominantly calcareous-argillaceous, allowing for taller vines and methods such as counter-espalier, with rows two metres high or more. These only allow a maximum of 3,500 vines per hectare; but quality-driven producers in Barolo, Barbaresco, Asti and Franciacorte are planting vines with a higher density. Lower rows of vines, which allow more plants per hectare and a smaller distance between rows, result in fewer grapes per plant, but maintain the same yield per hectare. For example: to achieve ten tonnes per hectare with 3,000 plants, each vine has to yield more than three kilograms of grapes. But with 6,000 plants, 1.5 kilograms per vine will suffice, and higher quality grapes will ensue.

Viticulturally, the Alto Adige, Trentino, some eastern parts of Lombardy (ie Bergamo and Brescia) and the vast area of the western Veneto – including Verona and Vicenza – are fairly similar. Here, the Trentino pergola prevails, an excellent system, particularly useful for vines grown on the terracing of the lowest slopes of the mountains, which

below A hot, arid vineyard near Sciacca, in the Agrigento province of Sicily. The method of growing vines as bushes, and not training them along wires, is typical of Mediterranean regions.

rise on both sides of the Adige and Isarco rivers. The system is open on one side, on which the vines are trained into the shape of a figure 7, allowing a high density of planting in each row. The Trentino pergola system is particularly effective when used on dry terraces that restrict productivity, especially on the calcareous soils common in the Trentino and Upper Adige. But in the

Valpolicella region of Veronese soils are a little richer, with more clay. Here, the vines' output must be kept under control, so vineyards are planted with rows that are less high and trained by the Guyot system, for a smaller yield from each grapevine and a greater density per hectare.

Tall rows trained in the Sylvoz or Casarsa style reappear as soon as the hills give way to the vast, well-

above This view of vineyards near Bolzano in the Alto Adige (Santa Maddalena Classico DOC) captures the surprisingly cool and Alpine aspect of some of Italy's wine regions.

above *Nets can be used to protect vines from an array of predators, typically birds and small animals.*

watered plains of central-east Veneto and central Friuli. The Casarsa system takes its name from the town of Casarsa della Delizia, the winemaking capital of Grave del Friuli. This is a wide, flat region distinguished by dry, gravelly soils and a continental climate. Similar climatic conditions are found in the Veneto regions of Piave, while towards the Adriatic coast – notably at Lison-Pramaggiore, Latisana and Aquileia – the sea tempers the harsh winter. However, the systems of vine-cultivation and soil types remain much the same.

The extreme east of Italy is marked by the hilly areas dividing the Friuli and Giulia regions from Slovenia. Low-growing vines reappear, using the training system known locally as Cappuccina and in other parts of Italy as "double

overhead". This is a variation of the double Guyot system, with the vine shoot bent down in an arch rather than extended parallel with the ground. This allows a good density of plants per hectare and gives high quality grapes – particularly white varieties – in the Friuli regions of Collio, Colli Orientali del Friuli and Isonzo. These latter regions are distinguished by *ponca* – calcareous-clay soils – and a climate customarily described as temperate-Mediterranean: the Gulf of Trieste is a few kilometres from the southernmost vineyards of the Collio, and forms the northernmost extremity of the Mediterranean basin, at a latitude of 45° 30' – similar to the Haut-Médoc.

The southern part of the Paduan plain – occupied by the enormous region of Emilia-Romagna – is a wealth of idiosyncrasies, an enduring legacy of the many disparate, partisan states that divided this region before unification in the mid-19th century. Vine-growing in the Colli Piacentini is fairly similar to that in the Oltrepò Pavese region of Lombardy, the Colli Tortonesi, Monferrato and Piedmontese Astigiano, revealing a greater similarity between these zones and Emilia than the latter and its neighbouring provinces.

The Emilian system of training, similar to the Trentino pergola but more widespread, is prevalent in the flatter regions of Parma, Reggio Emilia and Modena. Guyot-trained rows of vines are more common in Romagna, with Sylvoz training for the taller ones.

The difficult winegrowing region of Liguria has a typically Mediterranean climate and vines are grown on the terraced hills, often near-vertical or near the sea. This permits only narrow, non-spreading systems of training, such as *alberello* (sapling) and espalier.

Throughout central Italy – where you'll find Tuscany, Umbria, northern Latium and the Marches – there is an apparent uniformity in both climate and cultivation. Depending on the former, rows of vines are almost always trained by the "double overhead" or *archetto Toscano* (Tuscan bow) systems, variations on the Guyot. The soil is almost always calcareous-argillaceous, with slight differences between the coastal and inland areas. The climate of the Marches, Umbria and inland Tuscany is cooler, while the Tuscan coast and northern Latium are more Mediterranean.

The awning or pergola system is widespread in Abruzzi, Molise, central-southern Latium and Puglia. This allows high yields but can also ensure quality results, notably in Abruzzi. However, the terrain varies markedly – it's mainly volcanic in Latium, while the soils of Abruzzi and the lower regions towards the Adriatic are generally richer in clay and limestone. The climate is similarly varied: purely Mediterranean on the Tyrrhenian slopes, becoming increasingly continental and more exposed to the cold winds of the northwest towards the Adriatic. The high mountains in the Apennines, which divide Latium from Abruzzi, influence the climate of the entire eastern side of southern-central Italy.

Alberello is the main method of vine-growing in the Mezzogiorno, and is common to the southern regions of Puglia, Campania, much of Sicily and the whole of Sardinia. The vineyards and climate are reminiscent of Mediterranean Spain: nearly always dry and drought-ridden, but occasionally wetter and more sub-tropical. The soils are different – typically calcareous-argillaceous or, on the slopes of Mount Etna for example, volcanic tufa, which is very rich in potassium.

Our journey round the peninsula ends with a twist, in northern Campania, Massico, Campi Flegrei and the district of Aversa. Here, ancient methods persist, with vines running rampant over poplar trees and reaching four or five metres high. But the soils are typical of volcanic regions of central-southern Italy – very rich in volcanic ash. This allows vines to be grown on French rootstocks, as the soil is too loose and soft for phylloxera.

below *The black cable in the foreground is for irrigating the vines. Without this added water, these Pinot Bianco vines in the Castel del Monte DOC in Puglia might not survive the region's long, hot, arid summers.*

The Grapes of Italy

Red grape varieties

Aglianico This ancient *Vitis hellenica* was introduced by the Greeks into Campania, and spread into Basilicata and Puglia. Ages gracefully and produces full-bodied, well-structured and generous red wines with plenty of acidity and tannin, such as Taurasi (DOCG) and Aglianico del Vulture (DOC).

above *Aglianico grapes on a 25-year-old vine, Rionero in Vulture, Basilicata. This variety was introduced by the Greeks.*

Aleatico Grown in Portoferraio, on Elba, in Gradoli in the north of Latium, and in Puglia, this variety yields wines with all the strength of a great Mediterranean red. Sweet, strong and alcoholic, many are unknown gems.

Ancellotta Cultivated mainly in central Emilia, where it is also known as Ancellotta or Lancellotta, this is a richly coloured grape and considered a close relative of the vast Lambrusco family.

Barbera Native to Monferrato, Barbera is grown throughout Piedmont and Lombardy, and is being tested successfully elsewhere, including south-central Italy. Accounts for approximately half the red wine made in Piedmont, either on its own or in blends, and is at its best in classical appellations, such as Barbera d'Alba. In Oltrepò Pavese it is a DOC in its own right.

Blauburgunder See Pinot Nero

Blaufränkisch See Franconia

Bombino Nero Grown almost exclusively in Puglia, where it is used to make Lizzano Rosso (DOC).

Bonarda From Monferrato to Colli Piacentini and Colli di Parma, including Oltrepò Pavese, it is used alone or with other varieties to produce several well-structured red DOC wines, violet in colour and with a good capacity for ageing. In Oltrepò, it is also known as Croatina.

Bonarda Novarese See Uva Rara

Bovale Of Spanish origin, Bovale is now cultivated in south-central Sardinia, where it is one of the ingredients in the red Campidano di Terralba, made in the Oristano and Cagliari provinces.

Brachetto Fragrant red grapes, popular in Acqui Terme in the Asti province, and behind the famous red Brachetto d'Acqui (DOCG): a sweet, highly-scented wine, sometimes sparkling or semi-sparkling.

Cabernet Franc An "international" grape variety, indigenous to Bordeaux. Less popular than Cabernet Sauvignon, but more successful in Italy — especially in the northeast. It is popular in Friuli and especially in the Veneto, while in Trentino and the Alto Adige it is most often blended with Cabernet Sauvignon. Yields excellent reds which age extremely well.

Cabernet Sauvignon The mainstay of international winemaking. Another native of Bordeaux, Cabernet Sauvignon is cultivated all over the world in cool, temperate

regions, yet always maintains its varietal characteristics. In Italy it is grown almost everywhere, but mainly in Trentino, the Alto Adige and more recently in Tuscany, Umbria and Sicily, with excellent results. Features in one of the most famous wines of all: the Tuscan Sassicaia di Bolgheri (DOC).

Calabrese See Nero d'Avola

Canaiolo Nero A variety often used to add softness to Chianti wines, which is grown in parts of central Italy.

Cannonau With the ability to produce excellent yields even in dry climates and rocky soils, this grape of Spanish origin is grown successfully all over the world — Garnacha, Grenache Noir, Alicante or Roussillon are just a few of the synonyms. In Sardinia, Cannonau is cultivated everywhere. Produces wines with a very high alcohol content — indeed the regulations provide for 13.5 per cent alcohol by volume (abv) for standard wine, and 15 per cent abv for riservas.

Carignano In Italy, Carignano is almost exclusive to southwestern Sardinia,

above *Barbera is Italy's second most important red grape behind Sangiovese. It is grown throughout Piedmont and Lombardy and experimentally elsewhere.*

particularly in the region of Sulcis, where the eponymous DOC wine is produced. Also exists throughout the western Mediterranean, from the French Midi to Penedés in Catalonia, in the guise of Carignan or Cariñena.

Cesanese A typical variety of Latium, now grown in the Piglio, Affile and Olevano Romano regions, an area straddling the provinces of Rome and Frosinone. Produces alcoholic wines, very often sweet and semi-sparkling, designed to be drunk young.

Chiavennasca See Nebbiolo

Ciliegiolo Also known as Ciliegiolo di Spagna (Ciliegiolo of Spain), its probable homeland. Grown mainly in Tuscany, Umbria and Latium where it is used to make Montecarlo Rosso, Val di Cornia Rosso, Colli del Trasimeno Rosso, Colli Perugini Rosso, Colli Amerini Rosso and Velletri Rosso.

Colorino A richly coloured red grape. A small percentage may be used in Chianti, Rosso delle Colline Lucchesi and Montecarlo Rosso.

Corvina A star of the Verona region and one of the varieties used (with Molinara and Rondinella) to produce wines such as Bardolino, Valpolicella, Recioto Classico and Amarone, which are made in the area between the Veneto coast of Lake Garda and the hills of Valpolicella, to the north and northeast of Verona.

Croatina See Bonarda

Dolcetto Originally from Piedmont (where it is still common) and Liguria, where it is known as Ormeasco. Dolcetto is a most popular and traditional Piedmontese variety. Tends to produce beautiful violet-ruby coloured wines, fragrant and aromatic with a typically pleasant but slightly bitter aftertaste. Most robust and durable in Dolcetto d' Alba, Dolcetto di Diano d'Alba and Dolcetto di Dogliani.

Franconia (Blaufränkisch) Grown in a few parts of the Friuli, especially in Isonzo and the Colli Orientali.

Frappato Grown almost exclusively in south-central Sicily, Frappato is used to make the famous Cerasuolo or Frappato di Vittoria: a sweet, alcoholic red wine.

Freisa Probably the least pretentious of Piedmont's red varieties. Yields light, often semi-sparkling reds, little suited to ageing. DOC wines includes Freisa d'Asti and Freisa di Chieri.

Gaglioppo Probably of Greek origin and the most cultivated red variety in Calabria, but also grown in Abruzzi, Campania, Umbria and the Marches. Cirò is undoubtedly the most famous wine made from Gaglioppo, but it also goes into Donnici, Lamezia, Melissa and Savuto – all DOC wines.

Gamay French in origin, and the main Beaujolais grape. Because it flowers, fruits and matures early, it can be cultivated in cooler regions, such as the Valle d'Aosta.

Girò Not to be confused with the Cirò wine of Calabria, Girò hails from Cagliari. It goes into the DOC wine of the same name, a red sometimes offered in a sweet version.

Grignolino Very unusual grape, rich in tannin and low in colour. Cultivated almost exclusively in Monferrato and Asti, where it produces eponymous DOC wines.

Groppello Grown almost exclusively in the Garda Bresciano in Lombardy, where it is the basic ingredient of all rosso and rosato wines, including Groppello del Bresciano.

Guarnaccia Almost exclusive to the province of Naples and used to make Ischia Rosso (DOC).

Incrocio Manzoni See "White grape varieties"

Lagrein Cultivated around Bolzano, producing fruit with high levels of colouring. Yields a violet-coloured wine, Lagrein Dunkel, which has aromas of blackberries and bilberries. There is also a rosato version, Lagrein Kretzer.

Lambrusco A grape known to the Etruscans, and by far the most widely cultivated grape in the Emilian plain. Also grown in Bassa Mantovana, and in parts of Trentino, where it is used mainly in new-styled wines. Currently has about 60 sub-varieties, the most important being Lambrusco Salamino, Lambrusco Marani, Lambrusco Maestri, Lambrusco Montericco and, most famously, Lambrusco di Sorbara. Forms the basis of the four main Lambrusco DOC wines produced in Emilia: Sorbara, Grasparossa di Castelvetro, Salamino di Santacroce and Reggiano.

Malvasia See "White grape varieties"

Marzemino Semi-immortalised by Lorenzo Da Ponte, librettist of Mozart's *Don Giovanni*, this grape is cultivated almost exclusively in Trentino, especially in Isera, near Rovereto, and in some parts of eastern Lombardy. Marzemino tends to yield a medium-bodied, violet-red wine with an intensely herbaceous aroma.

Merlot Another native of Bordeaux, where it is more prolific than Cabernet. The first French variety to be planted on a large scale in Italy after the phylloxera disaster, it was originally introduced to the Veneto, Friuli and Trentino, and is now found in Lombardy, Latium, Campania, Tuscany and Umbria.

Molinara The name derives from its waxy bloom and flour-like covering. Grown almost exclusively in the province of Verona, to produce Bardolino, Valpolicella, Amarone and Recioto Classico.

Monica A typical red grape of the Cagliaritano region, it produces sweet red wines, sometimes liqueur-like, and very occasionally semi-sparkling.

Montepulciano After Sangiovese, Montepulciano d'Abruzzo is one of the most widespread native varieties in Italy. A native of Tuscany, it has been confused with Sangiovese, a close relation. However, the name is the only similarity between the Montepulciano variety and Vino Nobile di Montepulciano, which is produced from completely different grapes. Montepulciano thrives in Abruzzi, where it is the most cultivated variety, producing over 200,000 hectolitres of red and rosé wines such as Cerasuolo. Also grown successfully in Emilia, in the Marches (where it adds a touch of elegance to Rosso Conero) and in Latium, Molise and Puglia.

Morellino See Sangiovese

Nebbiolo Evokes the October mists which throw a shroud over the Langhe hills. Nebbiolo is undoubtedly the most cultivated variety in this part of Piedmont. Barolo and Barbaresco owe their pedigree to the perfect union between the local soil and this grape, a match that cannot be replicated

below *Nebbiolo grapes. This is the classic variety of the Langhe hills and is most famous for Barolo and Barbaresco.*

above *Negroamaro. This is the dominant grape in Puglia and literally means "black-bitter". As with most other southern Italian varieties, it was introduced by the Greeks.*

elsewhere. The most cultivated sub-varieties are Lampia and Michet in Langa, Spanna in the regions of Vercello and Novara, and Chiavennasca in Valtellina. Apart from those Piedmont superstars Barolo and Barbaresco, other DOCG and DOC wines made entirely from Nebbiolo include Roero, Gattinara, Spanna, Carema, Nebbiolo d'Alba and, in Lombardy, the wines of Valtellina. Also used in many other reds from Lombardy and Piedmont.

Negrara Characteristic red grape of Valpolicella, which takes its name from the district of Negrar, one of the best-known communes in the region.

Negroamaro Prominent in 80 per cent of the powerful reds and delicate rosés of Puglia. Probably introduced by the Greeks to the Ionian coastal regions, and now most widely cultivated around Lecce, Brindisi and in the province of Tarantino. Also plays an important role in wines from the DOC regions of Alezio, Brindisi, Copertino, Nardò Leverano, Matino, Cerignola, Salice Salentino and Squinzano.

Nerello Includes the sub-varieties Mascalese and Cappuccio and is grown almost exclusively in eastern Sicily, where it merits its "decent" image. The basic ingredient of Faro and Etna Rosso.

Nero d'Avola Also known as Calabrese, this is Sicily's best red grape and the most widely cultivated. Usually grown as a small tree or espalier, it produces a grape with a high sugar content, and wines which can easily reach 15 per cent abv. The wine is fragrant and full of flavour but lacks acidity, so Nero d'Avola is usually balanced with other varieties. Features in Cerasuolo di Vittoria and other DOC wines, including some Marsala; in Sicilian vini da tavola; and in the IGT of Corvo and Regaleali.

Ormeasco See Dolcetto

Ottavianello The name comes from Ottaviano, a region in the province of Naples. Today it is cultivated almost exclusively in Puglia, which has earned a special DOC for Ostuni Ottavianello.

Pascale di Cagliari Grown mainly in Campidano di Terralba, between the provinces of Oristano and Cagliari, though drifting onto the endangered list.

Per'e Palummo See Piedirosso

Perricone (Pignatello) Grown virtually everywhere in Sicily, in various guises, and used in Marsala Rubino and Eloro Rosso.

Petit Rouge Typical variety of the central-west region of Valle d'Aosta, and used in Enfer d'Arvier, Torrette and Valle d'Aosta Petit Rouge.

Piedirosso (Per'e Palummo) Typical red grape of Campania, found throughout Sannio Benevento, Solopaca and Ischia.

Pignatello See Perricone

Pignolo A rare red grape typical of certain sub-districts of Colli Orientali del Friuli and Buttrio. Produces excellent, well-structured red wines.

Pinot Grigio This copper-red variety is a genetic mutation of Pinot Nero, although at the base of the vine the grapes are almost white. Ostensibly lacks the credentials of its aristocratic rival, the Pinot Bianco, or the distinctiveness of a Tocai; but it has certainly introduced a new style of white to a wider public – fruity and pleasant, but not without structure. The presence of Pinot Grigio in Collio and in Colli Orientali del Friuli has given these wines their texture, while in Alto Adige (where it is known as Ruländer), its greater acidity enables it to be kept longer. In Tuscany, too, the results have been excellent.

Pinot Nero Considered the most aristocratic red grape and also the most difficult to interpret. It is native to Burgundy (Pinot Noir), where it underscores the greatest wines of the region, and has a bubbly presence in Champagne and California. In Italy, there are two types: the first is widely grown in the Veneto, Friuli and especially Oltrepò Pavese, and produces a neutral but excellent white, used as a "base" for spumante. The second is very different: it is extremely delicate, so that

below *Primitivo. This variety has its roots in Dalmatia, in the Balkans, and was later introduced to California, where it became better known as Zinfandel.*

even in perfectly situated vineyards the quality of wine depends very much on the vintage. This type is widely cultivated in Trentino and Alto Adige (where it is called Blauburgunder), in Lombardy – especially in Oltrepò, but also in Franciacorta – Veneto and Friuli. Results in Tuscany are also encouraging.

Primitivo California Zinfandel is none other than a transatlantic version of Primitivo, a variety still cultivated in Salento and a few districts of Campania. Originally brought to Southern Italy from Dalmatia, where it is known as Plavac Mali, Primitivo is used to produce Primitivo di Manduria and was probably an ingredient in ancient Falernum.

Prugnolo Gentile A close relative of Sangiovese Grosso, this is cultivated in Montepulciano for making Vino Nobile di Montepulciano and Rosso di Montepulciano.

Raboso There are two versions: Raboso del Piave and Raboso Veronese, both of which are widely cultivated in the region of Trevigiano. Both are used in Piave Raboso, while the Veronese version appears in Colli Euganei Rosso, from the Padua province.

Refosco dal Peduncolo Rosso Archetypal Friuli variety, cultivated mainly in the hilly parts of Collio, Colli Orientali del Friuli and on the flat land of Grave and Isonzo. In Carso it is called Terrano, while in Romagna it is the basic ingredient of Cagnina, a very sweet, famous red.

Rondinella Renowned red grape of the Veronese region, used in making Bardolino, Valpolicella, Amarone and Recioto Classico.

Rossese Typical of the Ligurian Riviera di Ponente, most effective in Dolceacqua, inland from San Remo. Mainstay of two DOC wines: Rossese della Riviera Ligure di Ponente and Rossese di Dolceacqua.

right *Sangiovese is perceived as the classic Italian grape variety and is inspiring a growing number of experimental plantings in the US and Australia.*

Ruchè Found almost exclusively in Astigiano, Ruchè is the basic ingredient of DOC wine Ruchè di Castagnole: a slightly aromatic, dry red.

Ruländer See Pinot Grigio

Sagrantino Virtually exclusive to the district of Montefalco, in Perugia, Sagrantino is the basis of a great red wine, Sagrantino di Montefalco, recently awarded a DOCG. Tannic and powerful, and one of the new stars of Italian winemaking.

Sangiovese One of the most widely cultivated grape varieties in Italy, from Emilia-Romagna to Campania, while the quantity of wine produced equals that of Barbera. Chianti, Sangiovese di Romagna, Brunello di Montalcino and Morellino di Scansano are just a few of the headline wines featuring this variety. Sangiovese's vast distribution has over the centuries inspired numerous clones. Produces a wide spectrum of wines, ranging from undistingished, inexpensive little reds to aristocrats such as Brunello di Montalcino.

Schiava By far the most widely cultivated red grape in Trentino-Alto Adige. The name may suggest a Slavic origin, or refer to an old form of cultivation whereby it was attached to a "master" tree as support – hence schiava, or "slave". In German wine regions it is known as Trollinger (a possible corruption of Tirolinger) and may be native to the southern Tyrol. Various clones of Schiava (Vernatsch in Alto Adige) include Schiava Grossa (Grossvernatsch), the most widely cultivated. Also features in most of the region's reds, almost single-handedly in DOC wines such as Lago di Caldaro, Alto Adige Schiava and Santa Maddalena.

Schioppettino Also known as Ribolla Nera. Virtually exclusive to the region of Colli Orientali del Friuli, where it yields well-structured wines that age well.

Spanna See Nebbiolo

Spätburgunder See Pinot Nero

Syrah or Shiraz, which should not be confused with the unrelated Petite Sirah, is one of the more noble black grape varieties. Still most at home in the Rhône, where it makes wines of almost incomparable elegance, such as Côte-Rôtie, Cornas and Hermitage; but Australia is also proving a pedigree outpost. A few Tuscan wines made from Syrah are of international standard.

Tazzelenghe (Tacelenghe) Rare red grape of the Colli Orientali del Friuli, cultivated mainly in Buttrio and Manzano. Inspires such levels of acidity that Tazzelenghe means "tongue-cutter" in Friulian dialect.

Teroldego Black grape from the Trentino region, similar to Lagrein and similarly undervalued for decades. It's an extraordinary grape, whose structure, strength and refinement soon became apparent when producers began cultivating it on a large scale.

Terrano See Refosco dal Peduncolo Rosso.

Uva di Troia Cultivated mainly in north-central Puglia, and the main ingredient in Castel del Monte Rosso and Rosato, Cacc'e Mmitte di Lucca, Rosso Barletta, Canosa and Cerignola.

Uva Rara Owes its name to its sparse bunches of grapes. Grown mainly in Oltrepò Pavese, where it is used in Oltrepò Pavese Rosso, Buttafuoco, Sangue di Giuda, and in the Novara region, where it is used to produce Ghemme, Fara, Sizzano and Boca. Uva Rara is also grown in the Colline Novaresi as Bonarda Novarese.

Vernatsch See Schiava

Vespolina (Ughetta) Grown mainly in the province of Novara, this is often confused with Uva Rara or Bonarda Novarese. It is used to make Lessona, Bramaterra, Fara, Ghemme and Boca, and constitutes a small percentage of the Gattinara DOCG. Has a specific DOC which observes the wine regulations of the Colline Novaresi.

White grape varieties

Albana Found almost exclusively in Romagna, Albana produces a white DOCG wine, Albana di Romagna, in several versions: dry, semi-sweet, sweet and passito (made from sun-dried grapes). The last is the most coveted.

Albarola Typical of the Cinqueterre region in Liguria, it crops up in Cinqueterre Bianco and the rare passito Cinqueterre Sciacchetrà.

Ansonica (Ansonaca) See Inzolia

Arneis Only recently saved from extinction, today it is increasingly cultivated in its native Piedmont. Often used to soften the sharpness of Nebbiolo and also used in Barolo Bianco.

Asprinio Ancient grape grown almost exclusively in the Aversa region, where it's the staple grape in the DOC wine of the same name.

Bellone Traditional variety of the Castelli Romani since Roman times, but now extremely rare.

Biancame (Bianchello) Similar to Trebbiano and probably distantly related to Greco, Biancame is cultivated mainly in the northern Marches, where it is the basic ingredient in the famous Bianchello del Metauro.

Bianco d'Alessano Native grape of Puglia, grown mostly in the regions of Locorotondo and Martina Franca, where it is used in eponymous DOC wines.

Biancolella Grown almost exclusively on the island of Ischia, although it probably originated in Corsica. Biancolella is the basis of Ischia Bianco and the pleasant, fragrant white wine Biancolella d'Ischia.

Blanc de Morgex Typical variety of the Valle d'Aosta, one of the very few strains resistant to the phylloxera louse. It is the basic ingredient of the eponymous DOC white wine produced in the northwestern corner of the region. Grows at 1,000 metres above sea level.

Bombino Bianco Prominent in central Italy, from Romagna to Puglia, this is the basic ingredient of many DOC white wines, from Pagadebit di Romagna to Leverano and San Severo.

Bosco One of the ingredients in the Cinqueterre DOC and the legendary Sciacchettrà, the region's rare and highly esteemed passito. Believed to be one of the few native Ligurian varieties.

Cacchione See Bellone

Canaiolo Bianco See Drupeggio

Carricante This grape is grown almost exclusively on the slopes of Mount Etna, in Sicily, often at altitudes in excess of 1,000 metres. It's the prime ingredient of Etna Bianco, an agreeable white wine with a complex, mineral fragrance and a strong, aristocratic flavour.

Catarratto One of Sicily's most classic grapes, grow in the central and western districts and used in the production of Bianco Comune and Bianco Lucido. Also used alongside Grillo and Inzolia to make Marsala and Alcamo.

Chardonnay A native of Burgundy. In Italy, Chardonnay was once confused with Pinot Bianco, a distant cousin. Now grown throughout Italy, it's an excellent base for sparkling wines, especially if grown in calcareous soil at medium altitude. A high-yielding variety which produces a light, delicately fruity wine.

Coda di Volpe Together with Greco and Falanghina, Coda di Volpe is used to produce the wines of Campania in the DOCG regions of Vesuvius, Taburno and Campi Flegrei.

Cortese A native variety of Alessandria, in Piedmont: the hills between Novi and Tortona are its favoured habitat. Rarely seen elsewhere, though there are a few Cortese vineyards in the province of Verona. But its true centre is Gavi – so much so that the name of the village has replaced that of the grape in the DOCG appellation. Wines from this region are among the best-known Italian whites. Pale, with light-green reflections and a fine fragrance, they are aristocratic but intense and very dry. Great typicity, some acidity and a good structure.

Drupeggio Variety typical of central Italy, particularly Umbria and Alto Lazio. Sometimes known as Canaiolo Bianco.

Erbaluce One of the very few white varieties from Piedmont. This is grown in the region of Caluso in Torino province, to underscore Caluso white wine and Caluso passito.

Falanghina Very traditional white grape cultivated in the regions of Campi Flegrei, Sannio Benevento and Massico, and all the regions of northern Campania. Recently introduced to the Sorrento peninsula, especially along the Amalfi coast. Produces wines with a firm body and a delicate aromatic fragrance.

Favorita Cultivated in parts of Piedmont and in Langhe, where it is the eponymous basis of the white DOC wine.

Fiano Descendant of the Roman Apianum, Fiano inspired some of the great whites of classical antiquity. Today it is cultivated mainly in Irpinia and small areas in Molise. Fiano di Avellino DOC is made exclusively from Fiano grapes.

Forastera Like Biancolella, a white grape grown on the island of Ischia, and the basis of Ischia Bianco and Forastera d'Ischia.

Garganega Much cultivated in the eastern part of Verona and in parts of Vicenza. The backbone of Soave and Gambellara.

Gewürztraminer See Traminer

left *Garganega. This vigorous variety is the mainstay of Veneto's most famous white wine, Soave, and of Gambellara.*

left *Malvasia. This versatile, aromatic variety was introduced by the Greeks and is now grown throughout Italy.*

Malvasia A variety with a long and eventful history. In ancient Greece, where it arrived from Asia Minor, it was named after the port of Monemvasia. The main Italian Malvasian varieties are: Istriana, from Friuli-Venezia Giulia, which yields a slightly aromatic wine of good alcohol content and a rich, full taste; Malvasia del Lazio, an intense and elegant grape, used in some of the local whites but seldom on its own; Malvasia di Candia, grown in Latium and Campania; and Malvasia Bianca del Chianti, which is delicate and fragrant and also used as a blending grape with other varieties. Malvasia flourishes in the Lipari islands, where it is made into one of the greatest Italian dessert wines. Malvasia Nera is grown in Piedmont (it is a DOC wine in Casorzo and Castelnuovo), in the Alto Adige region (also a DOC) and in Puglia, for red

and rosé wines. Sardinian versions range from sparkling to liqueur-like wines.

Moscato Better known simply as Muscat, this is among the most ancient of grapes and is cultivated all over the world. A native of Asia Minor, it was promoted throughout the entire Mediterranean by Greek and Phoenician sailors. The extended family of Moscati (Muscats) includes Moscato, with small fruit (also known as Muscat à petits grains), which itself has many variants. In Italy it grows mainly in the Piedmontese hills and Oltrepò Pavese, although it can be found virtually everywhere. It produces a wide range of wines, from the sparkling, unmistakably aromatic Asti, to the Goldenmuskateller and Rosenmuskateller of the Alto Adige, and the golden liqueur-like wines from Puglia.

below *Moscato Bianco. This is one of the oldest and most widely cultivated grapes in the world, and is generally called Muscat.*

Grecanico Grown almost everywhere in western and central Sicily, Grecanico is pivotal in the DOC regions of Menfi, Santa Margherita di Belice and Contessa Entellina.

Grechetto In its element in Umbria and northern Latium, and used in Torgiano Bianco from Orvieto. The only grape of the Colli Martani region.

Greco Of Greek origin and grown in Campania and Calabria, where it makes the Greco di Tufo DOC wine. Also used in doses in Lacryma Christi del Vesuvio, Frascati, and Torre Quarto from the Puglia region. One of the best Italian dessert wines is produced from the Calabrese sub-variety, while Cirò Bianco is also made from Greco. Greco Nero is the most common sub-variety.

Grillo Much cultivated in the region of Marsalese and Alcamo, in western Sicily, where it is the basic constituent in the respective DOC wines.

Grüner Veltliner See Veltliner

Incrocio Manzoni There are two versions of this grape: one is a cross between Riesling and Pinot Bianco, and produces a light, slightly aromatic white. Less common is the red: a cross of Prosecco and Cabernet Sauvignon. It's grown in a few parts of the Veneto, most notably in the Treviso province.

Inzolia After Trebbiano and Catarratto, Inzolia (also known as Ansonica) is comfortably the most widespread grape variety in Sicily, its homeland, where it is the main ingredient of Marsala. Also grown, to a lesser extent, in Tuscany.

Kerner A variety created from the crossing of Riesling Renano with Schiava (aka Vernatsch in Germany). This occasionally crops up in England and the Rhine, but in Italy it is grown almost exclusively in the Alto Adige region.

Müller-Thurgau This Riesling and Sylvaner cross was developed in the Geisenheim oenological research laboratory in Germany in 1882 by Professor Hermann Müller, a native of Thurgau in Switzerland. It is rare in Italy: there are a few dozen hectares in Lombardy, Veneto and Friuli, but the best wines come from the Valle Isarco in the Alto Adige and the Valle di Cembra in Trentino. The vineyards really need good sun, high altitude and a rather cool climate.

Nasco Native Sardinian variety, found mainly in the Cagliari area and especially in Campidano. Produces sweet white wines, sometimes liqueur-like.

Nosiola Native of Trentino and very rare, It yields fruity white wines with a distinctive, slightly bitter aftertaste.

Nuragus Cultivated in Sardinia for thousands of years and probably imported by the Phoenicians. It is grown almost everywhere here, mostly in the central and southern areas. With Vermentino, Nuragus is the main ingredient in the light, fruity, well-balanced and often frizzanti (semi-sparkling) wines for which the island is famous. In the Sardinian DOC classification, Nuragus di Cagliari is second in output only to Vermentino di Sardegna.

Ortrugo Native of Oltrepò Pavese and Colli Piacentini, this variety is used as a component in Trebbianino Val Trebbia, Monterosso Val d'Arda, Val Nure and on its own to make Colli Piacentini Ortugo.

Pampanuto Very similar to the Bianco d'Alessano, Pampanuto used in Castel del Monte Bianco, which is produced in a large part of the province of Bari.

Pecorino Cultivated in much of central Italy, particularly in the region of Osimo, in the central Marches, and in a large part of Umbria.

Picolit Rare variety grown mainly in the Colli Orientali del Friuli and, to a lesser extent, in Collio Goriziano. It suffers from "floral abortion" – only a few grapes in each bunch develop fully and mature. The eponymous wine is a delicately sweet white, pleasant and with a good concentration of flavours.

Pigato Cultivated mainly in the Ligurian Riviera of Ponente, and especially the commune of Albenga.

Pignoletto Grown almost exclusively in the region of Colli Bolognesi, in the commune of Zola Predosa and in a few neighbouring districts. The basis of a light, white DOC wine, sometimes in a frizzante version.

Pinot Bianco For decades, this variety was confused with Chardonnay (with which it shares many characteristics) – so much so that until 15 years ago it was known in Italy as Pinot-Chardonnay. It is grown in Lombardy, Veneto, Friuli and Trentino-Alto Adige. In the 18th century, the Lorena grand dukes of Tuscany encouraged its cultivation there; today, it is used in the Pomino DOC, although Pomino Bianco is also marketed widely as an expensive *vino da tavola*. The most popular Pinot Bianco wines are produced in the regions of Friuli and Alto Adige. Also used in the most famous spumanti, those produced in Friuli, Trentino and Franciacorta.

Prosecco Of uncertain origin, Prosecco probably came from the Venezia Giulia region, or further east. Popular in the Veneto and only slightly less so in the province of Padua. Yields a straw-coloured wine with a distinctive fragrance of apples, almonds and wisteria, boasting a delicate, slightly aromatic flavour but little structure. The most popular Prosecco DOC, in the wine region of Conegliano-Valdobbiadene, are frizzanti (semi-sparkling) and spumanti (sparkling) – paler with a delicate fragrance. A sweeter grape grows in the commune of San Pietro di Barbozza, on the hill of Cartizze, used for popular sweet spumanti. Their labels include the words Superiore di Cartizze, or simply Cartizze.

Ribolla Gialla An historical variety of Friuli, cultivated there since the end of the Middle Ages. Now used to produce light white wines with a floral bouquet and modest structure, particularly interesting in the region of Collio.

Riesling Together with Chardonnay, Riesling is considered one of the noblest white grape varieties in the world. This variety consists of two basic types: the Renano, or Rhein Riesling, and the Riesling Italico, or Welschriesling. The first is a native of the Rhine Valley and the Moselle region, and is undoubtedly the more valuable, producing great wines capable of extensive ageing. It is also sometimes used to make sweet wines, made from late-harvested or even frozen grapes (Eiswein), or botrytised fruit (Trockenbeerenauslese). Both Rieslings are cultivated in Italy, mostly in the north, although they are often confused. The Italico type is popular in Oltrepò Pavese, producing spumanti and light, fragrant wines. The Renano is grown in Trentino-Alto Adige, Lombardy, Veneto (especially Treviso) and Friuli.

Sauvignon Blanc A fashionable international grape and native to the Bordeaux and Loire regions of France. In Italy it has been cultivated for over a century, firstly in the province of Parma and Piacenza, then in the Veneto and above all in Friuli – in the districts of Collio, Isonzo, Aquileia, Grave and Colli Orientali. Now beginning to realise its potential.

below *Trebbiano dates from Roman times, when it was called Trebulanum. It is now grown throughout Italy and its quality has recently improved through reduced yields.*

Sylvaner Grown in Alsace, where it is the simplest, most economic variety at the bottom of the quality pyramid. In Italy, it grows quite successfully in the Alto Adige, producing simple, slightly fruity white wines.

Tocai Friulano Sometimes wrongly accorded Hungarian origin, due to that country's famous track record with Tokáji Aszú. To add to the confusion, in Alsace "Tokay" is synonymous with Pinot Grigio, which itself is also much cultivated in Friuli. Tocai is in fact a native Italian grape variety and the most widely cultivated white grape in the Veneto – although the soil and climate of Collio Goriziano are its ideal habitat. It is grown throughout Friuli, the Veronese and in Lombardy.

Torbato Probably belongs to the Malvasia family. Currently cultivated only in the region of Alghero in the Sassari province, where it is the basis for the white DOC wine of the same name.

Traminer Traminer probably originates from the region of Tramin (Termeno in Italian), a small region in the Alto Adige. French oenologists, however, believe it to be a sub-variety of the local Savagnin and native to the Jura, near the Franco-Swiss border. At any rate, there are two types: Traminer and aromatic Traminer, the latter better known under the name of Gewürztraminer ("spicy Traminer") from Termeno. Traminer is cultivated in the Alto Adige, to a lesser degree in Trentino, and very occasionally in the Veneto and Friuli.

Trebbiano Known to the Romans as Trebulanum, this prolific variety has the distinction of producing the largest quantity of wine in the world. Its origins are open to dispute, but it's known in France as Ugni Blanc and provides an ideal basis for the distillation of cognac and armagnac – and the best Italian brandy. From Lombardy to the south, it is used in an incredible number of wines and has adapted to particular conditions, often producing some interesting white wines with distinctive properties. It has also benefited from the drastic reduction in yield per hectare. Some

right Verdicchio. This variety is mainly grown in the Marches region and is rapidly increasing in popularity. Its name derives from the green colour of the fruit.

Lugana and Trebbiano d'Abruzzo wines are particularly good examples.

Veltliner The most common name of the Austrian white grape variety Grüner Veltliner. Usually yields wines of medium quality, pleasant but not particularly complex, though there are exceptions.

Verdeca Grown in parts of Puglia, especially on the plateau of the Murge and in the province of Bari. It forms the basis of two whites, Locorotondo and Martina Franca, both DOC.

Verdello Cultivated mainly in southern Umbria, especially round Orvieto.

Verdicchio Grown in the Marches from time immemorial, the wine of the same name has in the last few years become one of Italy's most popular whites. The name refers to the colour of the grape which, even when ripe, retains a green tinge. Experts still debate its relationship with the Trebbiano of Soave and Lugana, with which it shares important characteristics. Verdicchio is a DOC wine in the classic region of Castelli di Jesi and in Matelica.

Verduzzo Cultivated in northeast Italy, especially in Friuli where it is the basis of dry and sweet wines. Successful sweet wines (such as those from the Ramandolo region) are well-structured and balanced.

Vermentino Vermentino has spread from the Iberian Peninsula into Liguria, Corsica, Sardinia and, to a lesser degree, Tuscany. Vaguely related to Malvasia, especially to that grown in Madeira, its possible origin. There are three Vermentino DOCs in Sardinia: Vermentino di Gallura – traditionally better-structured and more alcoholic; Alghero Vermentino frizzante; and Vermentino di Sardegna, produced everywhere on the island. Ligurian

Vermentino wines are usually less well structured although elegant, though they have a DOC in Riviera di Ponente and at Colli di Luni. Pigato is widely considered to be a type of Vermentino. From Tuscany, Candia dei Colli Apuani, Montecarlo and Bolgheri Vermentino are DOC wines, and use Vermentino in varying capacities.

Vernaccia Probably takes its name from the Latin *vernaculum*, meaning "local" or "native", which explains the numerous grapes known by this name in Italy. The most famous is probably San Gimignano in Tuscany, which has been producing a famous wine since the Middle Ages. This Vernaccia is firm and full of character, dry and alcoholic, with a range of fragrances. Vernaccia di Orestano in Sardinia is made from overripe grapes from the Tirso Basin, using a method akin to the solera system in sherry – which it much resembles. To the west of Macerata in the Marches, a special spumante is made from red Vernaccia

grapes, Vernaccia di Serrapetrona DOC. It can be dry, semi-sweet or sweet, but the best are the traditional-method spumanti.

Vespaiolo Typical of the Breganze region in Vicenza. Used to make Breganze Vespaiolo DOC, and a small percentage appears in the famous Torcolato di Breganze, a sweet white wine made from dried grapes.

Viognier Among the most interesting white grapes in the world. Initially cultivated in Languedoc-Roussillon and the Rhône Valley, where it is the basis of Condrieu and Château-Grillet. Little known in Italy, but used experimentally in Tuscany and Latium.

Weissburgunder See Pinot Bianco

Zibibbo Also known as Moscatellone or Moscato di Alessandria, and now grown exclusively in Isola di Pantelleria, where it is the driving force behind the outstanding Moscato and Passito di Pantelleria.

The Northwest

Northwest Italy consists of four regions: two are small, the Valle d'Aosta and Liguria, and two are among the largest in the country, Piedmont and Lombardy. These winegrowing areas are wealthy, highly developed and industrial, and not surprisingly attuned to the quality end of the market.

In Valle d'Aosta, the cultivation of vines is on a small scale, given the mountainous terrain: not much wine is made but the quality is consistently high. The situation is similar in Liguria, a region dominated by the mountain ranges of the Appennines and the Alps, which restrict agriculture to the level strip hugging the coast and the lowland hills. Cultivation is all but limited to olives and grapes, carried out on land which is often terraced and very steep: this is an expensive process, as virtually all the work is done by hand. Here, the Riviera di Levante and the Cinqueterre are costlier to cultivate than the Riviera di Ponente, which lies parallel to the sea and has gentler hills.

However, it is the large regions which take centre stage. Piedmont may be prime territory for dairy and cattle farming, with rice, hazelnuts and fruit also in evidence, but wine remains the region's most important crop and is grown mostly on the mountains. The region also includes the Langhe, where approximately 80,000 hectolitres of Barolo and Barbaresco, the two most famous DOCG wines, are produced. These great reds are made from the Nebbiolo grape and are of vital importance to the regional economy, often reaching prices of 20,000 to 40,000 lire (approximately £7 to £13) per bottle at the winery, while the grapes reach 9,000 lire (£3) per kilo. Such is the international kudos enjoyed by Barolo and Barbaresco that the wineries now sell their produce in advance, before the bottles reach the market place – a privilege enjoyed by the best Burgundy vineyards.

Further comparisons with this French luminary are evident in Piedmont's vinous infrastructure. In Langhe, as in the Côte de Nuits or the Côte de Beaune, the vineyard owners are fragmented: producers are mainly winemakers who work on grapes they grow themselves, and the négociants – agents who buy the grapes and wines from the vineyard to sell on to others – are few in number, lofty in reputation. So, for Bruno Giacosa, Prunotto, Pio Cesare and Ceretto with Barolo or Barbaresco, read Drouhin, Latour and Jadot in Burgundy.

In Lombardy, the most eye-catching region is undoubtedly Franciacorta, near the Lago d'Iseo, in the province of Brescia. The achievement of DOCG status is fair reward for the efforts of a surprising number of entrepreneurs who have brought invaluable experience and resources from non-viticulture or agriculture backgrounds. Here, quality and ambition are the watchwords, and the spumante may be compared with some of the world's most stylish sparkling wines.

Yet in much of Lombardy, old agricultural farming traditions and conditions persist. Oltrepò Pavese represents a great reservoir of wine almost exclusively siphoned off to the Milanese market, while the Valtellina region – whose vineyards cling to the steep mountain slopes of the valley cut by the river Adda – is a difficult place for winemaking. The quality of wine is generally excellent, almost all of it red and made from the Chiavennasca grape (the local name for Nebbiolo); but it's hard to locate any of this produce outside of Lombardy, unless you live in one of the great Italian cities, or Switzerland – which lies just over the border.

The parochialism is shared by the red wines of the central region, such as Botticino, Cellatica and the wines of Garda Bresciano. The same applies to the whites of the Colli Morenici Mantovani and even to Lugana di Sirmione, which was once widespread but may have suffered from the demise of Italian white wines in the mid-late Seventies.

left *The stunning patchwork of vineyards* (crus) *surrounding the village of La Morra produces some of the finest Barolo wines. The greatest* crus *include Brunate and Cerequio.*

Valle d'Aosta

The Valle d'Aosta has been inhabited since the end of the prehistoric era. In historic times it was home initially to the Salassi, a people of Ligurio-Gallic origin who resisted Roman invasion for over a century. Then, in 25 BC, the troops of Aulus Terentius Varro managed to conquer the area and, having subdued its warlike people, built the city of Augusta Praetoria, the present-day Aosta.

In the early Middle Ages the Valle d'Aosta was invaded by the Ostrogoths, Burgundians, Byzantines, Lombards and Franks, until in 904 it was conquered by the King of Burgundy. When in 1032 Umberto Biancamano – regarded as the founder of the royal dynasty of Savoy – became Duca d'Aosta, the land was permanently annexed and joined to the family's estates. Subsequently, it became part of the Kingdom of Sardinia, and then of Italy.

Vinegrowing was introduced in 1272, at the behest of Federico Front, Bishop of Ivrea, who ordered the citizens of Val di Cly to turn all their suitable land into vineyards. Nevertheless, vine growing and winemaking remained marginal activities until about 1950, when the Institut Agricole Régional (both Italian and French are spoken in the Valle d'Aosta) was created as an experimental pilot enterprise. It duly became the blueprint for the seven cooperatives which soon followed and which now cover most of the wine region.

Wines and winemaking

The local wine industry is very small. Only 46,000 hectolitres of wine are produced, of which a little over 6,000 hectolitres is attributed to the regional DOC appellation, "Valle d'Aosta/Vallée d'Aosta". Many wines are produced from the various grapes grown in this region: Blanc de Morgex et de La Salle, for example, is made from the grape variety of that name in the northern part of the region, at an altitude of 1,000 metres on the slopes of Mont Blanc. It is a very light white wine and almost impossible to find elsewhere.

Red wines predominate further south: the most important are Arnad-Montjovet and Donnas, which have great body and are made mainly from Picotener, the local version of Nebbiolo. Chambave Rouge, Nus, Torrette and Enfer d'Arvier are made mostly from Petit Rouge grapes, while the rarer and more expensive dessert wines include Chambave Muscat and Nus Malvoisie, the latter a blend of Pinot Grigio and local Malvoisie. All these wines are named after specific geographic regions, but some are produced in such small quantities that they are seldom sold outside the valley.

Visitors to the area will discover several Valle d'Aosta DOCs, indicating both the grape variety and the regional denomination. There are wines such as Vallée d'Aoste Müller Thurgau, Pinot Gris, Chardonnay, Gamay, Pinot Noir, Petite Arvine, Petit Rouge, Premetta and Fumin. These are made from grapes cultivated in different areas, from varieties which do not appear in the more specific sub-regions. Even here there are some real surprises, such as relatively successful Pinot Noir and Gamay wines. But, again, they are sold almost entirely at a local level.

Several growers are now experimenting with French grape varieties, especially in the Valle del Rodano. Some excellent red wines made from 'adopted' Syrah and Grenache are likely to find a permanent home in the Valdostana hills, but most wines of Valle del Rodano are

below *Vines at Morgex, growing at over 1,000 metres. These are trained traditionally on low pergolas, to protect them from bitterly cold temperatures.*

classic "mountain wines". The whites have a subtle, aromatic fragrance and are light-bodied, dominated by slightly acidic tones. The reds are medium-bodied, pale and lacking both definitive strength and ageing potential.

Soil, climate and viticulture

The Valle d'Aosta is a very small region (less than 3,000 square kilometres) and is surrounded by the Alps. The only part where vines may be grown is in the valley of the Dora Baltea, the region's most important river, which flows almost diagonally across from its source on Mont Blanc to the southeastern border with Piedmont, at Valtournenche.

The vineyards are situated on the left bank of the river Dora, which catches plenty of sunshine and has an abundance of sandy, clay soils – an essential for high quality grapes. The grapes may be good, but tending vineyards in this part of Valle d'Aosta is no easy task. The practice is similar to cultivating vines in the Swiss Valais, where they are grown on terraces and situated on steep slopes, clinging to the mountainside.

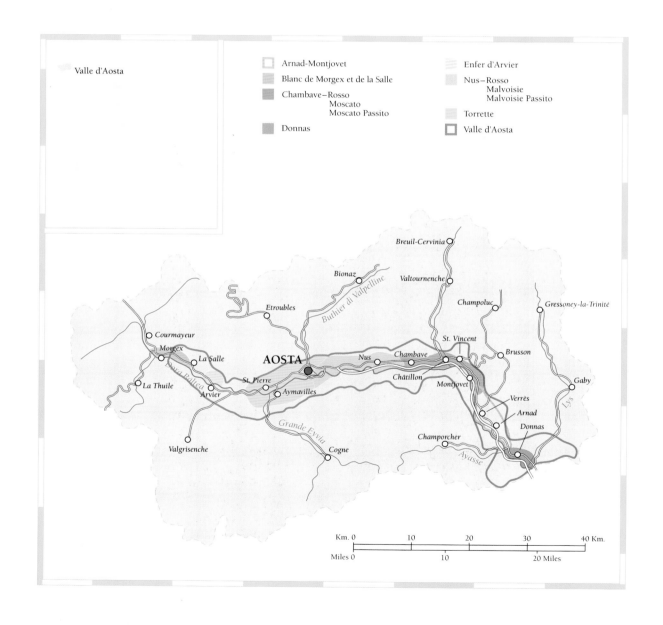

Valle d'Aosta

- Arnad-Montjovet
- Blanc de Morgex et de la Salle
- Chambave–Rosso
  Moscato
  Moscato Passito
- Donnas
- Enfer d'Arvier
- Nus–Rosso
  Malvoisie
  Malvoisie Passito
- Torrette
- Valle d'Aosta

right *In Valle d'Aosta vines can only be grown in the valley of the Dora Baltea river, such as these in the sub-zone of Chambave.*

There are three main winemaking districts: Valdigne, the furthest to the northwest, Valle Centrale and Bassa Valle. The main difference between the three is altitude, which is highest in the northernmost district and decreases quickly towards the southeast. The steep hills of the Valle d'Aosta face intensely cold weather during the long winter and blazing heat between July and the beginning of September – a typical continental climate, in other words, which is only suitable for growing early-maturing grape varieties such as Dolcetto, Gamay, Pinot Noir, Merlot and Petit Rouge.

The most popular system of cultivation is the low pergola, which is broadly similar to that used in the Trentino and Alto Adige regions. Alternatively, vines are trained on wires on the terraces, usually supported by poles or trained on small trees, especially in vineyards enclosed by stone walls – similar to those occasionally found in Burgundy.

Notable producers

Institut Agricole Régional, Aosta One of the most famous wineries in the region, the IAR offers a wide range of wines using avant-garde methods of production. The best are Trésor du Caveau, made exclusively from Syrah grapes, Vallée d'Aoste Chardonnay, matured in small casks, and Vin du Prévôt, produced from Cabernet Sauvignon and Merlot. Rouge du Prieur from Grenache grapes and Vallée d'Aoste Müller Thurgau also catch the eye.

Costantino Charrère, Aymavilles (AO) This small winery is run with great skill by Costantino Charrère, one of the region's most famous winemakers. His speciality is Vin de La Sabla, a red wine made from a blend of Fumin and Petit Rouge grapes. The Valle d'Aosta Prëmetta, a red wine made from grapes of the same name, and the Vin Les Fourches, made exclusively from Grenache grapes; in both cases, only a few hundred bottles are produced. Lighter and easier to drink is the Vallée d'Aoste Torrette, made predominantly from Petit Rouge grapes. Charrère is a French-speaking winemaker, as is apparent from his labels, but he follows the most authentic local traditions, with the emphasis on very densely planted vineyards and old, low-yielding grape varieties.

Les Crêtes, Aymavilles (AO) Among the most respected cooperative producers in the region, Les Crêtes offers a particularly wide range of local wines. The most prestigious is Coteau La Tour, made from Syrah; followed by Vallée d'Aoste Fumin and Vigne La Tour Cuvée Bois, both full-bodied reds. There are also two Vallée d'Aoste Chardonnay Cuvée Frissonière wines, one matured in wood for a year (the Cuvée Bois), and the other in steel vats. Finally there are the Vallée d'Aoste Petite Arvine Vigne Champorette, a white wine, and Vallée d'Aoste Torrette, a red wine made from Petit Rouge with a top-up of Fumin, Gamay and Pinot Noir.

La Crotta di Vegneron, Chambave (AO) La Crotta di Vegneron lies at the centre of the Chambave district and vinifies grapes grown by members in the neighbouring villages of Nus, Verrayes, Saint Denis, Châtillon and Saint Vincent. Their best wines are Vallée d'Aoste Chambave Moscato Passito, an aromatic sweet wine, the red Vallée d'Aoste Fumin and Vallée d'Aoste Nus Malvoisie, another sweet white.

Ezio Voyat, Chambave (AO) The best known producer in the region, Ezio Voyat wines have been gracing fine restaurants in Italy and abroad for over 30 years. His finest is the classic Moscato Passito, now called Vino Passito Le Muraglie, while the Moscato La Gazzella is fresher and lighter.

Cave du Vin Blanc de Morgex et de La Salle, Morgex (AO) Viticulture in the Valle d'Aosta is at its most hardy in Morgex and La Salle, at the foot of Mont Blanc. In some of the highest vineyards in Europe, between 900 and 1,200 metres above sea level, a small group of "heroic" winegrowers produce small quantities of one wine: Valle d'Aosta Blanc de Morgex et de La Salle, a unique, light, fragrant white almost impossible to find outside its own district.

left *Early winter, and these vines are about to be pruned of all their pale golden wood, in preparation for the following year's new growth. Only the old trunk will remain.*

Piedmont

above *Truffle hunting is one of the most popular (and indeed secretive) activities in Piedmont. Truffle-based dishes are perfect complements for the local wines.*

Literally the "foot of the mountain", Piedmont is defined by the Alps to the north and west, which separate it from Switzerland and France, and by the Appennines to the south, which form its border with Liguria.

In ancient times the people of Liguria used the area's natural defences to resist Roman invasion, until the reign of Augustus (27BC to AD14). After subduing the locals he developed "proper" viticulture in Piedmont, in the Etruscan fashion. While Charlemagne, the first Holy Roman Emperor (c742 to 814) and successive French kings invaded the Italian peninsula through this region, it was the prime minister of Savoy, Camillo Benso, Count of Cavour, who proved instrumental in the creation of Barolo, one of the greatest of Italian red wines.

Winemaking and wine styles

Piedmont is one of Italy's most prolific sources of high-quality wines, producing more than three million hectolitres, about half of which is DOC or DOCG quality. It is also home to more DOCG wines – seven – than anywhere else in Italy: Asti or Moscato d'Asti, Barolo, Barbaresco, Brachetto d'Acqui or Acqui, Gattinara, Ghemme and, since 1998, Gavi – the first white wine in the region to achieve this recognition.

The two most widespread grape varieties here are Barbera and Dolcetto, the latter providing the juice for ten DOC wines. Third most common but first in stature is Nebbiolo, used either as a varietal or a main constituent in the likes of Nebbiolo d'Alba, Roero, Barolo, Barbaresco, Gattinara, Ghemme, and many lesser DOC wines from around Novara and Vercelli.

The most widespread variety of all is a white, the Moscato or Muscat, from which most DOCs and DOCG whites are made, including Asti – the sweet spumante. Moscato d'Asti, the lesser-known semi-sparkling version, is a light, fragrant white and usually the preserve of small producers. Other Moscato wines are Loazzolo – a sweet white – and Brachetto d'Acqui, a fragrant sparkling red.

Asti is also home to two lesser sweet, semi-sparkling reds made from Malvasia Rosso: the Casorzo d'Asti and Castelnuovo Don Bosco are regarded as local specialities.

In flatter, central Piedmont there are three DOCs: Carema is a full-bodied red from Nebbiolo; Freisa di Chieri is a sparkling red made from Freisa; and Erbaluce di Caluso is a light white wine made from Erbaluce. A sweet passito version is made from shrivelled grapes.

Gabiano and Rubino di Cantavenna are two small but important areas in northern Alessandria. Both make a blend of Barbera and Grignolino, full-bodied reds with ageing potential. Grignolino is a grape unique to the provinces of Asti and Alessandria, producing red wines with a low colour concentration but distinct tannins. The best known is probably Grignolino d'Asti, but Grignolino del Monferrato Casalese, by Vercelli, is a worthy rival.

The most recent DOCs are Langhe and Piedmont, renowned for innovative viticulture and their balance of international and traditional grape varieties. Langhe covers almost the whole province of Cuneo, in the southwest of the region. It operates as a DOC *di ricaduta* ("relapsed") and includes all reds based on Nebbiolo or Dolcetto that cannot be included in other denominations. This more relaxed category permits different lengths of bottle ageing for Barolo or Barbaresco; less traditional maturation techniques; and experiments with non-traditional grapes in the region, such as Chardonnay, Sauvignon and Cabernet Sauvignon. In general, these are high-quality wines matured in small barrels, and play the same role in Piedmont as the "Super-Tuscans" in Tuscany.

Finally there is the Piemonte DOC, the denomination of all the smaller regions. It has to observe less stringent regulations than other DOCs and includes all the wines made from the region's myriad varieties. It also represents sparkling wines that do not qualify for the Asti DOCG.

Soil, climate and viticulture

Piedmont has a continental climate – the winters are cold and long and the summers hot and fairly wet. Vines are widely grown, but most densely planted in the southern band of hills that runs from the Ligurian border.

The best soils tend to have a high percentage of clay marl and calcareous matter – so thin, however, that vine-growing is almost the only feasible form of agriculture.

Grape-picking generally takes place from the end of September for the earliest varieties – such as Dolcetto, Chardonnay and Moscato – until the end of October for the latecomers, such as Nebbiolo, which ripens at the time of the first fog (*nebbie*) in the lowest parts of the region. The predominant form of cultivation is espalier with Guyot pruning and a density of up to 3,000 to 3,500 rootstocks per hectare. Experiments with greater densities and shorter vines are taking place, but the steep hills of the Langhe and Asti regions restrict the efficacy of these techniques.

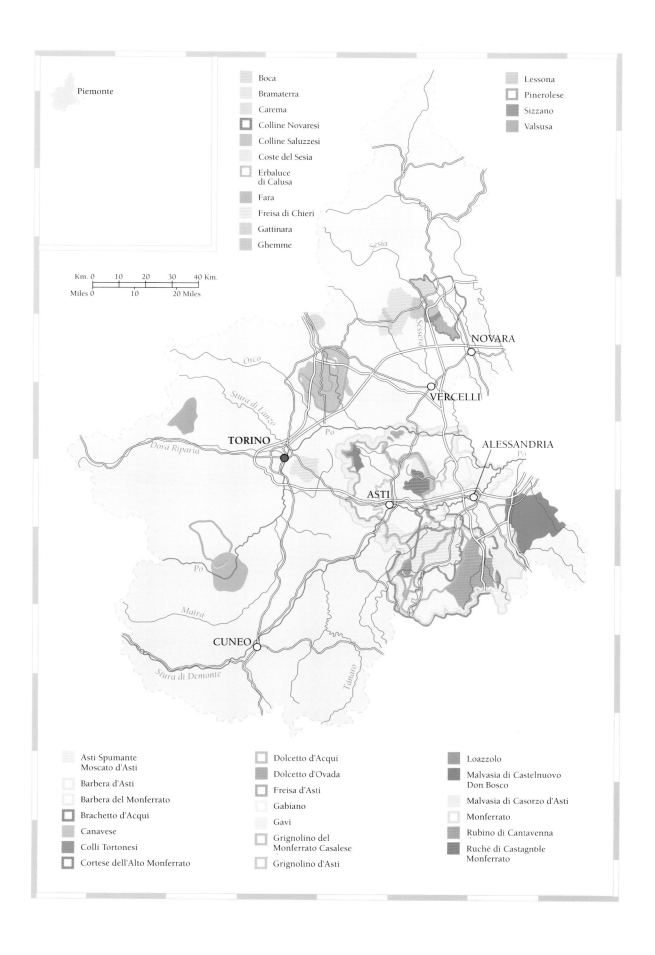

Piemonte

	Boca
	Bramaterra
	Carema
	Colline Novaresi
	Colline Saluzzesi
	Coste del Sesia
	Erbaluce di Calusa
	Fara
	Freisa di Chieri
	Gattinara
	Ghemme
	Lessona
	Pinerolese
	Sizzano
	Valsusa

Km. 0   10   20   30   40 Km.
Miles 0   10   20 Miles

NOVARA

VERCELLI

TORINO

ALESSANDRIA

ASTI

CUNEO

Orco

Stura di Lanzo

Dora Riparia

Po

Sesia

Sessera

Po

Po

Maira

Stura di Demonte

Tanaro

	Asti Spumante Moscato d'Asti
	Barbera d'Asti
	Barbera del Monferrato
	Brachetto d'Acqui
	Canavese
	Colli Tortonesi
	Cortese dell'Alto Monferrato
	Dolcetto d'Acqui
	Dolcetto d'Ovada
	Freisa d'Asti
	Gabiano
	Gavi
	Grignolino del Monferrato Casalese
	Grignolino d'Asti
	Loazzolo
	Malvasia di Castelnuovo Don Bosco
	Malvasia di Casorzo d'Asti
	Monferrato
	Rubino di Cantavenna
	Ruché di Castagnole Monferrato

Barbaresco

It may suffer slightly from living in the shadow of its more famous 'cousin', Barolo, but Barbaresco is a prestigious and exciting wine in its own right. This DOCG wine is also made from the Nebbiolo grape and its origins are contemporary with those of Barolo. It is aged for only two years before it goes on sale, one less than Barolo, or four years in the case of the rare and unusual Riserva. Annual production is between two and three million bottles.

Barbaresco's home is east of Alba and includes the districts of Neive, Treiso and of course Barbaresco. It first came to winemakers' attention at the beginning of the 19th century, when vineyards already covered over 40 per cent of the arable land. The man initially responsible for developing Barbaresco was Professor Domizio Cavazza, the first director of the School of Viticulture and Oenology in Alba. In 1894 he and a few friends set up the first

Below *The hilltop village of Neive overlooks some of the finest vineyards in Barbaresco and, indeed, Piedmont.*

cooperative in the region, the Cantina Sociale di Barbaresco. The wine they produced was fermented out so as to be completely dry, and aged in the cellars of the Castello di Barbaresco, owned by the professor.

Over the last few years this wine has achieved an international cult status, due mostly to the efforts of one winemaker – Angelo Gaja. The most important traditional Barbaresco vineyards, or "*crus*", are Basarin, Gallina and Santo Stefano in Neive, the vineyards of Montestefano, Martinenga, Montefico, Paglieri, Pora, Rabajà, Rio Sordo and Bricco Asili in Barbaresco, and those of Pajorè, Marcarini and Giacosa in Treiso.

Barbaresco's best vintages are the same as Barolo's and while the former has less body and greater elegance, only an expert on Langhe wines would be able to distinguish between the two.

Piemonte

Asti
Barbera d'Alba
Barbaresco
Barolo
Nebbiolo d'Alba
Roero

Km. 0   5   10 Km.
Miles 0   5 Miles

Tanaro

Asti

Monta

Canale

Nëive

Barbaresco

S. Stefano Belbo

Santa Vittoria d'Alba

● **ALBA**

BRA

Treiso

Diano d'Alba

La Morra

Barolo

Tanaro

Monforte d'Alba

Dogliani

Mondovi

Dolcetto d'Alba
Dolcetto delle Langhe Monregalesi
Dolcetto di Diano d'Alba
Dolcetto di Dogliani
Langhe

Notable producers

Bricco Asili, Alba (CN) The Ceretto brothers own vineyards in the most prestigious *crus* of the Langhe, producing wines sold under the labels Bricco Rocche, Bricco Asili, La Bernardina and Ceretto. Their Barbaresco Bricco Asili is a classic, stylish wine of great elegance. They also produce a range of excellent Barolos: Bricco Rocche di Castiglione Falletto, Brunate and Prapò di Serralunga.

Tenute Cisa Asinari dei Marchesi di Gresy, Barbaresco (CN) Situated in a splendid location in the valley of Martinenga in Barbaresco, this estate offers Barbaresco from various vineyards, distinguished by their elegance and pleasant drinking. The Gajun is the most structured, but the Camp Gros and Martinenga are also interesting.

Gaja, Barbaresco (CN) Angelo Gaja epitomises Italian winemaking to the rest of the world. Since the end of the 1960s, when he took over the reins of the family business with the help of oenologist Guido Rivella, he has striven relentlessly to achieve the highest quality, elevating his Barbaresco onto the world's top shelf of red wines. Today the French call him *le roi Gaja*, while in America he enjoys legendary status.

Following in the footsteps of his global success with Barbaresco Sorì Tildin, Sorì San Lorenzo and Costa Russi, Angelo Gaja has interests throughout the region (an excellent Barolo comes from the Sperss vineyard) as well as in Tuscany, Bolgheri and Montalcino.

Moccagatta, Barbaresco (CN) Some of the best Barbarescos of recent years are those produced by Franco and Sergio Minuto, under this label. Their wines are modern, with a firm body and structure and full of concentrated fruit aromas. The Barbaresco from the Bric Balin *cru* is a perfect example.

Albino Rocca, Barbaresco (CN) Rocca is a vine-grower who has completed a thorough renovation of his winery and vinification techniques. His wines are elegant and modern, full of intensity and long-lived. The Barbaresco of the Brich Ronchi and Vigneto Loreto vineyards is particularly impressive.

Bruno Rocca, Barbaresco (CN) The Barbaresco produced by Bruno Rocca reflects the typical characteristics of the local Nebbiolo grape. These wines possess a complex structure and striking elegance, and develop over time into refined selections, such as the Barbaresco Rabajà.

above *Angelo Gaja stepping out on the main street in Barbaresco. Gaja is both a remarkable ambassador for the wines of Piedmont and one of its finest producers.*

Fratelli Cigliuti, Neive (CN) Renato Cigliuti's wine benefits immeasurably from the location of the magnificent old vineyards of the *cru* Serra Boella, which produce grapes with abundant bouquet, alcohol and tannin: these qualities are the hallmark of Ciliguti's Barbaresco Serra Boella, Dolcetto d'Alba and Langhe Rosso Bricco Serra.

Bruno Giacosa, Neive (CN) Bruno Giacosa is a connoisseur of wines from the Langhe. His speciality is the Barbaresco, especially from the Santo Stefano vineyard. The Barolo Collina Rionda and Rocche di Castiglione Falletto are also striking.

Fratelli Giacosa, Neive (CN) Valerio and Silverio Giacosa own one of the largest winegrowing estates in the Langhe, producing over 600,000 bottles a year. The Barbaresco tops the list and their *cru*, Rio Sordo, has an intense aroma of spices and great consistency on the palate.

Paitin, Neive (CN) The Pasquero Elia family estate covers 15 hectares of vineyards between Alba and Neive – ten are on the splendid Serra Boella hill – and is famed for

its Barbaresco. The *cru*, Sorì Paitin, is a fascinating wine with a complex bouquet, a tangle of tannins and great balance.

Fiorenzo Nada, Treiso (CN) Bruno Nada produces an elegant and modern Barbaresco, rich in fruit and with a firm structure. But his best wine is the Langhe Rosso Seifile, made from Barbera grapes with 30 per cent Nebbiolo must. The wine combines an attractive aroma with great strength and a complex taste.

Pelissero, Treiso (CN) One of the Langhe estates to make considerable strides in quality. The Barbaresco from the Vanotu vineyard, one of the best appellations, is a perfect example, with spicy aromas on the nose and great breadth on the palate.

above *Cellaring is vital, for these wines require several years' bottle-ageing before the tough Nebbiolo tannins will soften.*

left *Pruning is performed mostly during the winter months, as here in Barbaresco. It can also be carried out later in spring and early summer, when it may be necessary to remove bunches of grapes in order to reduce yields even further.*

Barolo

When one thinks of a great red wine, powerful and full-bodied, ideal for long ageing, Barolo inevitably springs to mind. Barolo has its origins in the early 19th century, when a young French noblewoman, Giulia Vittorinin Colbert, married the Marchese Carlo Tancredi Falletti. They subsequently employed the French wine technologist Louis Oudart on the Marchesa Falletti's Barolo estates of Serralunga and La Morra. At the same time, the young Conte di Grinzane, Camillo Cavour, left the royal palace of Turin and turned his mind to the modernisation and rationalisation of agriculture on his estates. Turning his back on the sweet red wines which came from Langhe, Cavour planted new Pinot Noir vines and adapted the Nebbiolo variety to make a red wine in the French style. Crucially, he then enlisted Louis Oudart, and after a period of experimentation Barolo took on the characteristics which, to a great extent, it retains today.

below *The vivid contrast in these colours shows the importance of the aspect of individual vineyards. Those that receive the most sunlight are more highly valued.*

The Marchesa's wine proved overwhelmingly successful at the court of Carlo Alberto, a success which has continued without interruption from the era of Cavour and Victor Emmanuel II through to the present. But it was on the cusp of the 20th century that Barolo enjoyed its greatest international fame. The arrival of phylloxera in the 1920s, the economic crises of the 1930s and the Second World War sorely tested the tenacity of the vine-growers of the Langhe and led to certain sacrifices, but the DOC designation was achieved in 1966 and their subsequent progress has been slow but irresistible. Recognition as a DOCG in 1980 inspired an extraordinary decade for Barolo, which was studded by great years and the integration of a new wave of small producers alongside the great traditionalists. Barolo is once again the undisputed king of Italian wines, with its prestige now beyond question.

The "cru" of Barolo

To earn the DOCG designation, Barolo must be made exclusively from Nebbiolo grapes of the Lampia, Michet and Rosé sub-varieties, and must be aged for at least three years, or five in the case of Riserva. The yield of grapes must not exceed 8,000 kilos per hectare.

These Nebbiolo grapes are grown in various communes in the Langhe, with the finest and most traditional/ historical vineyards located mostly in six communes – in Barolo, the vineyard of Cannubi and Sarmassa; in La Morra, the Brunate and Cerequio vineyard; in Verduno, the Monvigliero vineyard; in Castiglione, the vineyards Falletto Rocche and Villero and Monprivato; in Monforte, those of Bussia Soprana, Bricco Cicala and Pianpolvere; and in Serralunga, the vineyards of Vigna Rionda, Ornato, Briccolina, Vigna Francia and Lazzarito.

Many of these commune names are combined on the label with the Barolo denomination, to emphasise the provenance of the grapes.

Barolo and Barbaresco – tradition and innovation

The most passionate debate on Italian wine in recent years has raged between producers of Barolo and Barbaresco. On one side stand the likes of Angelo Gaja and the modern winemakers, and on the opposite side are the traditional producers or "fathers of the country",

such as Bartolo Mascarello, Giovanni Conterno, Battista Rinaldi and Bruno Giacosa.

At the end of the 1970s the local industry suffered an image crisis, both on the domestic and international front, because the use of traditional methods had rendered its wines unfashionable. Producers would use large, ancient casks for maturation, following a long fermentation and maceration on the skins – and their wines soon became virtual archeological finds in the market place. One had to wait years before drinking them and the bottles had to be opened hours before the wine was served, in order to allow adequate oxygenation. One could only hope that the cork held true.

Vintages such as 1958, 1961 and 1964 produced a few unforgettable, complex, powerful wines, but for those used to the refined balance of a great Bordeaux, or the elegance and beauty of a great Burgundy, they were hard to appreciate. A school of young winemakers realised that while the regions of Barolo and Barbaresco were not in Pomerol and that the Nebbiolo grape was not a Pinot Noir or a Merlot, this should be turned to their advantage. Sensing the need for change, those on the leading edge – Angelo Gaja, Elio Altare, Domenico Clerico, Roberto Voerzio, Enrico Scavino and Luciano Sandrone – began experimenting with new methods, including a shorter maceration period and the use of smaller barrels. In a short space of time, these producers had revolutionised the style of their wines and rapidly won the support of critics and public alike.

A similar transformation had taken place ten years earlier in Bordeaux, when all the major producers decided to modernise. But in the Langhe, a very traditional region with a predominantly rural community, these new style Barbarescos and Barolos have unleashed endless debates and controversies. Barolo and Barbaresco now have their greatest ever following and command unprecedented prices, but – paradoxically – they also retain a devoted cult following. Today, both traditional and innovative producers are creating the finest wines ever to emerge from this region.

The lesson has evidently been salutary.

right *The village of Grinzane Cavour was home to the 19th century pioneer of Barolo – Conte di Grinzane, Camillo Cavour.*

Notable producers

Pio Cesare, Alba (CN)
Owns some of the best vineyards in Alba and produces a range of sophisticated modern wines, including Barolos from the Ornato di Serralunga, Barbaresco Bricco and a super Langhe Chardonnay Piodilei.

Marchesi di Barolo, Barolo (CN)
One of the best-known Piedmontese names, both in Italy and abroad, offering an enormous range of wines, from Dolcetto d'Alba to Gavi. Especially noteworthy are the prestigious Barolos, among them the Estate Vineyard, a softly structured wine with a long finish.

Bartolo Mascarello, Barolo (CN)
Bartolo Mascarello is acclaimed by enthusiasts on the lookout for a more traditional Barolo. Its wines are austere and marked by the incisiveness of tannins created by a long maceration – they acquire elegance and complexity over the years.

Giuseppe Rinaldi, Barolo (CN)
This producer owns vineyards in some of the best positions in the region, such as Cannubi San Lorenzo, Le Coste, Ravera and Brunate. The grapes are vinified and aged by traditional means (long maceration and large casks), leading to a fascinating range of Barolos.

Luciano Sandrone, Barolo (CN)
The legendary Barolo Cannubi Boschis of Luciano Sandrone is for many the quintessential modern style of Barolo. Sandrone draws the best from this variety, creating a structured wine, long-lived and rich in soft fruit flavours. The Barbera and the Dolcetto d'Alba are also recommended.

Azelia, Castiglione Falletto (CN)
Luigi and Lorella Scavino make an excellent range of reds which culminates in their Barolos: the Barolo, Barolo Bricco Fiasco and Barbera d'Alba Vigneto Punta. All are soft and rotund but not short of structure or longevity.

Paolo Scavino, Castiglione Falletto (CN)
Enrico Scavino has been a leading Barolo producer for years. Behind his success are his magnificent vines and genuine passion for excellence. The Barolos from the Cannubi, Bric del Fiasc and Rocche dell'Annunziata vineyards combine concentration and power with a sophisticated elegance. The sumptuous Barbera d'Alba Carati is another outstanding wine.

Vietti, Castiglione Falletto (CN)
One of the best expressions of the terroir of Castiglione Falletto, interpreted in the modern manner. A range of Barolos with few rivals, from Cru Lazzarito, Brunate, Castiglione and Vallero. Barbera d'Alba Scarrone, Dolcetto d'Alba Tre Vigne and Lazzarito are also excellent.

Elio Altare, La Morra (CN)
A few years ago, Robert Parker named Elio Altare as one of the ten winemakers of the year, and today he is widely recognised as the founder of a progressive school of winemaking. The Barolo 1983 was revolutionary and could be drunk with the ease of a great Burgundy. Other notable successes include the barrel-matured Langhe Arborina and Langhe Larigi (Nebbiolo and Barbera respectively).

Corino, La Morra (CN)
The brothers Giuliano and Renato Corino make concentrated Barberas and Barolos, full of colour and fruit. The Barbera d'Alba Vigna Pozzo is rich in ripe cherry and liquorice flavours, but in the best years the Barolo Vigna Giachini and Vigneto Rocche are outstanding.

Marcarini, La Morra (CN)
This historic enterprise, run by Luisa and Manuel Marchetti has 12 hectares of vineyards, *cru* Brunate, La Serra and Boschi di Berri. Elegant, long-lived Barolos are made from the first two, while the third, a 100 year-old vineyard of original rootstock, makes a fascinating Dolcetto d'Alba.

Mauro Molino, La Morra (CN)
For several years now, Mauro Molino has been making wine instead of selling his grapes and has been very successful, particularly abroad. His Barolo Vigna Conca and the striking Barbera d'Alba Vigna Gattere are superb.

Cordero di Montezemolo, La Morra (CN)
Positioned in the Monfalletto region of La Morra, the best location for Barolo, this historic winery is surrounded by 26 hectares of vines. It also has three hectares in the *cru* Villero at Castiglione Falletto, which provides the grapes for another Barolo, Enrico VI. All its wines are excellent, including the simple Dolcetto d'Alba.

Roberto Voerzio, La Morra (CN)
The rising star of the Barolo and on the cutting edge, Roberto produces wines with a modern outlook, drinkable between three and four years after the vintage. Helped by the grapes of the *crus* Cerequio and Brunate,

the bitter, harsh tannins typical of old Barolo are reduced, by limiting the period of contact between grape skins and the must, and by using barrels of French oak at maturation stage. The Brunate and Cerequio wines of the 1990s are probably his best yet, and an Italian response to the great Pinot Noirs of Burgundy. Vignaserra, made from Nebbiolo grapes and a sprinkling of Barbera, is a delicious barrel-matured red, as is the Barbera d'Alba Vignassa.

Gianfranco Alessandria, Monforte d'Alba (CN)
From four hectares of vineyards Gianfranco Alessandria makes some remarkable wines. His Barolo has a winning modern style, even in lesser years, and the Barbera d'Alba Vittoria is superlative.

Domenico Clerico, Monforte d'Alba (CN)
Domenico Clerico is a great "interpreter" of the wines of the Langhe hills. His Barolos from the *cru* Ciabot Mentin Ginestra and Pajana epitomise the new age, with an elegance and complexity owing to the fabulous blend of Nebbiolo, Barbera and Cabernet. A masterly ability to integrate modern oenological techniques with local traditional practices.

Poderi Aldo Conterno, Monforte d'Alba (CN)
Aldo Conterno now makes wines at Monforte in the region of Bussia, one of the historic *crus* of Barolo. These are decisive and unusual, partly innovative and partly traditional in style – striking a chord with lovers of traditional Barolos, with their tannins and long-ageing capacity, and those fascinated by elegant wines that may be drunk during the first years of their life. His Barolo Gran Bussia is made from the best grapes in his vineyards and only in the greatest vintages. The 1988 is a tremendous red which will stand undefeated for at least two decades. The complex bouquets and decisive flavours are bound to remind Barolo enthusiasts of Violante Sobrero or Battista Rinaldi from the early seventies.

Giacomo Conterno di Giovanni Conterno, Monforte d'Alba (CN)
The wines of Giovanni Conterno are uncompromising – they change for nobody. His Barolo Monfortino is one of the greatest traditional Italian wines and probably this family business's signature wine. One would be mad to drink it before it was ten years old: those most ready to drink now date to the early 1960s. Over 30 years in the bottle are needed to tame the rebellious tannins, which eventually harmonise with 14 per cent of alcohol, to transform the bouquets into splendid aromas of liquorice and withered roses. Barolo Cascina Francia follows in the traditional style, as does the Freisa delle Langhe – the simplest, which seems a fuller-bodied and higher-class red than similar styles now produced on a vast scale in Piedmont.

Conterno-Fantino, Monforte d'Alba (CN)
Consistently one of the best outfits in the Langhe. Diego Conterno take great care over their wines and Guido Fantino looks after the winery. This cooperation has led to the outstanding Barolo Sorì Ginestra, Cabernet and Langhe Rosso Monprà, made from Nebbiolo and Barbera grapes with a touch of Sauvignon.

Elio Grasso, Monforte d'Alba (CN)
Elio Grasso has a very personal style and a shiny, new and efficient cellar. His wines are distinguished by their structure, longevity and concentration: the Barolo of *cru* Ginestra Vigna Casa Matè and Gavarini Vigna Chiniera stand out.

Podere Rocche dei Manzoni, Monforte d'Alba (CN)
Valentino Migliorini has in the course of a few years restructured his vineyards and winery, producing a series of surprising wines: among them the Barolo Vigna Big and Vigna d'la Roul, as well as one of the best Italian sparkling wines, Valentino Brut Zero Riserva. The Barbera from Mosconi is also a serious contender.

Elvio Cogno, Novello (CN)
Run by Walter Fissore with the help of consultant oenologist Beppe Ca' Viola. Their range of wines are modern and fruity, and include a good Barbera and Dolcetto d'Alba, an interesting Langhe Rosso Montegrilli and a very promising Barolo Ravera.

above *Giovanni Conterno of the long-standing and traditional Cantina Giacomo Conterno, Monforte d'Alba. His finest wines come from the historic Cascina Francia vineyards.*

Fontanafredda, Serralunga d'Alba (CN)
This 100-year-old estate was presented to the Contessa Mirafiori by King Vittorio Emanuele II and is one of the most famous in the region. Its strongest wine is the Barolo from the vineyards of La Villa, La Delizia and Lazzarito. Also produces young-drinking Chardonnay and Gavi.

Vigna Rionda-Massolino, Serralunga d'Alba (CN)
This winery takes its name from an historical *cru* in the commune of Serralunga and produces excellent traditional wines. It offers two classic Barolos from Vigna Rionda and Parafada.

Fratelli Alessandria, Verduno (CN)
Verduno is famous for the voluptuous, rounded style of its Barolo and the *cru* Monvigliero is a perfect example. A ruby-coloured wine with a peppery taste and a strong bouquet of red fruits, it's rich in the mouth with a long after-taste. Verduno Pelaverga is an attractive red wine from the vineyard of the same name.

Alba and Roero

Roero Rosso is made predominantly from Nebbiolo grapes and was only awarded DOC status ten years ago. It represents a new development in winegrowing in Alba. Many producers (generally small in size) take a modern approach by using small casks for maturing in wood, without excessive ageing. Barbera d'Alba is among the more distinguished Barberas, although in the more prestigious districts of Alba the most favourably exposed vineyards tend to be reserved for the great Nebbiolo, Barolo and Barbaresco varieties. The Dolcetto d'Alba is a Piedmont red riding the crest of a wave. Besides its familiar name, it owes its success to its attractive characteristics such as low tannin and acidity, and is ready after only a few months' maturation.

A few kilometres south of Alba, the small commune of Diano d'Alba produces an exciting Dolcetto that boasts important structure and impressive alcoholic strength. The Dolcetto of Dogliani, however, is probably the most traditional variety – its reputation enlarged by the fact that one of its producers was Luigi Einaudi, the president of the Italian Republic after the Second World War.

Two other Dolcetto wines are produced in Alba. The first is Langhe Dolcetto, which is made throughout the region and is typical of a basic, drinkable style. The other is Langhe Monregalesi, which has a less imposing structure and originates near Mondovi, the furthest vinous outpost in the region.

The renaissance of Alba wines is reflected in the large number sold with the Langhe DOC. Many of these are extremely innovative by local standards. Chardonnay or Cabernet Sauvignon are fermented or matured in small casks and wines of traditional varieties, such as Nebbiolo and Barbera, are vinified on their own, or alongside the non-native Cabernet Sauvignon, Syrah and Merlot. When international grapes are used, they are sold under the Langhe Rosso label.

Naturally, the aim of this recent DOC, which tends to emphasise terroir rather than grape variety, is to create production regulations for all those wines which first developed experimentally but are now famous and/or highly prized abroad. They include: Darmagi, Chardonnay Gaia & Rey and Sauvignon Alteni di Brassica from Angelo Gaja, Arte from Domenico Clerico, Arborina and Larigi from Elio Altare, and Favot and Bussiador from Aldo Conterno. Of course Alba still produces traditional regional wines such as Barolo and Barbaresco, but they should not be confused with the newcomers.

above *Alba and its environs are home to a range of innovative wines bearing the Langhe, Roero and Alba labels. Traditional grapes such as Nebbiolo, Barbera and Dolcetto feature alongside non-native varieties like Chardonnay, Cabernet Sauvignon and Merlot.*

The town of Alba lies in the heart of the hilly Langhe region, the pinnacle of Piedmontese winemaking. This ancient city and regional capital dates back to Roman times. Like Beaune in the Côte d'Or, a number of wine companies have set up shop in the town, which is a thriving commercial centre and has earned a reputation for its nut-enriched chocolate, chocolate cream – *gianduja* – and white truffles.

But wine is the lifeblood of the local economy. Wines whose DOCs include the names Alba or Roero are mostly reds, based on Nebbiolo, Dolcetto and Barbera. The only white grape variety in Roero is Arneis, which gives its name to a light, white, slightly aromatic wine that's become a marketing sensation in these parts. The rest is a sea of reds, usually noble.

Notable producers

Matteo Correggia, Canale (CN) This winemaker has been one of Piedmont's leading producers and oenologists for several years. Although he owns no vineyards in Barolo or Barbaresco, he produces some extraordinary wines, such as Barbera d'Alba Marun and Nebbiolo d'Alba La Valle dei Preti, which benefit from painstaking methods of cultivation. His modern, innovative wines are concentrated and full of colour and fruity aromas. They result from a relentless selection of grapes in the vineyard and winegrowing techniques, which would seem practically revolutionary to a traditional Piedmontese producer: vinification involves rapid maceration of the grapes, made possible by new equipment, and the use of small casks of new French oak. The outstanding quality of these wines is due to the Barbera and Nebbiolo grapes. Great value for money, too.

Malvirà, Canale (CN) Massimo and Roberto Damonte are key figures in the Roero renaissance. Their range of their wines is varied and of a high quality. Their quality whites include Langhe Bianco Tre Uve, Roero Arneis and *cru* Renesio, and the reds include Roero and the outstanding Roero Superiore, in a class of its own.

Quinto Chionetti & Figlio, Dogliani (CN) Today, Dogliani is considered one of the emerging terroirs in Piedmont, but winegrower Quinto Chionetti has long produced a firm, vigorous Dolcetto di Dogliani with concentrations of fruity aromas and elegance, made from grapes cultivated in his Briccolero and San Luigi vineyards.

Poderi Luigi Einaudi, Dogliani (CN) This historic winery – once owned by Luigi Einaudi, the second president of the Italian Republic – has undergone a complete reconstruction, and recently acquired part of the famous Cannubi vineyard in Barolo. The excellent Dolcetto di Dogliani I Filari still stands out in an impressive range of wines.

Fratelli Pecchenino, Dogliani (CN) Attilio and Orlando Pecchenino are among the young producers who have changed the face of winemaking in Roero. Their excellent Dolcettos, such as the Sirì d'Yermu, are the result of careful selection in the vineyard. Their Chardonnay Vigna Maestro and Langhe Rosso La Castella are also good.

San Fereolo, Dogliani (CN) Nicoletta Bocca has entrusted the fate of her winery to some of the best oenologists in Piedmont: Federico Curtaz and agronomist and oenologist Beppe Ca' Viola. The results are extremely modern wines, warm and concentrated, while the Dolcetto di Dogliani San Fereolo is a beauty.

San Romano, Dogliani (CN) Bruno Chionetti has reshaped this Dogliani-based winery and transformed it into a model estate. A firm believer in the great potential of Dolcetto di Dogliani, he produces a spectacular Vigna del Pilone, a wine with the concentration and fascination of a great Merlot.

Giovanni Battista Gillardi, Farigliano (CN) This small winery only produces 25,000 bottles per year, but the wines made by Giovanni's son Giaculin are the result of careful methods of cultivation. Besides the Dolcetto di Dogliani Cursalet and Vigneto Maestra there is also a very successful Syrah, curiously named Harys, which has plenty of spice and fruity aromas.

Il Colombo – Barone Riccati, Mondovì (CN) A respected Professor of Philosophy at the University of Turin, Carlo Riccati has an undying passion for viticulture, which he shares with his wife Adriana. Their wines, produced exclusively from Dolcetto grapes, are at the top of the range of Langhe Monregalesi wines. The *cru* Il Colombo is simply out of this world.

Ca' Viola, Montelupo Albese (CN) Oenologist Beppe Caviola is one of the most famous names in Piedmontese wine. Having begun his career in a laboratory for oenological research, he became consultant winemaker to several wineries in the region, and now also produces wines in his own winery. His Dolcetto d'Alba Barturot and the Langhe Rosso Bric du Luv are two mini-masterpieces.

His expert hand can also be detected in wines produced by Angelo Rocca, Eraldo Viberti, Gian Alessandria and, as if that were not enough, he also works with Villa Sparina in Gavi and Luigi Einaudi in Dogliani. His approach is based on low yields per hectare, thinning out the grapes, the recuperation of the oldest vines, shorter maceration times and the use of casks made from new oak. He shares the same philosophy as the new wave producers of Barolo in the Langhe region, who have found in Caviola an outstanding consultant.

below *Matteo Correggia topping up barrels in his cellar in Canale. With his minute attention to detail, Correggia has earned a reputation for outstanding and innovative wines that offer remarkable value for money.*

Asti and Barbera d'Asti

above *Despite its worldwide renown for light, grapy sparkling wines, the Asti area produces an array of styles. These vineyards are planted with a local favourite, the Freisa variety.*

Vineyards gently trace the outline of the rolling hills of Asti, creating an impressive landscape stretching for kilometre after kilometre from Acqui Terme and Canelli, almost to the cities of Asti and Alba. This patchwork of green, concentric lines conceals a white, arid soil for much of the year, and which turns to mud with the first rains.

This is the land of liquid gold, of one of the greatest and most famous Italian wines: Asti. Strangely enough, nearly 80 per cent of Asti – almost 500,000 hectolitres per year – is exported. While the Germans and Americans are big enthusiasts, many still think of it as a sweet sparkling wine drunk at Christmas with panettone, or a bottle won at the fairground.

This sweet-tasting, aromatic sparkling wine is intrinsically tied to the culture and people of southern Piedmont. The white Moscato di Canelli was already being grown throughout the region in the early 16th century, producing a cloudy, sweet, semi-sparkling Moscato. This had to be drunk before the spring following the grape harvest, for fear that it might start fermenting again.

In the centuries that followed, early attempts at bottling wines that were too young and lively caused an endless series of explosions, similar to those which occurred in Champagne or the Rheingau. Renewed fermentation and the consequent formation of carbon dioxide built up incredible pressure inside fragile glass bottles. Villagers in Asti tried instead to filter the must through bags made of hemp and to decant their Moscato wine several times, as soon as it started to ferment again. But the wine never remained stable.

The situation changed in 1865 with the arrival of Carlo Gancia, a great technician. He introduced avant-garde technologies which enabled Asti's winemakers to produce a sweet, stable and clear semi-sparkling wine using the Champagne method, while preserving all the characteristics of fragrance and aroma that distinguish the Moscato grape. Thus Asti Spumante was born, under the name Moscato Champagne. The system used by Gancia was based on perfect filtration of the must and patient, repeated filtrations carried out after every secondary fermentation, however small.

Success was such that after a few years many other wineries in the region, from Cinzano to Contratto, from Cora to Martini & Rossi, from Bosca to Riccadonna, began to produce this fascinating sparkling wine.

Today, Asti is synonymous with Italian wine, and enjoys such a high international profile that a DOCG has been awarded. However, there is also a less 'technological' non-sparkling version, even more steeped in local tradition. The Moscato d'Asti, or Moscato naturale d'Asti, is a semi-sparkling version of Asti; a very light white wine with barely 5.5 per cent alcohol, it's intensely sweet and fragrant and available only from the medium-to-small wineries.

Completing the range of sweet, aromatic wines from this corner of Piedmont are Brachetto d'Acqui, Malvasia Rossa di Casorzo, Malvasia di Castelnuovo Don Bosco, and Loazzolo. The first is a sweet sparkling red with delicate aromas of fruits of the forest and roses. A recently-awarded DOCG has significantly improved its quality, but has also raised its price. Made from Brachetto grapes, this variety resembles a red Moscato, full of fragrance. The sparkling version, complete with the champagne-style cork, is more elaborate than the ordinary semi-sparkling, which is more traditional and 'rustic'.

The next two wines are semi-sparkling reds, but they are very difficult to locate outside the region: Malvasia di Casorzo d'Asti and Castelnuovo Don Bosco are produced in the province of Asti, though the latter is occasionally found in Alessandria. These reds are very similar and somewhat reminiscent of Brachetto d'Acqui, albeit in a slightly less fragrant form.

Loazzolo is a different proposition. A white wine produced from Moscato grapes and named after the town of Loazzolo, this is distinct from other Piedmontese Moscatos as it's a still wine. The best versions of Loazzolo are produced from partially withered grapes, giving a succulent dessert wine with plenty of fragrance and complexity.

Barbera d'Asti

Asti's extensive terrain offers more than just a huge Moscato harvest. In recent years a number of wineries have been making strides towards quality cultivation, notably with Barbera d'Asti, a well-structured red. This trend began 15 years ago, when a visionary winemaker, Giacomo Bologna, realised that lower yields from the best vineyards could produce excellent wine, which could be matured in small casks. The result was wines such as Bricco dell'Uccellone, Bricco della Bigotta and Ai Suma, fabulous wines made from Barbera grapes. The late Bologna understood the basic characteristics of Barbera, in particular the high level

below *Tending to Barbera vines at Casorzo. During the spring months vines are tied up in order to be trained correctly.*

of fixed acidity, high concentration of polyphenols and early ripening when compared with Nebbiolo. His intervention paved the way to international success for Barbera d'Asti wines.

Giacomo Bologna may have pioneered this movement, but many since have flourished in his wake: wineries such as Prunotto, Michele Chiarlo, Coppo, Bava, Vietti, Boffa and Scarpa, and winemakers of the calibre of Angelo Sonvico of Cascina La Barbatella, Franco Martinetti, Delfina Quattrocolo of Tenuta La Tenaglia, and Franco and Mario Scrimaglio.

The Barbera d'Astis of the past, often semi-sparkling and lacking structure, have been transformed. But there is still frustration in Italy, because the DOC does not provide clear distinctions to help the consumer identify various wines. Everything is termed "Barbera d'Asti", or, at best, "Barbera d'Asti Superiore". A well-intended DOC Piemonte classification – treated as a basic appellation – has only succeeded in fudging the issue: imagine if the producers of *premiers crus* in the Haut-Médoc were obliged to use only the Bordeaux AOC and not the names of the communes. This paradox could only exist in Italy.

right *Huge pressure tanks (autoclavi) in the cellars of Martini and Rossi. These are used in the production of Asti Spumante.*

Notable producers

Prunotto, Alba (CN) This company is a century old and has a long and distinguished tradition. For decades it has produced great Barolo wines from *cru* Cannubi and *cru* Bussia Soprana, as well as a spectacular Barbaresco from the Montestefano vineyard. The star creation of this winery (now owned by Antinori) is Barbera d'Asti Costamiole, an outstanding, well-structured wine.

Michele Chiarlo, Calamandrana (AT) From Gavi to Barolo Cannubi, there are no wines of Langhe or Asti which do not appear in the catalogue of this prestigious company. The Moscato d'Asti Nivole and Barbera d'Asti Superiore la Court are superb.

Contratto, Canelli (AT) This ancient house, owned by the Bocchino family, has made a brilliant comeback and offers fine Asti and Langhe wines, including some great spumanti, including the exceptional Asti de Miranda Metodo Classico.

Coppo, Canelli (AT) The Coppo family makes some of the most interesting Barbera d'Asti in barriques, with grapes from single vineyards, such as Camp du Rouss and Pomorosso. They also produce some excellent sparkling white wines.

Gancia, Canelli (AT) With an output of 15 million bottles a year, Gancia is one of the most famous Italian sparkling wine producers. Besides an excellent Asti Atto Primo, it also produces the Brut Mon Grande Cuvée Riserva Metodo Classico.

La Spinetta, Castagnole Lanze (AT) Giorgio Rivetti is one of the most important people in Piedmontese wine. At the end of the 1980s he attracted popular and critical acclaim with his exceptional Moscato d'Asti, placing him among the best producers in the region.

However, this eclectic, passionate winemaker did not want to rest on his Moscato laurels. His desire to make great

wine saw Giorgio Rivetti become a key force behind Piedmont's renaissance in the 1990s, creating a host of unforgettable wines, such as Monferrato Rosso Pin. Made from Nebbiolo, Cabernet Sauvignon and Barbera, and matured in barrels of new oak, it boasts great depth and strength. Today, the company also owns vineyards in Neive in the Barbaresco region, where it produces a fascinating Barbera d'Alba and a Barbaresco from the Gallina vineyard.

Caudrina – Romano Dogliotti, Castiglione Tinella (CN) Romano Dogliotti is a specialist with the Moscato grape and makes an excellent trio of wines: Moscato d'Asti La Caudrina and La Galeisa, and the hugely aromatic Asti Spumante La Selvatica.

Paolo Saracco, Castiglione Tinella (CN) Paolo Saracco is renowned in the Asti region for his great Moscati d'Asti wines, and innovative whites such as the Langhe Bianco Graffagno, made from Riesling, Chardonnay and Sauvignon grapes.

Martini & Rossi, Chieri (TO) As well as the most famous vermouth in the world, Martini also makes an excellent range of spumanti. Pick of the bunch are Asti and the wines produced under the Montelera label, using the *metodo classico*, ranging from Brut to Riserva.

Bava, Cocconato d'Asti (AT) This large, famous winery has built a solid reputation on its wide range of *vini di territorio*, such as the Barbera d'Asti Stradivario, and on the spumanti produced under the Giulio Cocchi label.

Forteto della Luja, Loazzolo (AT) In a region known for its spumanti and semi-sparkling wines, Giancarlo Scaglione delights with the elegance and fruity concentration of his Loazzolo Piasa Rischei, produced from late-harvested Moscato grapes, and Brachetto Pian dei Sogni. Scaglione is without doubt the master of Loazzolo, and the driving force behind the clamour for a DOC – his years of fighting for one finally paid off.

Cascina La Barbatella, Nizza Monferrato (AT) Angelo Sonvico specialises in Barbera d'Asti and offers two selections from the *crus* La Vigna dell'Angelo and La Vigna di Sonvico: these are wines of breathtaking complexity and among the best in the region.

Franco and Mario Scrimaglio, Nizza Monferrato (AT) This traditional, family-run Asti winery is distinguished by its continuous research and development of Barbera d'Asti. The wines from the *crus* Bricco San Ippolito, Vigneto Roccanivo and Croutin are impressive.

Braida, Rocchetta Tanaro (AT) In the 1970s the Bologna family launched the Asti revival with the *cru* Bricco dell'Uccellone. With Giacomo Bologna at the helm, the Bricco dell' Uccellone was followed by other excellent wines, such as Bricco della Bigotta and Ai Suma (which means 'we are' in Piedmontese dialect). Today these rank among the supreme Piedmontese wines.

Piero Gatti, San Stefano Belbo (CN) From just under four hectares of vineyards Piero Gatti produces three sweet wines with plentiful aroma and fragrance, a perfect expression of the terroir. Piemonte Moscato

above *Barbera vines to the north of the Asti region. Barbera d'Asti has been transformed in recent years.*

is fragrant and appley, and the Langhe Freisa La Violetta is fruity and sweet. There is also a decent Piedmont Brachetto.

Tenuta La Tenaglia, Serralunga di Crea (AL) One of the leading wineries in the region, offering some excellent Barbera d'Asti such as Emozioni and Selezione Bricco Crea, and Paradiso, an unusual Syrah of great breadth.

Cinzano, San Vittoria d' Alba (CN) Cinzano is the oldest winery in Piedmont, and now produces 30 million bottles a year. On first-name terms with the rest of the world for its excellent vermouth and its sweet spumanti, Asti in primis and Asti metodo classico.

Franco M Martinetti, (Calliano, Asti) The Barbera d'Asti Superiore Montruc produced by Franco Martinetti is an exquisitely refined wine with a substantial, rich bouquet. It's reminiscent of Sul Bric, made from a blend of Barbera and Cabernet and matured in small barrels.

Monferrato and Gavi

The southeastern parts of the region slope downwards towards the plains, where the hills are more rolling and the landscape less rugged than in the Langhe and most of the Asti wine region. The two most famous districts in the southeast are Monferrato and Gavi, the latter having recently been awarded DOCG status. Monferrato mostly produces red wines, predominantly from the central-northern part of the province of Alessandria, where Barbera, Grignolino, Freisa and Cortese, the white grape variety, are most prevalent.

As well as the grape-attributed DOCs, it is also possible to find some Monferrato Bianco and Monferrato Rosso, usually the result of a different style of vinification. The region also includes the sudsidiary appellation, Monferrato Casalese, looking after wines from the southernmost district, near the town of Casale

below Winter vines in Gavi DOCG, to the south of Piedmont. Here, the influences of coastal Liguria are stronger – hence the prominence of light, crisp wines.

Monferrato. The wines of this vast area are, without exception, easier to drink and less complex than those produced elsewhere in Piedmont. It's not unusual to find semi-sparkling Cortese or Barbera accompanying much of the region's tasty cuisine.

Gavi is situated further to the south of Piedmont, close to Liguria. The town, which has given its name to the DOCG, used to be part of the Republic of Genoa. Its cultural, gastronomic and oenological traditions are more tied to Liguria than Piedmont, which would explain the preference for fruity, light white wines made from Cortese grapes. Gavi, or Cortese di Gavi, is the only dry white wine of significance in Piedmont. The production zone includes 13 communes in the province of Alessandria, chiefly those of Gavi, Novi Ligure, Serravalle Scrivia and Arquata Scrivia.

Notable producers

Liedholm, Cuccaro (AL) Carlo Liedholm's winery offers a rigorous, clean interpretation of wines in the Monferrina tradition, Barbera d'Asti and Grignolino del Monferrato Casalese. The Rosso della Boemia is also excellent.

Nicola Bergaglio, Gavi (AL) Gianluigi Bergaglio's wines are produced in a rather traditional style. His Gavi di Gavi Minaia is very popular, its good acidity and firm structure making this a complex wine with good ageing qualities.

Gian Piero Broglia, Gavi (AL) Gian Piero Broglia's wine estate of some 73 hectares is an historic name in Gavi wines, produced here in many versions. The Selezione Bruno Broglia and the Spumante Extra Brut are worthy of note.

La Giustiniana, Gavi (AL) With its state-of-the-art winery, La Giustiniana makes two notable versions of this famous white – one using grapes from the Vigneto Centurionetta and the other with those from the Vigneto Montessora. There are also two notable reds: Brachetto d'Acqui Contero and Dolcetto d'Acqui Contero.

La Scolca, Gavi (AL) Gavi di Gavi Etichetta Nera from Giorgio Soldati's winery is one of the most sought-after Italian white wines of the last 20 years. The company also produces excellent Gavi Spumante metodo classico.

Villa Sparina, Gavi (AL) Specialising in Gavi wines, the Moccagatta family is transforming this famous company into a real experimental laboratory, with the advice of oenologist Ca' Viola and agronomist Curtaz.

Abbazia di Valle Chiara, Lerma (AL) The famous Italian actress Ornella Mutti makes a small range of excellent *vini da tavola* here, in collaboration with winemaker Elisabetta Currado. Top of the bill are an outsanding Dolcetto di Ovada and the red Due Donne made from Dolcetto, Lancillotta and Barbera grapes.

Banfi Vini, Strevi (AL) This Piedmont-based wine estate of the famous Montalcino cantina offers an excellent range of wines from Asti and Alessandria. Gavi Principessa Gavia is absolutely outstanding, one of the best interpretations of this wine. Other distinguished wines include the Bracchetto d'Acqui Spumante, Moscato d'Asti and Dolcetto d'Acqui Argusto.

Bricco Mondalino, Vignale Monferrato (AL) Mauro Gaudio is responsible for a quintessential version of the rare and very distinctive Grignolino del Monferrato Casalese. This is a wine made from slightly overripe grapes, with aromas of red fruit, a firm structure and a typical – slightly bitter – aftertaste. The good, rich body is sound enough to marshal the tannins.

above *Cortese vines near Gavi. Gavi, made from the Cortese grape, is one of the very few significant dry white wines produced in Piedmont.*

Novara and the Vercelli Hills

above *Rice fields are as important to the local Vercelli economy as vineyards. These fields in the Po flatlands produce some of the finest rice in the world.*

Probably the least-known region of Piedmont stretches across the provinces of Vercelli and Novara. The area has a decidedly Nordic and continental climate. Almost all of the wines produced here are generally red and very rough during the first years of their life, and require long periods of bottle ageing.

The most famous is Vercelli's Gattinara, a DOCG since 1990. Gattinara is made from Spanna grapes – the local name for Nebbiolo – with up to 14 per cent Vespolina and Bonarda di Gattinara, from the vineyards around the town of Gattinara. Aged for at least three years, or four in the case of the Riserva, this is best left in the cellar for another two or three. The wine owes its reputation to an imposing longevity, drawn from the large quantity of tannins (the essence of Nebbiolo) and the high acidity, which is greater than that of its Langhe cousins, Barolo and Barbaresco. Its more dilute colour is typical of the northern wines.

Ghemme is produced in the province of Novara. It is also a DOCG, very similar to the Gattinara and with even greater longevity. Again, Spanna grapes provide the backbone, with additions of Vespolina (ten to 30 per cent) and Bonarda Novarese (up to 15 per cent). Ghemme is initially aged for at least four years, but any residual astringency will decrease with a few more years in the winery.

There are numerous DOC wines in Novara and Vercelli, produced from Spanna grapes topped up with varying amounts of Vespolina, Croatina and Bonarda Novarese. Their styles are very similar, but each wine is named after the place of production: thus, there are Boca, Fara and Sizzano wines in the Novarese region, and Bramaterra and Lessona in Vercelli. These are all reds with firm body, but are decidedly less enduring than Gattinara and Ghemme.

Finally, the DOC Colline Novaresi is a recent creation, producing wines which are usually less complex and less concentrated. They are made in the region of Novara, in the district of Borgomanero and as far as the shores of the beautiful Lake Maggiore.

Notable producers

Antoniolo, Gattinara (VC) Rosanna Antoniolo and her children Lorella and Alberto produce some of the best Gattinara wines. The *cru* Vigneto Osso San Grato is a perfect example of the Vercellese Nebbiolo: an austere wine with a firm body and rich in tannin, it has a bouquet of raspberries and currants, with complex mineral traces.

Nervi, Gattinara (VC) Giorgio Agliata and Carla Ferrero make around 90,000 bottles of red wine a year, including some outstanding Gattinaras. That from the Molsino vineyard is appreciated for its ruby colour and orange reflections, its spicy fragrance and tannic structure. Spanna Coste della Sesia is also recommended.

Giancarlo Travaglini, Gattinara (VC) Giancarlo Travaglini has promoted this noble, austere Piedmont wine worldwide. He has developed his wines over the years, reflected in a very sophisticated Gattinara and Riserva Numerata, which combine power and a rich bouquet.

Antichi Vigneti di Cantalupo, Ghemme (NO) Alberto Arlunno is the most convincing producer of Ghemme, whose potential he has exploited to the full, creating various versions. The best is Collis Breclemae, aged for a long time, which convinces with its harmonious structure, fine tannic flavour and persistent aromatic finish.

Sella, Lessona (VC) This winery is a real reference point, with two typical geographical wines – Lessona and Bramaterra, which bear the hallmark of consultant oenologist Giancarlo Scaglione. Lessona della Selezione San Sebastiano allo Zoppo is recommended, a powerful and austere wine with a fully developed character.

right *The cellar belonging to Giancarlo Travaglini in Gattinara, producer of sophisticated, austere wines.*

Lombardy

Raethic wines produced around Valtellina and Lake Garda were widely known in Roman times, but this region has an even older vinous imprint. Today, the province of Pavia shows the quality bias of the Ligurians, who were influenced by Greek viticulture in the south of France: their vines were pruned and grafted and grown as saplings or, if the ground was too moist, supported higher by stakes. The Etruscans, meanwhile, favoured quantity.

Lombardy's main market is Milan. In medieval times the proximity of such an important marketplace encouraged winemakers to resume cultivation after the most damaging periods of invasion, and by the 14th century the Milanese were quaffing approximately 30,000 hectolitres of wine a year. Several centuries of success were then followed in the 19th century by oidium wilt, peronospora and phylloxera, and many areas never recovered. But winegrowing in the best regions has always found the strength to survive.

above *Steep, terraced Valtellina vineyards just below the Santuario della Sassella. These are some of Italy's most northern Nebbiolo vines.*

below *The supply of high quality rice has always been as important as wine to the people of Lombardy, especially the Milanese.*

Lombardy wines and wine regions

Lombardy is a large, important and complex Italian wine region. Its annual production is about 1.5 million hecto-litres. Several different sub-regions follow the traditions inherited from the many conquering tribes. Thus, for instance, the sizeable region of Oltrepò Pavese, known for its sparkling wines – as well as some fine whites and reds – was to a great extent ruled by Savoy, and has similarities with Monferrato and Asti. Valtellina, with its Chiavennasca

(Nebbiolo) grapes, shares many of the traditions of northern Piedmont. The wines from around Brescia and Bergamo have a likeness with those of Verona and Trento.

There is one region, however, that stands out from the rest. Franciacorta, best known for spumante wines and which was awarded its DOCG in 1995, is distinguished by its modern entrepreneurial spirit. Also on the ascent are wines from the west bank of Garda: Garda Classico DOC. In the area of Mantua are Lambrusco Mantovano and Garda Colli Mantovani, an autonomous DOC. The lively reds are made from Rondinella, Merlot and Cabernet, and whites from Tuscan Trebbiano, Garganega and other local white varieties. There is also a wide range of varietal wines.

The region of Lugana stands up proudly. It may have built its fortune on a more "noble" variety of Trebbiano, but it is now recognised for its *vini da tavola* made from international grape varieties. Some of the finer Cabernet and Merlot wines come from the heights of the Bergamo Pre-Alps in Valcalepio, a region which is also producing some good Pinot and Chardonnay. And there are signs of the revival of a valuable sweet passito, Moscato di Scanzo.

The Bresciano region has many "imported" wine traditions, adapted to suit many small DOCs. Among the whites are Capriano del Colle Trebbiano, and San Martino della Battaglia from Tocai Friulano grapes. The reds include Botticino, Capriano del Colle Rosso and Cellatica, made with a blend of Barbera, Schiava Gentile and Marzemino, with additions of Sangiovese for Botticino and Capriano (in place of Schiava) and Incrocio Terzi for Cellatica.

Lombardo-Piemontese Barbera, Schiava and Marzemino Trentini, and Sangiovese Romagnolo are quite rustic, medium-bodied reds – showing little relation to their grape varieties. The only Milanese DOC among these wines is the San Colombano, a traditional red wine made from Croatina, Barbera and Uva Rara.

Soil, climate and viticulture

Lombardy is a quilt of mountains, hills and plains, with vineyards concentrated around the higher parts of Oltrepò Pavese, Franciacorta and half of Valtellina. The shores of Lake Garda have been vine-friendly for thousands of years.

Lombardy is positioned in the centre of the Alpine crescent and is influenced by a variety of microclimates. In the Alpine regions, such as Valtellina, the vines cling to terraces at an altitude of some 600 metres. But as the landscape changes, from the hills of the Pre-Alps through

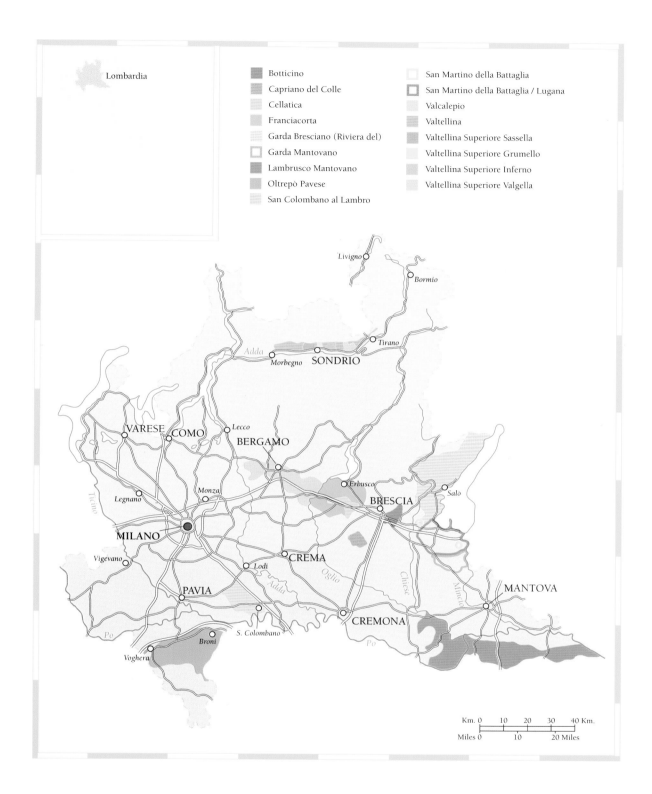

Lombardia

- ▉ Botticino
- ▉ Capriano del Colle
- ▉ Cellatica
- ▉ Franciacorta
- ▉ Garda Bresciano (Riviera del)
- ▢ Garda Mantovano
- ▉ Lambrusco Mantovano
- ▉ Oltrepò Pavese
- ▉ San Colombano al Lambro
- ▢ San Martino della Battaglia
- ▣ San Martino della Battaglia / Lugana
- ▉ Valcalepio
- ▉ Valtellina
- ▉ Valtellina Superiore Sassella
- ▉ Valtellina Superiore Grumello
- ▉ Valtellina Superiore Inferno
- ▉ Valtellina Superiore Valgella

to the valleys of the great Italian lakes, the conditions become temperate and, once on the lower flood plain of the river Po, continental. Here there are wide variations in temperature between winter and summer.

In Oltrepò the vines are trained as espaliers, or on the single or multiple Guyot system, while in Bresciano and Bergamasca vinegrowers opt for Trento pergola and Sylvoz methods. Franciacorta has a minimum planting density of 3,300 rootstocks and a maximum yield of 10,000 kilograms per hectare. Most recent plantings have been denser, on the Guyot method, as used on the terraces of Valtellina.

Oltrepò Pavese

Oltrepò Pavese is possibly the most traditional winegrowing region in Lombardy where, for several centuries, the House of Savoy ruled supreme. This ensured a close relationship between the Pavese wine production and that of Monferrato, Colli Tortonesi and Astigiano – their main wines are similar and the vines grown are practically the same. There is even an element of continuity and similarity in the tradition of sparkling wine. Production is widespread across this vast area, which continues as far as Colli Piacentini and includes a large part of Emilia.

Twenty wines have been nominated to the Oltrepò Pavese DOC, and divide into the traditional and the innovative. The former includes: Rosso, Rosso Riserva, Rosato, Buttafuoco and Sangue di Giuda (or Judas's Blood, made from a traditional blend of Barbera, Bonarda – aka Croatina – and Uva Rara), as well as Barbera and Bonarda. Among the whites, Moscato and Malvasia almost always occur in sweet and sparkling versions, and on occasions Cortese.

The second group consists of spumante wines and those made from non-native grapes: Cabernet Sauvignon and Pinot Nero, often matured in small barrels, represent the reds, with the whites numbering Chardonnay, Sauvignon, Pinot Nero, Riesling Italico and Riesling Renano. Finally, there is spumante, made by the traditional method or fermented in an autoclave (a method invented in Italy), which uses Pinot Nero vinified as a white, with possible additions of up to 30 per cent Pinot Bianco, Pinot Grigio or Chardonnay. Of course, this abundance of markedly different grape varieties invites different interpretations on the part of the region's producers. An Oltrepò Pavese Bonarda might be a sparkling red to accompany a Varzi salami, or it might be an imposing red, matured in small barrels and ideal with a saddle of veal alla Orloff.

Innovation and ingenuity are commonplace in this part of Lombardy, but Oltrepò is still regarded as a reservoir of acceptable wines, where less attention is paid to the quality of production than to the size of the yield. It is the source of supply for the great Piedmontese wineries, which retain an exclusive grip on this homeland of the Italian Pinot Nero. According to the statistics, more hectares of this variety are grown here than in any other Italian region.

The Pinot Nero is, of course, used as a base for spumante rather than for an international-style red wine.

The local decision to sacrifice quality over quantity is certainly not the fault of the land, which – with its cool, sunny hills exposed to the mezzogiorno, and the well-drained soil rich in clay and calcareous marl – seems to provide the ideal habitat. In the replanted vineyards where the vines are trained on denser systems and are grafted with quality red wine clones, it is possible to produce elegant Pinot Nero varietals which mature well in new wood. But the process is just beginning.

Notable producers

Frecciarossa, Casteggio (PV) This historic Oltrepò winery has recently undergone a comprehensive overhaul of its vineyards and cantinas, and with interesting results. Try the fine Pinot Nero, the Riesling Renano with a fine bouquet, or a good Oltrepò Pavese Rosso.

Le Fracce, Casteggio (PV) Le Fracce gives its name to several of the most attractive wines of the region, such as the intense, fruity Pinot Grigio, Oltrepò Pavese Rosso Bohemi, and an interesting Riesling Renano – another vine which has found its second home in this locality.

Casa Re, Montecalvo Versiggia (PV) The estate of the Casati family has the best vines in the Valle Versa and some truly exceptional wines, such as Chardonnay and Riesling Italico from the Il Fossone vineyard. Also offers good reds and a promising Brut made using the traditional method.

Vercesi del Castellazzo, Montù Beccaria (PV) The Vercesi brothers make some of the most interesting wines here, particularly reds, among which the position of honour goes to Pinot Nero Luogo dei Monti, a wine which hints at the potential of this great terroir.

Ca' di Frara, Mornico Losana (PV) The diversity of the Oltrepò vines is confirmed with the Pinot Grigio Vendemmia Tardiva, a remarkable wine produced at a fine young estate. Also on offer are a great Chardonnay and a superb Riesling Renano.

Anteo, Rocca de' Giorgi (PV) The pride of this estate is its superbly positioned Pinot Nero vines, which produce an excellent, traditional-method spumante, and two Pinot Nero Ca' dell Oca wines matured in new wood: the red is good, but the white is even better.

La Versa, Santa Maria della Versa (PV) Founded in 1905 as a cooperative winery, La Versa is the chief winemaking establishment in Oltrepò, with about 100 members who control a good 1,300 hectares of vineyards. Its traditional-method spumante is excellent; and the vintage Extra Brut vintage is outstanding. The ordinary wines are also very good.

Monsupello, Torricella Verzate (PV) Monsupello is one of the most interesting cantinas in Lombardy. Carlo Boatti and his son Pierangelo grow some of the finest vines in Oltrepò, and own perhaps the only winery in the region to employ a full-time agronomist.

Selected clones of traditional and innovative varieties are planted according to the nature of the soil and the conditions of the microclimate. From these vines come excellent traditional-method spumanti, such as Pinot Nero Nature and a vast range of wines, from the compelling Oltrepò Pavese Rosso Great Ruby Vivace – a lively traditional Bonarda and Barbera – to the excellent Riesling Renano, one of the best among the few grown on Italian soil. Both the Pinot Nero and Chardonnay Senso are matured in high-quality new oak, and are delicious. The Sauvignon di Monsupello has a condensed bouquet and is fresh and structured, while the elegant passito La Cuenta Passito Giallo is made from no fewer than seven varieties of white grapes.

Il Bosco, Zenevredo (PV) This winery is part of the large Zonin group, the pre-eminent producer of 'private' wine in Paese. With over 125 hectares it makes elegant traditional-method spumante and still wines – the Barbera Teodote is particularly good.

below *While a swathe of grape varieties are grown in Oltrepò Pavese – including Barbera, Croatina, Riesling Italico and Moscato – the region is home to more Pinot Nero than anywhere else in Italy.*

Valtellina

The mountain wines of Valtellina are similar to the reds of the Valle d'Aosta. Only one grape variety is grown here, Chiavennasca, the local name for Nebbiolo. The inclement climate and near-vertical vineyards with their stony soil make cultivation difficult. This region is, in effect, a strip 40 kilometres long with an altitude of 400 to 1,000 metres. It runs along the sunny side of the valleys of the river Adda, from Ardenno to Tirano in the province of Sondrio, not far from the Swiss border and about 100 kilometres from Milan.

Thanks to the hard work of the *terragne* over the centuries, the vineyard terraces have been constructed among the woods and churches which cling to the rock face. Mechanisation is impossible, so everything is done by hand. Even the soil, which every so often is needed for earthing up the vines, is carried to the terraces on the shoulders of the labourers. In the more precipitous regions, little *téléfériques* (cableways) make the harvest easier by carrying the grapes down into the valley.

The vines are planted on a perfectly drained, gravelly and silica-rich soil, at an altitude of between 800-1,000 metres. The variation between night and day temperature ensures that the grapes are infused with a fragrant delicacy, and they benefit from the milder air currents drifting in from the vicinity of Lake Como. Reds of great character are made in this region, full-bodied and blessed with extraordinary longevity.

Valtellina is divided into two categories: Valtellina, and Valtellina Superiore. Both have been DOCGs for some time but can also carry the sub-region of the producer as a further denomination. Here, then, are the wines of Grumello, Inferno, Sassella, Valgella and, finally, Riserva. The grapes must come from vines with a yield of not more than 8,000 kilograms per hectare, and the wine must have a minimum alcoholic content of 12 per cent. It is aged for at least two years, the Riserva for three. Though the grape specified for use is Chiavennasca, ten per cent of other red wine grapes may be added.

The outstanding local wine is Sforzato or Sfursat, a full-bodied red with over 14 per cent alcohol, made from Chiavennasca grapes which are left to dry for several months. It is an extremely long-lived wine and an ideal companion for some of the world's great cheeses. In recent years, the planting of new vines closer together and the use of small barrels or barriques made of new wood, has given an extra touch of depth and complexity to these great reds, whose status is firmly on an upward curve.

above *These baskets are borne on the backs of agile vineyard workers, whose grape picking often requires them to work on sheer terracing.*

Notable producers

Nino Negri, Chiuro (SO) Nino Negri is one of the historic estates of Valtellina and for some years has been part of the Gruppo Italiano Vini, the greatest establishment in Italian winemaking. Casimiro Maule is at the helm, a very experienced oenologist and a great 'conductor' of this terroir, not to mention president of the Valtellina Wine Consortium.

The estate's production covers the whole range of the DOCs, from Inferno to Valtellina Superiore Fracia, but it also has a real gem in Sfursat 5 Stelle, one of the best Italian reds of recent years. It has a deep ruby-purple colour and an elegant bouquet, fruity and balsamic, opening up with notes of well-blended oak and a touch of juniper. In the mouth it is warm, fruity and alcoholic, with a perfect touch of new wood – a real triumph. The white Sauvignon Ca' Brione, one of the few made in the region, is also worth a look.

Rainoldi, Chiuro (SO) The wines of Giuseppe Rainoldi have been among the best in Valtellina for some time. His Sfursat in particular has achieved considerable critical success. Giuseppe is a master of the process of drying grapes, evident in his Sfursat Ca' Rizzieri – which is fermented and matured in French oak barriques. It's concentrated, rich in red fruit flavours, elegant, harmonious and long-lasting. His Valtellina Superiore is classy, as are his Inferno Riserva, also matured in new wood, and his Valtellina Superiore Crespino.

Fay, Teglio (SO) Sandro Fay is a skilful oenologist and makes wines which are a perfect expression of Nebbiolo in this high-altitude enclave. His Sfursat is thrilling, but he's at his best with the superb Valtellina Superiore Sassella. From the best-known sub-region, this takes its name from the Cappella di Sassella, between Castione Andevenno and Sondrio, whose wines display a particular refinement and complexity. The Sassella Il Glicine is another elegant wine, with a shrewd use of oak, while the Valgella Ca' Morei is excellent.

above *Casimiro Maule, the winemaker at the Nino Negri estate in Chiuro, checks the progress of his wines in barrel.*

Conti Sertoli Salis, Tirano (SO) The emblem of Sertoli Salis is among the oldest in Valtellina, but the wine enterprise was itself was founded fairly recently. In the process, the magnificent 17th-century villa in the centre of Tirano has been restored and the picturesque old cantinas now boast the most modern equipment. Winemaker Claudio Introini makes an interesting range of wines, including a Sforzato Canua, which is concentrated and harmonious. The Valtellina Superiore Corte della Meridiana is also delicious, as are the two *vini da tavola* Saloncello, the red, and Torre della Sirena, the white.

Triacca, Villa di Tirano (SO) Domenico Triacca is a conscientious researcher and experiments in the vineyard and winery, driven by a rare perfectionism. His vineyards are among the best maintained in the valley and the cantina has recently installed ultra-modern equipment. His Valtellina Prestigio, matured in small barrels made of new oak, is among the best in the region, and is appreciated for the richness of its red fruit tones and balanced oak flavours. The Sforzato, with its tobacco notes and firm palate, is coming along nicely.

Franciacorta and Terre di Franciacorta

Franciacorta derives from "Franzacurta", which was mentioned for the first time in a statute of 1277 and appears in turn to be derived from *corte franca* or "free land" – at least, it was free of duty. Wine has enriched this region of gentle morainic hills since time immemorial.

The soils are mainly alluvial, with a prevalence of stony soil on sand, perfectly drained and ideal for vine growing. In the western and eastern parts the soil becomes chalky, while the heights of Mount Alto di Adro and Mount Orfano are mainly rocky. The climate is modified by the Lago d'Isea or Sebino, which acts as a thermal flywheel, warming the winters and even enabling olives to survive in the cool northern region. In summertime, on the other hand, the temperature in these hills is several degrees lower than on the plains, because of the Alpine air currents which fall from Val Camonica and cross the lake.

A recent survey of the soils and regional micro-climates carried out by the local winemakers association, in collaboration with the University of Milan, provided the producers with an incredibly structured amount of data: now, anyone planting (or replanting) a vineyard today can select the right grape variety and type of planting best suited to the production of high-quality wines.

If there is a downside to this emerging area, it is the vine-growing itself. Most of the planting is rather old and was done to meet lesser standards to those which prevail in the region today. In spite of this, significant progress has been achieved, due to producers refusing to compromise when it comes to the viticultural development. Impressive heights have already been scaled with the likes of spumante, in particular; indeed, the definition "little Champagne of Italy" is far from comical, as demonstrated in many blind tastings in which Franciacorta has compared favourably with its French cousins.

Franciacorta appears in one of the first ever publications on the technique of preparing wine for natural fermentation in the bottle, and its effect on the human body. Printed in Italy in 1570, this invaluable manual on sparkling wine was written by Girolamo Conforto, a doctor from Brescia who had the significant title *Libellus de vino mordaci*. Sadly, however, the brilliance of this precursor to Dom Pérignon was not matched by production in the region until recently, although Franciacorta is exceptionally well-suited to this type of wine.

Paradoxically, the modern success of Franciacorta

results from the absence of a great winemaking tradition. Early achievements were blown away at the turn of the century by phylloxera, and then ordinary wine production was reintroduced to satisfy the needs of the local market. In this respect, Franciacorta can be compared to California, a region tailor-made for viticulture and developed by entrepreneurs free from the spectre of tradition. Unbridled winemakers were able to discard obsolete techniques and, as most of these producers came from non-agricultural sectors, introduced fresh ideas and strategies to both the production and marketing of these wines.

The DOC was awarded in 1967 and modified in 1984 and 1992; Franciacorta finally earned its DOCG status in 1995. From that moment, the name Franciacorta alone signified spumante. Produced from Chardonnay and Pinot Bianco grapes, with up to 15 per cent of Pinot Nero, it has

a minimum ageing of 25 months from the date of harvesting, of which at least 18 months are in the bottle, on the lees. Vintage Franciacorta, made only in the best years, must be aged for at least 37 months, of which 30 are on the lees. Franciacorta is made in all grades, from Brut Nature (or Dosage Zero, no sugar added) to Extra Brut, Brut, Sec and Demi-Sec, not forgetting the Rosé (which has a minimum of 15 per cent Pinot Nero).

A style of wine which has acquired even greater importance in the region is Crémant, known in this part of Italy as Satèn, a name patented by producers from the Consorzio of Franciacorta, and which indicates certain specific characteristics of a Brut. Made only from white grapes, it has a lower carbon dioxide pressure (of four atmospheres or less) compared with the five of a normal Brut made by the traditional method. This is a wine much appreciated for its very fine bubbles, creamy foam, lovely

above *Stainless-steel tanks in the cellars of Ca'del Bosco, one of the most famous Italian wine brands in the world.*

greenish-straw colour and its bouquet, which opens with yeasty notes, spices and hints of ripe dried fruit. It's softly elegant in the mouth, fresh and with a notable smoothness, and signifies a distinct maturity of style for the region as a whole.

Other impressive wines include a pair defined by the regulations as Terre di Franciacorta: the Bianco is made from Chardonnay and/or Pinot Bianco, and the Rosso comes chiefly from Cabernet Sauvignon, with Cabernet Franc, Barbera, Nebbiolo, Merlot and other additions of authorised local varieties. These are excellent blends, particularly the Bianco. The superior examples have a better structure and complexity, resulting from longer

maturation than the basic DOC wines, part of which usually takes place in oak barriques.

Under the Sebino IGT denomination, thirsty drinkers can get stuck in to a new fruttato, a passito made from white grapes (Chardonnay, Trebbiano or Pinot Bianco combinations), and some varietal wines - Pinot Nero, which is in its element in this region, Merlot, and the white Riesling and Pinot Grigio.

Franciacorta is ideal for international varieties, and Nebbiolo and Barbera will most likely make room in the long run for Cabernet and Merlot. Some producers are also experimenting with the acclimatisation of Sauvignon Blanc, with mixed results.

Notable producers

Contadi Castaldi, Adro (BS) Like Bellavista, Contadi Castaldi is the property of the Moretti family. The winery makes a fine range of Franciacorta and Terre di Franciacorta, almost entirely from grapes brought in from outside vineyards. High quality is ensured by efficient technical control and ultra-modern equipment.

Ricci Curbastro, Capriolo (BS) This cantina has made an impression with the polished, attractive style of its Franciacorta, best shown in its Satèn, and by the fruity rounded style of its still wines, in particular the Sebino Pinot Nero.

Monte Rossa, Cazzago San Martino (BS) One of the most important establishments in the region, where beautiful vineyards have long provided the best material for a range of prestigious Franciacorta and other wines. The Rabotti family makes several variations, but it is the vintage Franciacorta Brut Cabochon which stands out, with rare elegance and complexity. Broad and endearing in its creamy effervescence, it is also full, dense, harmonious and packs a long finish. The Satèn di Monte Rossa is among the most successful of its kind, and the rest of the production is also excellent.

Guido Berlucchi & C., Cortefranca (BS) With its five million bottles a year, this is one of the best-known names for Italian spumante. If Franco Ziliani had not founded this winery in 1964, it is possible that Franciacorta would not be revelling in its current spotlight. Berlucchi makes a range of excellent non-DOC spumante, and a Franciacorta named Antica Cantina Fratta.

Bellavista, Erbusco (BS) Bellavista is one of the region's blue-riband producers. Its elegant cuvées are made with grapes from the Bellavista vineyards, which are scattered over the best-exposed parts of Franciacorta. Owner Vittorio Moretti has entrusted the running of the winery to Mattia Vezzola, an excellent oenologist. As well as the prestige Franciacorta wines, such as Gran Cuvée Pas Operé and Riserva Vittorio Moretti – both vintage wines rich in yeast notes and complex flavours of vanilla and spices – Bellavista also has some of the best Terre di Franciacorta, such as Bianco del Convento dell'Annunciata, from a vineyard with ideal exposure on the south side of Monte Orfano, and Chardonnay Uccellanda. Notable among the reds are Solesine, in the Bordeaux style, and the fine Pinot Nero Casotte.

Ca' del Bosco, Erbusco (BS) Maurizio Zanella is the founder of this beautiful establishment which, 30 years after it was founded, is now one of the most famous Italian wine brands in the world. The winery, which became a joint venture with Santa Margherita from the Veneto a couple of years ago, is an incredible showcase of the most advanced 'natural' wine technologies.

Years of research, travel and experimentation have given Maurizio Zanella an insight into the most celebrated wine regions in the world. This has enabled him to make some of the best Italian spumante wines, such as Franciacorta Cuvée Annamaria Clementi, vintage Dosage Zero, and the granddaddy of all Satèn. No less distinguished are Terre di Franciacorta Chardonnay, a wine of international standing, and structured reds such as Maurizio Zanella, a Bordeaux-style wine of notable power and subtlety.

Cavalleri, Erbusco (BS) Cavalleri follows a tradition going back to the 15th century, although the modern establishment dates from 1967. Giovanni Cavalleri controls over 30 hectares of lovely vineyards, some of them his own property and others rented, with Chardonnay the star performer. This winery has always believed in using the best vineyards, and he was the first to offer the best Terre di Franciacorta from single vineyards, such as the whites Rampaneto and Seradina and the red Tajardino. Top Franciacorta wines such as the excellent vintage Selezione are also on offer.

Ferghettina, Erbusco (BS) Much could be said about this small winery. Roberto Gatti is a winemaker with 20 years' experience who, a little while ago, set his winery the declared objective of making great wines and excellent Franciacorta. His Chardonnay Favento and Merlot are very good indeed.

Gatti, Erbusco (BS) The brothers-in-law Lorenzo Gatti and Enzo Balzarini, with the help of their respective wives Sonia and Paola, are working with incredible dedication at this small winery. To judge from their best Franciacorta, fragrant and fruity, and their notable Gatti Bianco and Gatti Rosso, they are well on their way.

Uberti, Erbusco (BS) Agostino Uberti and his wife Eleonora have performed a great service for the smaller family wineries of Franciacorta, by putting their name to some of the region's finest wines. Their 14 hectares of vines are situated in the heart of Erbusco, the little capital of Franciacorta. With the advice of oenologist Cesare Ferrari they make a prestigious range, which includes Franciacorta Magnificentia and Comarì del Salem, and in particular the whites Maria dei Medici and Bianco dei Frati Priori. The reds are excellent too.

Il Mosnel, Passirano (BS) Il Mosnel is one of the most interesting properties in this region. Giulio and Lucia Barzanò are reaping excellent rewards from their 35 hectares of vineyards, in the form of a very wide, meticulously made range of wines. The Franciacorta vintage Brut stands out.

below Besides sparkling wines, Ca' del Bosco produces many other fine wines. The Maurizio Zanella is a Cabernet blend named after the company's founder, here on the left.

Garda and Lugana

The region of Garda is in the process of being classified at DOC level. This extremely beautiful corner of Lombardy, which has an easy revenue from tourism, has recently been trying to raise a pulse in its wines. The new Garda DOC includes the provinces of Brescia and Mantua in Lombardy and Verona in the Veneto. A "Classico" region is envisaged, restricted to wines made on the Brescia side of the lake. Until now, these wines have been found under the DOC Riviera del Garda Bresciano.

Here, the whites use Riesling Italico or Riesling Renano grapes, rich with fresh fruity notes. The Chiaretto, a smooth, fragrant rosé is made from Groppello, Sangiovese, Marzemino and Barbera grapes and is a highly traditional Garda wine. The Rosso from the same grapes is distinguished by its gentle acidity and subtle tannins; it has a little more body than a Chiaretto and should be drunk young, ideally throughout a meal. Still in the traditional region, the straight Groppello – a full-bodied red, rich in tannins – is not completely tamed by the selection of clones or the techniques of the cantina. The grape has the potential to shine with modern winemaking technology and it has a healthy future. The best vines in this area are those which clamber up the slopes of the Valtenes, between Puegnago and Polpenazze.

Besides these native varieties, a long series of red and white varietals have been introduced which occupy all or almost all the vines grown in the three provinces. From Garganega to Pinot Bianco, from Riesling to Cortese and Pinot Grigio, virtually nothing is left out. Among the reds the story is very similar, ranging from Pinot Nero to Cabernet Sauvignon, from Marzemino to Corvina and Barbera. These are all grapes which have long found an excellent position in the hills overlooking the lake.

One of the fruitier and more pleasing Italian white wines is produced on the southern side of the lake. Lugana is made from Trebbiano di Lugana grapes, and has long been commercially successful. It is produced in a small area between the communes of Peschiera and Desenzano, and in parts of Lonato, Pozzolengo and Sirmione, all located in the Brescia province, where Trebbiano grapes flourish. These are used to make a wine with a rich, full body and fruity essences, delicately acidic, fresh in taste and nicely balanced.

In medieval times the grape was familiar to the likes of Pietro Aretino and Andrea Bacci, but it acquired a discrete fame between the two world wars. This was when Italians were breaking air speed records in seaplanes over the smooth waters of the lake, and when many journalists who had been sent to cover the gala indulged instead in the white wine of the local trattorias. Even today, besides a number of specialist producers who offer interesting versions of spumante, many great wineries of the Veronese include Trebbiano on their labels.

The region is rich in a mainly morainic terroir, which seems well suited to many other white varieties. In a small enclave near Lonato, for example, San Martino della Battaglia is still made, although this varietal, made from Tocai Friulano in dry and fortified sweet versions, has yet to savour real success.

below *Gardone on Lake Garda. Garda is most famous as a tourist destination, but the region is now the source of a variety of wines, including the popular Lugana.*

Notable producers

Visconti, Desenzano del Garda (BS) This winery began operating in the early years of the 20th century. Today it still selects and buys grapes from local vinegrowers, which are then vinified in its cantinas to create a range of quality wines, sold at reasonable prices. Examples include Lugana from the Santa Onorata vineyard, the selezione Ramoso and the fine Brut, made in the traditional method.

Trevisani, Gavardo (BS) Giampietro and Mauro Trevisani manage this beautiful estate in the vicinity of Lake Garda. Their vines grow at an altitude of 370 metres and benefit from an excellent microclimate. The air flow from the nearby lake ensures mild temperatures even in winter, while preserving a good variation between day and night temperature. The Cabernet Due Querce, matured in barriques, and the Chardonnay Bali are both interesting, as is the Rosso del Benaco.

Costaripa, Moniga del Garda (BS)
The *azienda* of the Vezzola family makes a series of interesting Garda wines, from the amiable reds Groppello Le Castelline (black cherry fruit) and Marzemino Le Mazane (blueberries and bilberries) to the white Lugana and the fragrant Chiaretto del Garda Rosamara. These are wines with a good bouquet, produced from vines with the best exposure – and the result of careful experiments. However, one might expect them to pack a greater concentration and power in the future.

Cà dei Frati, Sirmione (BS) For years the Dal Cero brothers have striven feverishly to promote the Lugana and its wines, both in Italy and abroad. They have gradually turned the traditional fruity white into a bestseller, a champion of the quality-price ratio, and created a convincing spumante version with bouquet and body: this Cuvée dei Frati Brut can hold its own against spumante from more celebrated regions. The cru Brolettino has notable body and complexity, a good advert for vineyard selections, while a fascinating Tre Filer Chardonnay and

Sauvignon with noble rot are added to Trebbiano di Lugana. The final ace in the pack is Pratto, an unusual blend of Chardonnay and Sauvignon Blanc matured in new wood, one of the most interesting Italian white wines of the last few years.

Cascina La Pertica, Picedo di Polpenazze del Garda (BS) The re-qualification of Garda wines is a subject close to the heart of Ruggero Brunori. He lavishes great care on his traditional and international varieties and in the handsome cantina there are French

barrels and modern equipment to make a complete range of wines. Especially recommended are the Garda Rosso Le Sincette and Garda Bresciano Groppello.

Cominciolì, Puegnago del Garda (BS) Giovanni Battista and Gianfranco Cominciolì produce a well-selected range of Garda wines. For years their best has been Chiaretto, one of the finest in the local DOC portfolio, with a fine cherry red colour and an intensely fruity bouquet. They also make an excellent Groppello.

above *An old basket-press at Cà dei Frati in Sirmione. This estate is owned by the Dal Cero brothers, who have striven to promote Lugana and its wines. Their enviable local reputation rests on a wide and exciting range of good value wines.*

Liguria

below *This view of Vernazza in the Cinque Terre zone, to the east of Liguria, demonstrates spectacularly how the vined terraces cascade down to the sea.*

Liguria is a small region dominated by hills which descend almost vertically to the sea. It's not an ideal place to grow vines, but grapes have been cultivated here for over 25 centuries, initially by Greek merchants or the Etruscans. In the Roman era the most famous wines came from the magnificent area known today as the Cinque Terre (Five Lands), in the extreme east of the region, while the Animea grape assumed pole position. The Riviera di Ponente, which adjoins the French Côte d'Azur, came to prominence only in the late Medieval period, when the Republic of Genoa became a sea power – varieties such as Rossese and Pigato appeared, with the former earning Napoleon's approval on his "visit" to the region in 1797. These varieties remain the basis of regional production.

Ormeasco, the Ligurian version of Piedmontese Dolcetto, also has ancient origins and is most probably indigenous. Vermentino is of indeterminate origin – some point to the Iberian peninsula, others to ancient Greece, and others to Lunigiana – but it is undoubtedly the signature grape of the region, making well-structured whites in both the eastern and western zones.

Wines and wine regions

Winemaking in Liguria is a heroic activity: in some areas vines cling to steep slopes which rise almost vertically above the sea and must be cultivated entirely by hand, as it is impossible to use machinery. Nonetheless, viticulture is essential for managing the land and preventing soil erosion and landslides, while wine output reaches 260,000 hectolitres a year – a little over seven per cent of it DOC.

Cinque Terre is situated between La Spezia and Tigullio, and is famous for its magnificent landscapes and a celebrated white wine made from Bosco, Albarola and Vermentino. Harvesting is carried out using monorails which transport the grapes from the vineyards to the nearest road, where they are loaded onto trucks and taken to the winery, an expensive process which is scarcely concealed in the price of the wines.

The situation is slightly more straightforward in the DOC region of Colli di Luni, which stretches towards the eastern boundaries of Liguria, into the southernmost part of Lunigiana. Its gently rolling hills are home to wines which resemble those from the Tuscan coast: Colli di Luni Rosso is made from Sangiovese grapes with small amounts of local varieties, like many of its Tuscan counterparts. Colli di Luni Bianco, made from Vermentino and Trebbiano Toscano, is a medium-structured wine,

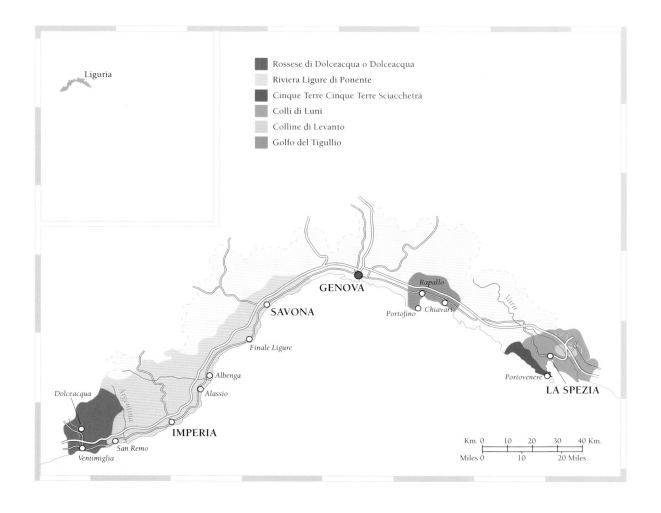

Liguria

Rossese di Dolceacqua o Dolceacqua
Riviera Ligure di Ponente
Cinque Terre Cinque Terre Sciacchetrà
Colli di Luni
Colline di Levanto
Golfo del Tigullio

GENOVA
Rapallo
SAVONA
Portofino Chiavari
Vara
Finale Ligure
Albenga
Portovenere
Dolceacqua
Argentina
Alassio
LA SPEZIA
IMPERIA
San Remo
Ventimiglia

Km. 0   10   20   30   40 Km.
Miles 0   10   20 Miles

right *A typical Ligurian view of terraced market gardens and vines, in the Cinque Terre district. Vine planting is understandably dense and compact.*

reminiscent of those of Montecarlo and Bolgheri, a few dozen kilometres to the south. Finally there is Colli di Luni Vermentino, perhaps the archetypal wine of the district – with the structure and concentration of a Bianco and a perfect accompaniment to local dishes such as testaroli (wholemeal dumplings with pesto).

Some 200 kilometres east is Riviera Ligure di Ponente, a vast DOC which boasts some of the most famous wines in Liguria. Vermentino and Pigato are the two premier whites, and are rather similar: well-structured and mellow, perfect with traditional Ligurian cuisine, such as pasta with pesto and cappon magro (a salad of mixed vegetables, fish and crustacea).

Red wines include Ormeasco, from Dolcetto grapes and vaguely reminiscent of its Piedmont cousins – there is a rosé version called Sciac-trà, not to be confused with the Sciacchetrà delle Cinque Terre – and the Rossese, which has two DOCs: Riviera Ligure di Ponente and the more famous Dolceacqua, grown inland from Ventimiglia on the Via del Sale, the ancient thoroughfare. This is a fascinating wine with a good structure, and an ideal match for mushroom-based dishes and white meats.

Soil, climate and viticulture

Liguria's viticulture is determined by the mountainous aspect of the region. Terraced vineyards are built on sheer slopes overlooking the sea, while the hillsides inland – which are only marginally less steep, especially in the west of the region – allow only compact, dense planting. The main training systems are alberello ('sapling') and espalier: the former is more frequent in Riviera Ligure di Ponente and Dolceacqua, and is used with a few local variations in the eastern part of the Cinque Terre district. In Colli di Luni, most growers favour a system of espalier and wires with Guyot training, similar to those used in neighbouring northern Tuscany.

The Ligurian soil is poor and stony almost everywhere, so vines and olive trees are often found together. The climate is pretty uniform – with typically Mediterranean conditions of fairly hot summers and mild winters. What ultimately distinguishes this from other Mediterranean areas are the autumn rains, which are often more abundant than elsewhere, and the constant presence of westerly winds.

Notable producers

Anfossi, Albenga (SV) One of the best "interpreters" of the Pigato della Riviera Ligure di Ponente – a rich, mellow white wine from the western hills (a superior version bears the name of the Le Caminate vineyard). The Vermentino from Riviera Ligure di Ponente is also worth a look.

Cascina Feipu dei Massaretti, Albenga (SV) Bice and Pippo Parodi are the leading producers of Pigato della Riviera Ligure di Ponente. Theirs is a fragrant white, with a delicate aroma of sage and cedar and a mellow taste. Notable, too, is Rossese della Riviera Ligure di Ponente, with a fragrance of raspberries, a firm taste and excellent concentration.

La Vecchia Cantina, Albenga (SV) Umberto Calleri's functional winery produces one of the most spectacular Pigato della Riviera Ligure di Ponente wines, from grapes grown in vineyards at Salea, near Albenga. It has a strong bouquet of musk, ripe peach and sage and a full, mellow taste which improves with at least four or five years' ageing.

Tenuta Giuncheo, Camporosso (IM) Marco Romagnoli is an eminent producer of Vermentino and in alliance with Donato Lanati, the well-known Piedmontese oenologist, produces a reliable stock of wines. Le Palme is a selection matured in barriques; there is a basic Vermentino and an excellent Rossese di Dolceacqua Vigneto Pian del Vescovo.

Ottaviano Lambruschi, Castelnuovo Magra (SP) One of the Colli di Luni's greatest Vermentinos. Several versions are offered, from a basic white to selections from the classic vineyards of Sarticola and Costa Marina. Hallmarks are the vegetal fragrances, a faintly aromatic nose and a concentrated taste in the mouth.

Enoteca Bisson, Chiavari (GE) Piero Lugano, winemaker and wine merchant in Chiavari, offers a vast selection of wines, from the rare Sciacchetrà delle Cinque Terre to whites of the IGT zone of Golfo del Tigullio, Vermentino and Bianchetta Genovese.

Maria Donata Bianchi, Diano Castello (IM) Emanuele Trevia makes one of the best Vermentinos of recent years, although it lacks a DOC status: Eretico ("heretical") runs counter to tradition, as it is fermented and matured in barriques of oak from Allier. This is a powerful, mellow white, with the typical perfumes of Vermentino and the structure of a Condrieu.

Giobatta Mandino Cane, Dolceacqua (IM) The greatest interpreter of Rossese di Dolceacqua is undoubtedly Giobatta Mandino Cane. He produces two styles from individual vineyards bearing the Superiore denomination. The first comes from Vigneto Morghe and is usually the better. The second is from Vigneto Arcagna: it has less concentration but is easier to drink.

Terre Bianche, Dolceacqua (IM) Paolo Rondelli and Franco Laconi became the owners of this winery after the death of its founder, Claudio Rondelli. They produce some of the region's best wines, including two verions of Arcana: the white is made from Pigato and Vermentino grapes; and the red from Rossese and Cabernet Sauvignon. Rossese di Dolceacqua from the Bricco Arcagna vineyards is deservedly famous.

Tommaso e Angelo Lupi, Pieve di Teco (IM) Perhaps the most famous winery of the region, the Lupi brothers offer a vast selection of beautiful wines. Ormeasco Superiore Le Braje, Pigato Le Petraie and Vermentino Le Serre are Ligurian wonders, boasting outstanding complexity.

A Maccia, Ranzo (IM) *La macchia* means "patch" or "spot", a reference to this small estate that produces only 17,000 bottles a year. Yet Loredana Faraldi still produces a Pigato della Riviera Ligure di Ponente which is rightly and regularly rated one of the best.

Bruna, Ranzo (IM) Le Russeghine di Bruna is a classic example of Pigato della Riviera Ligure di Ponente: a white wine with a mature, resinous fragrance and a rich, mellow taste, as the best local tradition demands.

Coop. Agricola di Riomaggiore, Manarola, Corniglia, Vernazza e Monterosso, Riomaggiore (SP) A cooperative of highly skilled small growers. Cinque Terre Sciacchetrà, a sweet white wine made from *appassito* (shrivelled) grapes, is a feast of fragrances and flavours. The basic Cinque Terre is a well-made dry white wine, pleasant and with fruity fragrances.

Walter De Batté, Riomaggiore (SP) Walter De Batté is a vinous craftsman and the best interpreter of Cinque Terre Sciacchetrà, an extremely rare wine and difficult to produce. His version combines fragrances of dried apricots and cocoa with a delicately sweet taste. The basic Cinque Terre is also excellent, a dry white wine with fragrances of ripe fruit and a mellow, long-lasting taste.

Rodolfo Biamonti, San Biagio della Cima (IM) Rodolfo and Clelia Biamonti produce an excellent Rossese di Dolceacqua: a red wine with fragrant perfumes, fruity and easy to drink.

Claudio Vio, Vendone (SV) Claudio Vio is a specialist in the production of both Pigato and Vermentino in the Riviera Ligure di Ponente. He owns just five hectares of vineyards, but is a winemaker of great sensitivity – his wines are true to their varietal characteristics and rich in taste.

below *A vineyard of young Vermentino vines. This variety is used throughout Liguria to increasingly good effect.*

The Northeast

The northeastern quarter of Italy is traditionally known as the Tre Venezie ("three Venetias"), and encompasses the regions of Friuli-Venezia Giulia, Veneto and Trentino-Alto Adige. These have much in common, from geological and geographical features to the historical events which have united them over the centuries.

Today this is one of the richest parts of the country. This is also unquestionably the area which has spearheaded the dramatic revival in Italian winemaking in recent years, resulting in new, modern-style wines and the resurgence of ancient traditions. This began with white wines in the 1970s, cold fermentations, the selection of yeasts and the novel approach to planting vineyards more densely and with quality in mind. The time had also come to make room for international varieties as well as traditional grapes.

It was already obvious by the 1970s that change would come hard and fast, once a successful publicity campaign had propelled the sales of Pinot Grigio to giddy heights. This triggered a widespread replanting of white grapes, which has only recently started abating.

Winemaking and wine styles

Before the advent of phylloxera, production was largely confined to traditional native red wines, but its arrival led to mass replanting. At the time, the easiest obtainable scion stock, which had proven best at taking root and was subsequently widely planted, came from France. So, in the early years of the 20th century, Merlot, Cabernet Franc, Sauvignon and the Pinot family became popular in the Veneto, as did wines made from direct hybrids.

It was the northeast, too, that eventually encouraged great vine nurseries. It also gave rise to wines developed for the modern palate, the result of technical innovation. The only institute specialising in teaching oenology and viticulture had been in Alba, Piedmont; hence, in 1876 the prestigious Scuola Enologica di Conegliano Veneto was founded and is still thriving. There are now two other important institutions in the Venezias: the Istituto Agrario Sperimentale di San Michele in Adige and that of Laimburg, Vadena.

It was in the northeast again, particularly in Trentino-Alto Adige, that large cooperative organisations began to change their winemaking strategies. In the mid-to-late seventies, they shifted their emphasis towards high-quality wine.

The northeast is still a region of substantial production, and accounts for about 15 per cent of Italy's entire output. The Veneto alone is the third largest region after Sicily and Puglia, but in terms of Italy's total DOC production it is the foremost, producing almost 11 per cent. The Trentino-Alto Adige boasts the highest DOC wine percentage of the total produced: in the province of Bolzano it is thought to be over 85 per cent, and in Trento over 70 per cent. Friuli remains out in front in terms of sheer quality, and today there is a revival of reds, which are making a very good impression in tandem with the local whites.

Protected from the cold winds of northern Europe by the Alps, the Tre Venezie are gently sloping and mostly sunny, with warm air currents arriving from the Adriatic and the great rivers, the Po, the Adige and the Piave, which take the edge off the hardest winters.

At the crossroads of the north, east and south of Europe, this region has always had a cosmopolitan air, which is reflected in its wines – typical Slav and German grape varieties appear next to native vines and those imported from France.

Many varieties are cultivated in this region, and often a large variety of wines will come under the auspices of a single DOC, particularly in the Alto Adige and Trentino DOCs. However, as the two provinces have distinct histories, cultures and languages, they will be treated individually in the following chapter.

right *Vineyards in front of the eastern shore of Lake Garda, Bardolino DOC. Bardolino is made from the same blend of grapes as Valpolicella – Corvina, Rondinella and Molinara.*

Veneto

above *Prosecco grapes can be used for both still wines and the sparkling styles that are so popular in and around Venice.*

The Veneti and Reti were producing excellent wines long before Rome was founded. Retico, for example, originated in the hills just north of the Padua-Veneto plain. A concentrated and elegant red passito wine, its history has been amply recorded and its fine tradition preserved in Recioto della Valpolicella and Recioto di Soave.

In the Middle Ages the best grape varieties and wine regions were demarcated and two kinds of wine emerged: an inexpensive style produced on the plains, and another in the mountains, which was good enough for export. Between the 14th and 15th centuries a flourishing wine trade developed, supported by many laws and regulations and prompting wines markedly different from those we know today. The most cultivated white grapes were the Bianchetta Trevigiana, Verdiso and Vespaiolo, while Marzemino and Raboso led the reds. All the vineyards had to be completely reorganised after the terrible frost of 1709, which destroyed all but the most chill-resistant vines. These varieties still exist today, alongside those which arrived post-phylloxera. Since then Garganega, Prosecco, Tocai, Verduzzo and Trebbiano di Soave have been the most popular white grape varieties, and Corvina Veronese, Rondinella, Raboso, Negrara, Merlot and Cabernet the preferred reds.

Wines and winemaking

The Veneto produces around seven million hectolitres of wine per year, with DOC wines accounting for over 30 per cent of this vast production. The cream is represented by Valpolicella, Amarone and Recioto della Valpolicella, which are produced a few kilometres north of the city, on the foothills of the Monti Lessini.

The Soave region lies southeast of Verona. Produced mainly from Garganega grapes, this is probably the most famous Italian white wine in the world. There is a Classico version, historically from the best-known area; a fascinating sweet version – Recioto di Soave; and two sparkling versions, one Soave and the other Recioto, which is also sweet. Bardolino, a red wine, and the white Bianco di Custoza from the Veneto shores of Lake Garda, are both produced from Valpolicella and Soave varieties; these are light and pleasant to drink. Colli Euganei is the sole quality wine from a small district in the province of Padua, while the volcanic soils of the prominent hills can yield respectable wines such as the Fior d'Arancio, one of the best Moscatos in Italy.

Vicenza is quietly producing some high-quality varietals. Its best known DOC is probably Gambellara, which boasts a Classico; a Recioto, either sweet – similar to the Recioto di Soave – or spumante; and a Vin Santo.

In the southern part of Vicenza is the DOC of Colli Berici, which is home to a vast range of wines – almost all from non-local varieties. South of Colli Berici lies Bagnoli di Sopra, a very recent DOC comprising 15 communes in the Padua province which are responsible for white and red blends and a few varietal wines, including Raboso.

In Breganze, north of Vicenza, Vespaiolo takes centre stage, creating fruity, pleasant white wines including Torcolato di Breganze – one of Italy's finest sweet whites – Breganze Bianco, made predominantly from Tocai, and Pinot Bianco and Pinot Grigio.

Foremost among an exceptional array of reds is the excellent Breganze Rosso (which is in fact a Merlot) and a clutch of impressive Cabernet and Pinot Nero wines. The eastern part of the region has produced many DOCs, such as Montello e Colli Asolani, while the right bank of the Piave produces varietals including a white, a red and a Prosecco Spumante. On the left bank is the district of Conegliano Valdobbiadene, where Prosecco rules supreme, and the more recently created Colli di Conegliano, home to still wines. Further down-river lies the Piave DOC and Lison-Pramaggiore, which focus on modern, value-for-money varietals. Merlot and Cabernet are dominant in Piave, but Tocai, Pinot Grigio and Pinot Bianco lead the way in Lison-Pramaggiore.

Soil, climate and viticulture

Veneto's most intensely cultivated vineyards are on the Alpine foothills: from Lake Garda to Conegliano Veneto, including Colli Berici and Colli Euganei – where the soil is rich, volcanic and calcareous. These hills in turn surround the fertile plain, with its rich alluvial soil, the wetlands of the Po delta and the Venetian lagoon.

The climate on the coast is much influenced by the Adriatic, while the central plain is hot in summer and harsh and foggy in winter. Those regions situated at the base of the Alps are particularly at risk from rain and hail.

The grape varieties planted post-phylloxera were mainly French, and introduced so widely that in the east of the region the only remaining native vines are Prosecco and Raboso. For quality wines in this part of Italy, head for the northern mountainous regions and the central hills.

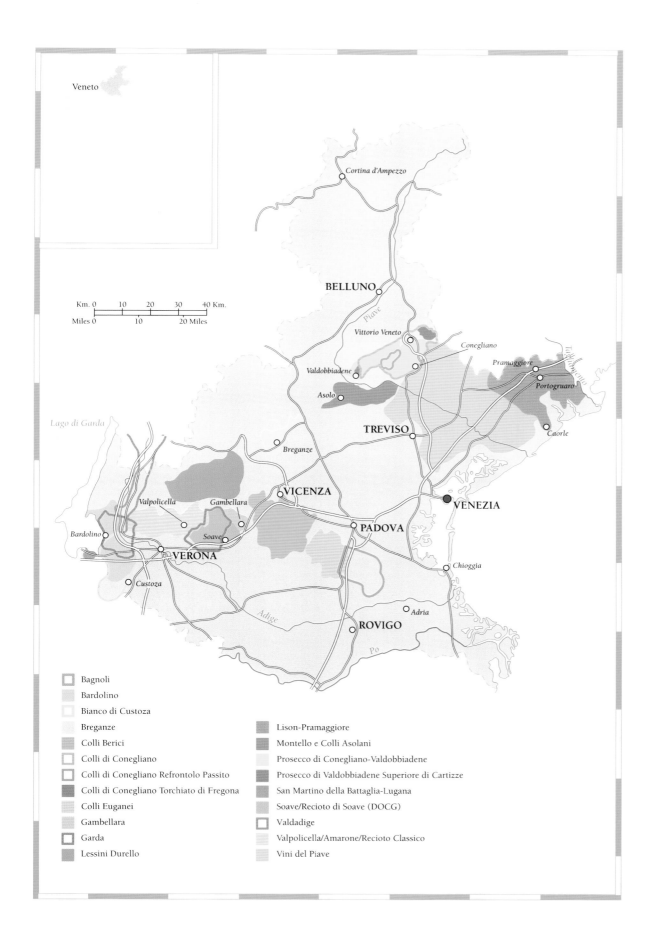

Veneto

BELLUNO

Piave

Cortina d'Ampezzo

Vittorio Veneto

Conegliano

Valdobbiadene

Pramaggiore

Portogruaro

Asolo

TREVISO

Caorle

Lago di Garda

Km. 0   10   20   30   40 Km.

Miles 0   10   20 Miles

Breganze

VICENZA

Valpolicella

Gambellara

VENEZIA

Bardolino

Soave

PADOVA

VERONA

Chioggia

Custoza

Adria

Adige

ROVIGO

Po

☐ Bagnoli

▨ Bardolino

☐ Bianco di Custoza

▨ Breganze

▨ Colli Berici

☐ Colli di Conegliano

☐ Colli di Conegliano Refrontolo Passito

▨ Colli di Conegliano Torchiato di Fregona

▨ Colli Euganei

▨ Gambellara

☐ Garda

▨ Lessini Durello

▨ Lison-Pramaggiore

▨ Montello e Colli Asolani

▨ Prosecco di Conegliano-Valdobbiadene

▨ Prosecco di Valdobbiadene Superiore di Cartizze

▨ San Martino della Battaglia-Lugana

▨ Soave/Recioto di Soave (DOCG)

☐ Valdadige

▨ Valpolicella/Amarone/Recioto Classico

▨ Vini del Piave

Verona, Valpolicella, Soave, Gambellara and Vicenza

The headline wine in Verona is Soave, a dry and fruity white named after the city of Soave. Produced from Garganega and either Trebbiano, Chardonnay or Pinot Bianco from vineyards in the hills southeast of Verona, this easy-drinking wine is available in three versions: Soave Classico is produced in the most "ancient" area. If the alcohol content reaches 11.5 per cent or more, then it gains a Superiore appellation. The trio is completed by a sweet passito version, Recioto di Soave, whose name is derived from the Venetian "rece", or "ears". Only the outer grapes (or "ears") of the bunch are used, and are placed on mats for the drying process, known as *appassimento*.

Soave has struggled to promote its genuinely class acts above an often insipid supporting cast. A handful of producers have succeeded through selective bottling, but there is still a degree of dross to cut through.

North of Verona, Corvina, Molinara and Rondinella are the main ingredients of Veneto's most famous red wine, Valpolicella. The classic heartlands of Fumane, Marano, Negrar and Sant'Ambroglio have a good track record in turning out ruby-rich all-rounders, but the Valpolicella DOC has arguably encompassed too large a region, and conferred the same DOC status to a widely varying collection of wines.

The distinctions between Classico and Superiore are conferred on the same basis as for Soave, but so are some of the familiar Italian image problems. In both Soave and Valpolicella, some of the less stringent producers have upgraded with modernised wineries and a production policy based on better-quality grapes. The temptation to pass these overheads onto consumers has been widely resisted, but when it comes to separating the good and good value from the cheap and cheerless, Soave and Valpolicella still pose a consumer conundrum.

Veneto's great reds

The king of Veneto's reds is Amarone della Valpolicella. This uses the same grape varieties as Valpolicella, but these have been left to dry on mats, under cover, until the end of March. Amarone is a very powerful wine which can reach a strength of 15/16 per cent and is traditionally drunk with red meat roasts, game and mature cheeses. Recioto or Recioto Classico della Valpolicella, on the other hand, is a sweet, sometimes sparkling wine, produced in the same region from the same grapes and using identical vinification methods to the Recioto di Soave.

Ripasso is a wine made according to traditional vinification methods, which consist of subjecting Valpolicella to a second fermentation on the lees drawn from Amarone, for fortification purposes. Some producers achieve better results by adding dried grapes to the wine, the same as those used in Amarone.

Wines from around Lake Garda

A few kilometres to the west are the shores of Lake Garda, the largest of the Italian lakes. Vineyards covering the hills around the lake are planted with the same grape varieties as those used for Valpolicella, and produce Bardolino – a

below *High-trained vines of Corvina, one of the three grape varieties grown in Valpolicella and Bardolino. These baskets are full of harvested grapes ready to go back to the winery.*

deliciously light and easy-drinking red wine with delicate fruity fragrances and a mellow, well-balanced taste. The Bardolino "Novello" version, awarded the DOC a few years ago, is achieved by subjecting the grapes to carbonic maceration, similar to that used by the French in Beaujolais Nouveau.

Bianco di Custoza originates in the Veronese hills on the southern shore of Lake Garda, where Trebbiano, Tocai, Garganega, Cortese, Riesling, Pinot Bianco, Chardonnay and Malvasia Toscana are grown. This is a classic wine, to be drunk with food or as an apéritif, and is increasingly popular with critics and consumers. Gambellara is a white wine produced from Garganega grapes: it's intensely fruity and complex, with interesting Recioto and Vin Santo versions offering great refinement and a good, long finish. Lessini, meanwhile, is home to a white wine and a spumante from Durello grapes. The Gambellara appellation lying adjacent to Soave is famous not only for its wines, but for one of its residents – the Zonin winery is one of the largest in the country, and occupies about half of the town centre.

Not far from Gambellara, Colli Berici produces a wide range of white wines (Garganega, Tocai, Sauvignon Blanc,

above *The romantic city of Verona has always been a vital market for the wines of Veneto, particularly the Soave and Valpolicella from the nearby Lessini hills.*

Pinot Bianco and Chardonnay) and reds (Merlot, Cabernet Sauvignon and the rare Tocai Rosso, which is believed to be a close relative of the Sardinian Cannonau and the French Grenache). These are mellow and well-structured wines, especially when produced from grapes cultivated in the higher vineyards. The microclimate of Colli Euganei is very similar, but there's a wider choice of varietals. Here, too, the prime vineyards are located higher up on the slopes. Finally, there is the delightful Fior d'Arancio ("orange blossom"): a fragrant, aromatic and sweet wine.

Finally, the high plains of Breganze are associated primarily with fruity whites, but – thanks to the efforts of the distinguished Maculan winery – there is renewed optimism that the vast potential of this region can now be exploited. It is certainly an ideal home for very good white wines, from Chardonnay to Sauvignon Blanc, as well as impressive reds from Cabernet to Pinot Nero – and not forgetting the Marzemino grapes. Anyone who has tasted the superb Torcolato di Breganze, or the rare and much sought-after Acininobili – Italy's nearest equivalent to the great Sauternes – produced by Maculan, will testify to the riches of this region.

below *Harvesting Corvina grapes for Valpolicella. Traditionally the ripest grapes (often from the outer part of the bunches) were set aside for Recioto and Amarone wines.*

Notable producers

Vignalta, Arquà Petrarca (PD) A model small establishment with some of the best vineyards in the Colli Euganei and, thanks to Franco Zanovello, some of its best wines, including Colli Euganei Gemola from Merlot and Cabernet Franc grapes.

Fratelli Zeni, Bardolino (VR) This large outfit makes a complete range of Valpolicella and Garda wines, from the Bardolino to the Valpolicella. These are all extremely well-made and some are outstanding, such as the best of the Amarone Classico.

Maculan, Breganze (VI) The Maculans express the great potential of the local terroir in their range of great wines. Torcolato and the expensive Acininobili are two of Italy's greatest sweet styles, but their Cabernet Sauvignon Ferrata is just as noble.

Allegrini, Fumane (VR) This winery played a major role in the recent revival of Valpolicella, and now ranks among the most distinguished names in Italian winemaking. It was founded 30 years ago by Giovanni Allegrini, father of the present owners, brothers Walter, Franco and Marilisa. Some of the family's success is due to the excellent position of their vineyards, which are fastidiously tended like gardens, the low yields per hectare and a perfectly equipped winery where every possible innovation is tested – this sounds almost de rigeur today, but at a time when Valpolicella was sold everywhere by the gallon, this kind of vision was at a premium. Besides a fine Amarone and a superb Recioto della Valpolicella, the Allegrinis offer a Valpolicella Superiore from the La Grola vineyard – a wine of incredible depth. Their innovative red, La Poja, a Corvina Veronese varietal, is a pedigree wine.

Zonin, Gambellara (VI) A real family company and the most important private producer in Italy, with many companies nationwide and in the United States. The main winery at Gambellara produces an admirable range of Gambellara DOC wines, from Classico to Recioto Spumante, as well as Soave, Amarone, and other still and spumante wines.

Dal Forno, Illasi (VR) Romano Dal Forno is one of the great personalities of Valpolicella and his mission is to express all the unfathomed potential of the land and its grapes. To this purpose, he divides all his time between the vineyard and the winery

above *In these cellars owned by Masi, grapes are slowly drying out to be used in Recioto and Amarone wines. The water in the grapes evaporates, leaving a rich, complex and concentrated juice.*

he transforms the best material into a range of world-class wines. His Recioto di Soave I Capitelli is unanimously feted as one of the best sweet Italian wines.

Ca' Rugate, Monteforte d'Alpone (VR)

Ca' Rugate, owned by the Tessari family, is a "boutique" winery which has recently produced a range of Soaves of great elegance and complexity. Among the best are the *crus* Monte Alto and Monte Fiorentine.

Gini, Monteforte d'Alpone (VR)

It is impossible to fully appreciate the tremendous potential of the Garganega and Trebbiano grapes and terroir without tasting the Soave Classico Superiore Contrada Salvarenza Vecchie Vigne, a mouthful in every sense. Made by Sandro and Claudio Gini, this is a wine of unbelievable concentration, balance and complexity. All Gini wines are sublime, from the Recioto di Soave to the Soave Classico Superiore La Froscà.

La Cappuccina, Monteforte d'Alpone (VR)

The Tessari family makes innovative regional wines, such as Sauvignon and an exceptional Cabernet Franc Campo Buri, as well as fine Soave from the Fontégo and San Brizio vineyards.

Umberto Portinari, Monteforte d'Alpone (VR)

Umberto Portinari has put his name to some of the best Soaves of recent years, the result of careful experimentation. His Soave Vigna Albare Doppia Maturazione Ragionata (a long name, indicating that some of the grapes have been dried) is an intriguing wine, with compelling richness and complexity.

Cav GB Bertani, Negrar (VR)

Bertani is an historic name in the Veneto. Its wineries are among the few in the world to store thousands of bottles from long-ago vintages in perfect drinkable conditions. From the legendary Acinatico of 1928 to the latest Amarone, they form a fascinating collection. But the innovative wines, such as Cabernet Sauvignon Villa Novare, are also a class apart.

above *Romano Dal Forno and his three sons in the cellar of his estate in Illasi. Romano produces tiny quantities of exemplary Valpolicella, most notably Amarone Vigneto di Monte Lodoletta.*

and has replanted traditional varieties, with surprising results. His Amarone Vigneto di Monte Lodoletta is one of the best ever Italian reds, even in lesser years, and reflects Dal Forno's exemplary vineyard management.

Santi, Illasi (VR)

Santi is at the heart of Gruppo Italiano Vini, the largest wine producer in Italy. This huge enterprise produces millions of bottles of wine from a dozen establishments scattered around the very best wine regions of the country, and boasts a range renowned for its high quality and good value. Among many other

excellent wines, Santi's star attractions include an excellent Soave Classico and a fine Amarone.

Corte Sant'Alda, Mezzane di Sotto (VR)

A small establishment owned by the Camerani family, who produce Valpolicella and Amarone of the highest quality.

Anselmi, Monteforte d'Alpone (VR)

Roberto Anselmi has been instrumental in the Soave renaissance. An enthusiastic experimenter, Roberto is dedicated to creating excellent vineyards. Vinified by *cru*,

Cantina Sociale Valpolicella, Negrar (VR)
Even this great establishment has bent slightly into the wind of change. Today, it offers excellent wines from some of the best vineyards in the region, the Amarone della Valpolicella Classico Vigneti di Jago Selezione a typical example.

Le Ragose, Negrar (VR) In the heart of the traditional Valpolicella region, Le Ragose makes wines of the greatest merit, whether Amarone, Valpolicella or the new Cabernet. In a good vintage the Amarone achieves an unmistakable distinction.

Quintarelli, Negrar (VR) Small quantities and very high prices are the only arguable drawbacks of the wines from this great Valpolicella winemaker. Its Amarone Riserva has the breadth and depth of some of the world's greatest wines, while the Cabernet Alzero and Valpolicella Superiore are also attractive and stylish.

Zenato, Peschiera del Garda (VR) Sergio Zenato is a négociant with an incredible nose, and has the crucial knack of acquiring the best grapes for his wide range of vines. Standards are high: there is a pear-tinged Lugana and an excellent Cabernet, but the Amarone Riserva stands out.

Masi, San Ambrogio di Valpolicella (VR)
This historic Veronese establishment, owner of magnificent vineyards such as Campolongo di Torbe and Serego Alighieri, has firmly established itself in the front wave of the Valpolicella renaissance, and has carried out invaluable research into the terroir, grapes and winery techniques. The Amarone and Valpolicella are striking, world-class wines. Check out the Osar too, an unusual blend of Oseletta and Corvina.

Inama, San Bonifacio (VR) In the last few years, Stefano Inama has been the brains behind some of the most interesting white wines of the Veneto. His Soave and his Sauvignon are wines which fully vindicate Inama's substantial research into vineyard and above all winery techniques, where long maturation, maceration of the skins and new oak confer a distinctive character on every wine. Among a strong selection, the Soave Classico Superiore Du Lot and the Sauvignon Vulcaia Fumé are particularly recommended.

Stefano Accordini, San Pietro in Cariano (VR) Stefano and Tiziano Accordini make some excellent Valpolicellas and Amarones from their own vineyards. The Selezioni Amarone and Recioto from the Acinatico range are particularly attractive, and the Amarone Classico del Vigneto Il Fornetto is sometimes spectacular.

Angelo Nicolis e Figli, San Pietro in Cariano (VR) Beppe Nicolis works hard with excellent varieties to best express this great terroir. His Amarones are excellent, in particular the dark, brooding Ambrosan, which is manna to those who love juicy fruit and depth and has few equals in the region.

Fratelli Speri, San Pietro in Cariano (VR) The Amarone della Valpolicella Classico del Vigneto Monte Sant'Urbano is a mouthful in every sense, and a standard-bearer of winemaking in Valpolicella. It's an extremely well-made wine, like all Speri's offerings, and displays extraordinary concentration, refinement and complexity.

Fratelli Tedeschi, San Pietro in Cariano (VR) Buoyed by a long winemaking tradition and some of the best vineyards in the region, Tedeschi's Valpolicella and Amarone are of rare elegance, particularly those from single vineyards. Most noteworthy are the Amarone Classico Capitel Monte Olmi, the Capitel della Fabriseria and the Recioto della Valpolicella Capitel Monte Fontana.

Leonildo Pieropan, Soave (VR) The wines of Leonildo Pieropan were revolutionary in the Soave region. When this wine was still known as a very modest white, Leonildo created wines capable of lasting 20 years in the cellar. His selected wines, such as Soave Vigneto La Rocca and Soave Vigneto Calvarino, are exceptional and his Recioto di Soave Le Colombare and Passito della Rocca are some of the best sweet Italian wines.

Bolla, Verona A grand establishment in the Veronese tradition. Its millions of bottles can reach high levels of quality, and there are signs of further improvement. The Amarone Riserva and an excellent Valpolicella Superiore Le Pojane stand out.

Fratelli Pasqua, Verona One of the most important enterprises in the Veneto, with traditional and innovative styles — the Soave Classico Sagramoso and Amarone Vigneti di Casterna are worth a look.

below These grapes for Bardolino have come straight from the vineyard and will be transported to the crusher via the screw mechanism. This operation is carried out as quickly as possible, to prevent the grape juice from oxidising.

Veneto Orientale

The Upper Treviso is a region with a great vinous tradition, and is divided into two parts by the river Piave. South of the river is Montello e Colli Asolani, while to the north is Conegliano Valdobbiadene. The common denominator linking the two regions is Prosecco wines, but the Montello region now seems to specialise in the production of full-bodied reds, especially Merlot and Cabernet Sauvignon, which prosper in the clay-rich, stony soil. The recent DOC, Colli di Conegliano, produces a Bianco (from Incrocio Manzoni, Riesling and other grape varieties) and a Rosso (from Cabernet Sauvignon, Merlot, Marzemino and Incrocio Manzoni). There are also two sweet wines to recommend: the Refrontolo Passito made from Marzemino grapes, and Torchiato di Fregona, a white wine made from Prosecco, Verdiso and Boschera.

There are three basic types of Prosecco in the various DOCs: "still" Prosecco, a little-known light white wine; a semi-sparkling, which nearly always comes in bottles with a flat cork or champagne-like cork, traditionally secured not with wire but with string; and the Prosecco spumante, which is produced according to the Italian method of secondary fermentation in an autoclave, and is regarded as the finest wine in both DOC regions.

Prosecco di Valdobbiadene DOC is produced to the tune of nearly 25 million litres a year. It includes a sub-region, Cartizze, which is home to the Prosecco di Valdobbiadene Superiore di Cartizze, or simply Cartizze – a sparkling wine, slightly sweet and very fragrant, which has a reputation for finesse and commands three times the price of Prosecco. However, there are more "Cartizze" wines produced than the regulations permit. Despite its name, Extra Dry – the most commonplace Prosecco – is sweeter than a Brut according to European regulations, and the Dry is even sweeter. This makes it an excellent sparkling dessert wine.

Treviso and Piave

The hilly Treviso wine district stretches down to the well-watered plains of the eastern part of the region, towards the Venetian coast. Here the view changes completely: drivers on the Venice-Trieste motorway, which skirts the wine regions of Portogruaro and Cessalto, can look over to the pergola-trained vines of Lison-Pramaggiore, a DOC region synonymous with three wines. Tocai is a white wine that clearly reveals its links with the adjacent region of Friuli: indeed, the DOC straddles the two regions. Then there are the Merlot and Cabernet Sauvignon, which on these thin, stony soils manage to express themselves with an unrivalled subtlety – this is, in fact, a land reminiscent of the plain of the Haut-Médoc in Bordeaux.

Further north, across the provinces of Venezia and Treviso, is the very large DOC region of Piave, which is home to an enormous range of wines, almost all made from international varieties and all in keeping with popular demand: namely Pinot Bianco, Pinot Grigio, Pinot Nero, Chardonnay, Merlot and Cabernet Sauvignon. But more homespun wines have survived since the pre-phylloxera era: Verduzzo among the whites, and the famously powerful Raboso, among the reds, are perhaps the most traditional.

below *Treviso forms the hilly hinterland of Venice. It is home to many small family plots and numerous grape varieties.*

Notable producers

Carpenè Malvolti, Conegliano (TV)
Antonio Carpenè, father of Italian spumante, founded this establishment in 1868. It now produces 3.5 million bottles a year and some of the best spumante. The traditional-method Talento and the excellent Prosecco di Conegliano are the pick of the bunch.

Zardetto, Conegliano (TV)
Pino and Fabio Zardetto are true believers in wines with typicity, as shown by their Prosecco dei Colli di Conegliano, which they make in several versions. The Prosecco Brut, Zeroventi Dry and Colli di Conegliano Bianco are all excellent.

Santa Margherita, Fossalta di Portogruaro (VE)
One of the most important Italian wineries, responsible for launching Pinot Grigio in the 1970s, and with a range of varietals from the Veneto – from Müller Thurgau to Chardonnay and Malbec. From its HQ in Lison-Pramaggiore it exports wine all over the world.

below Prosecco grapes. In the past, Prosecco wines would cease fermenting during the cold winters, leaving residual sweetness in the wine. New fermenting in spring added the sparkle.

Serafini & Vidotto, Nervesa della Battaglia (TV)
Francesco Serafini and Antonello Vidotto are keen to exploit the hitherto little-known terroir of Montello to its full potential. Their Rosso dell'Abazia, a blend of Cabernet Sauvignon, Cabernet Franc and Merlot, has spectacular power and complexity.

Ornella Molon Traverso, Salgareda (TV)
Ornella Molon and her husband Giancarlo Traverso make very interesting wines from the Piave region. Conspicuous among them are an excellent Piave Merlot, a Piave Cabernet of the Ornella range and very good whites, such as Traminer.

Desiderio Bisol & Figli, Valdobbiadene (TV)
The Bisol brothers are among the best spumante producers in Italy. They have a property of 25 hectares, with 13 more rented, divided between the most favourable parts of Santo Stefano, with the Fol and Cartizze *crus*, and the locality of Rolle. Besides Prosecco grapes, the likes of Incrozio Manzoni, Pinot Nero and Pinot Bianco, Chardonnay, Sauvignon and Verdiso have been planted. Outstanding wines include an excellent Cartizze and Prosecco from the Fol, Garnei, Colmei and Salis, each with its own rich personality. The traditional-method Talento is made in several versions, but the vintage dedicated to the founder, Eliseo Bisol, stands supreme.

Canevel, Valdobbiadene (TV)
A Treviso stalwart: grapes from its 12 hectares are combined with those from 60 others, which are rented, to make an admirable range of Italian-method spumante wines, led by the smooth, fruity Prosecco Extra Dry.

Cantina Produttori di Valdobbiadene, Valdobbiadene (TV)
A very large cooperative, with 750 members controlling over 600 hectares of vineyards. Two million bottles a year are sold under the Val d'Oca label and the quality is excellent.

Ruggeri & C, Valdobbiadene (TV)
Great care taken in selecting the grapes, which are mostly brought in, and modern technology in the winery enables this establishment to produce the highest quality Prosecco. The Selezione Oro, an Extra Dry of which about 600,000 bottles are made each year, is sensational.

Adami, Vidor (TV)
This winery has only 2.5 hectares of vineyards and a total production of about 300,000 bottles a year, but the Adami brothers are shrewd 'readers' of Treviso wines: their Prosecco di Valdobbiadene Vigneto Giardino Dry is already a classic.

above The hilly inland area of Venezia is beautiful, and awash with art, architecture and history. But it's often given short shrift by tourists, due to the proximity of Venice.

Trentino

A copper bucket celebrating Bacchus and a situla of Etruscan origin, both discovered in the mid-19th century in Val di Cembra, are among relics of a Trentino wine culture that stretches back to the 6th century BC. In the Middle Ages Augustine monks of the abbey of San Michele all'Adige codified winemaking practices, the dates of vintages, checks on production and even the prices of wine in their "books of rules", while in the mid-16th century Michelangelo Mariani, the historian of the Council of Trent, made a valuable record of the wines and grape varieties of the region.

But it was after the annexation of this region by the Austro-Hungarian Empire in the 19th century that wine first became a focal point of life in the Trentino. Then in 1874, the coordination of regional wine production and the training of oenologists and agronomists was entrusted to the Istituto Agrario di San Michele all'Adige, which replaced the venerable Augustine abbey. The Istituto is one of the best winemaking schools in Italy and educates dozens of specialised technicians each year. While many graduates are now plying their trade across the country, most remain loyal to the local wine industry. This initiative

right *Trentino's vineyards are often found clinging to steep mountainsides, but the Alpine climate encourages producers to focus on refined wines.*

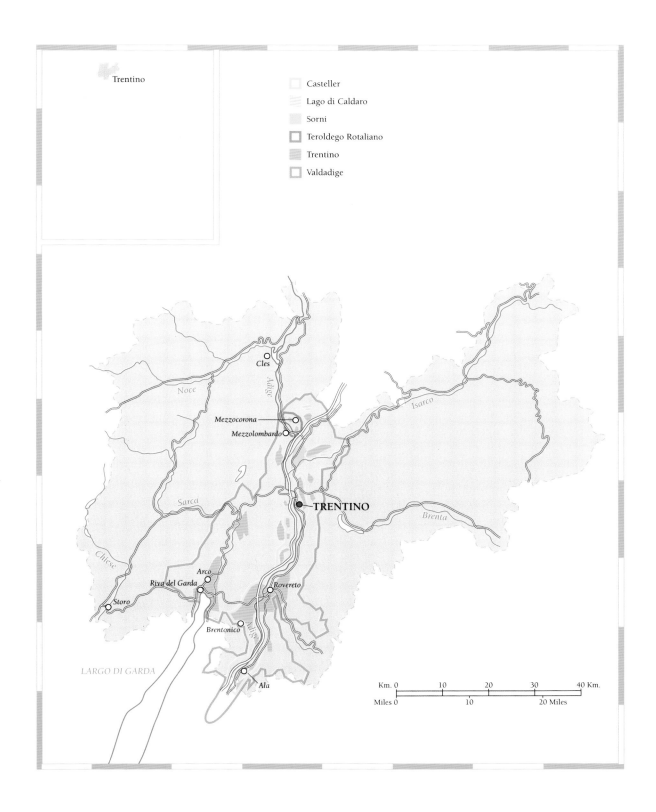

Trentino

Casteller

Lago di Caldaro

Sorni

Teroldego Rotaliano

Trentino

Valdadige

Cles

Noce

Adige

Isarco

Mezzocorona

Mezzolombardo

Sarca

TRENTINO

Brenta

Chiese

Arco

Riva del Garda

Rovereto

Storo

Brentonico

Adige

LARGO DI GARDA

Ala

Km. 0   10   20   30   40 Km.

Miles 0   10   20 Miles

medium-bodied red. The other vineyards are located between Avio and Mezzolombardo, following the course of the river and the narrow valley. Vines are grown on steep terraces and trained on the Trentino pergola system.

Nosiola was once the main grape here, but this white variety was savaged by phylloxera in the early 20th century and is now rare. Today, the most widespread white variety is Chardonnay, used to produce Trentino Chardonnay or as a base for DOC *metodo classico* sparkling wines, under the name Trento Classico. These are some of the best Italian sparkling wines, and are marketed by well-known enterprises such as Ferrari, Cavit and MezzaCorona.

The rest of the production – almost all covered by the Trentino DOC and comprising over 60 per cent of a total of approximately 700,000 hectolitres – is mostly wines from international varieties, including Müller-Thurgau, Pinot Grigio and Sauvignon Blanc. More traditional wines survive, such as Nosiola and Sorni, in both Rosso and Bianco form. All these wines are extremely well made by the graduates of the Istituto.

However, most of the production in Trentino is now controlled by large, modern cooperative wineries – Cavit is a perfect example – which deliver decent but slightly simple styles. Exceptions to this rule include Teroldego Rotaliano, a red DOC hailing from outside the Trentino appellation and made from Teroldego grapes. This is the finest wine in the region, with a spicy fragrance and remarkable balance. Also with its own DOC, Casteller is a red wine made from Schiava Grossa, Lambrusco and up to 20 per cent Merlot, Lagrein and Teroldego.

Soil, climate and viticulture

Differences in altitude, exposure of the vineyards and the orientation of the valleys create a variety of microclimates – some hostile, others favourable. In the more southern parts along the northern shores of Lake Garda, the climate is Mediterranean, while more northern regions, such as the hilly Mezzolombardo and Mezzocorona, are similar to the Moselle. Here, even a precocious grape variety such as Chardonnay may find it difficult to fully mature.

The soil is more uniform: vines are concentrated in the valley of the Adige, where soils are sandy and gravelly with patches of calcareous soil. The Trentino pergola is found almost everywhere, but the Guyot system is increasingly popular in newly-planted vineyards, especially on estates striving for very high quality wines.

has thus helped to ensure that the average standard of Trentino wines is among the highest in the country, while promoting the formation of the region's influential and numerous cooperative wineries.

Wines and wine regions

In wine terms, Trentino and Alto Adige are completely distinct entities. Trento is clearly influenced by the neighbouring Veneto and most of its vineyards are situated along the valley of the Adige: an exception is the district of Isera, the home of Marzemino – a fragrant,

Notable producers

Tenuta San Leonardo, Avio (TN) Carlo Guerrieri Gonzaga is probably Trentino's best interpreter of Cabernet Sauvignon. His San Leonardo is a gem, made from his finest grapes. The best vintages display sophisticated elegance and a harmonious, smooth taste like few other Trentino reds. Also produces a strikingly fragrant Merlot.

Maso Cantanghel Civezzano (TN) Talented winemaker Piero Zabini's modern winery offers highly innovative wines matured in small oak barrels. Choice selections are Trentino Cabernet Rosso di Pila, Trentino Merlot Tajapreda and Trentino Pinot Nero Piero Zabini.

Pojer & Sandri Faedo (TN) Fiorentina Sandri and Mario Pojer's partnership of 20 years has produced extraordinary wines. Whites include an aromatic, floral Traminer and a voluptuous Bianco Faye, a Chardonnay matured in new barriques. But the reds are now ascendant: the Pinot Nero is one of the best in Italy, but the Rosso Faye – a Cabernet, Merlot and Lagrein blend – is breathtaking, a dark red with a nose rich in eastern spices and jam, and a harmonious, silky palate.

Cantina d'Isera, Isera (TN) This small cooperative specialises in technically irreproachable wines at reasonable prices. Its Trentino Marzemino Etichetta Verde is one of the best versions of this fragrant red.

de Tarczal, Isera (TN) The most famous Marzemino: an intensely fruity fragrance, light and easy to drink.

Pravis, Lasino (TN) Perhaps rather simple wines, but well-made, personal and good value. The Trentino Nosiola Le Frate is a deliciously fruity white with a clean taste.

Cesconi, Lavis (TN) Paolo Cesconi and his sons' small but successful winery turns out technically proficient and highly innovative wines, especially whites. The Sauvignon, Chardonnay and Pinot Bianco DOCs are excellent.

La Vis Lavis (TN) Perhaps the best large cooperative in Trentino, producing very well made wines – modern and innovative. The most interesting is the Ritratto, made from Teroldego and Lagrein: a red with an intense, complex bouquet, with hints of blackcurrant and wild black cherries. Trentino Cabernet Sauvignon Ritratti and Trentino Chardonnay are also interesting.

MezzaCorona, Mezzocorona (TN) A large, well-known cooperative with a very modern plant for its sparkling wines, and soon to become the largest producer of Trento Classico. High point is Rotari Brut, a Trento Classico of the highest quality.

Foradori, Mezzolombardo (TN) Elisabetta Foradori has been producing extraordinary, elegant red wines for several years now. These are modern and innovative, with superb structure: the Teroldego Rotaliano Vigneto Sgarzon and Vigneto Morei are the best in their category, while Granato, another Teroldego, is simply outstanding.

Castel Noarna, Nogaredo (TN) Marco Zani's estate is based in a medieval fortress, but its modern history began in the mid-1970s, when the Zani family took over the holding from the counts of Lodron. Courageous modernisation has delivered extremely reliable white wines; from the fragrant Nosiola to Sauvignon Leverini and Campo Grande, a Chardonnay. The reds have depth and body, with elegance and firmness in good years. Pick of the bunch are the Schiava Scalzavacca, fresh with a clean taste, and Cabernet Romeo, a wine of wonderful tannic depth. All wines are Trentino or Valdadige DOC.

Cavit, Trento A consortium of cooperative wineries which bottles and markets wines produced from the grapes of 6,000 growers, almost half of the region's production. Valuable names in this sea of wine include Trento Classico Graal, an outstanding sparkling Chardonnay.

Cesarini Sforza, Trento Makes all its wines from grapes bought from local growers. Count Lamberto produces about 1.2 million bottles of sparkling wine each year: the magnificent Brut Riserva dei Conti has an aristocratic mousse and firm, harmonious taste; the Brut has lively acidity; while the Blanc de Blancs Chardonnay displays class and well-balanced aromas.

Spumante Ferrari, Trento This prestigious "maison" was founded in 1902 by Giulio Ferrari, one of the pioneers of spumante. Today it is owned by the Lunelli brothers, who make three million bottles a year across five labels. Most prestigious is the Giulio Ferrari Riserva del Fondatore: a vintage blanc de blancs of incredible complexity and elegance. There is spumante from Chardonnay and Pinot Nero; Trento Brut, the vintage Trento Perlé, Maximum Brut, and Trento Rosé, all wines of outstanding quality.

Concilio Vini, Volano (TN) Size is most definitely important here, for this large and well-known winery thrives on producing inspired wines – across four labels. Most notable are the Trentino Cabernet Sauvignon Riserva and Trentino Merlot Novaline Riserva.

below *Carlo Guerrieri Gonzaga at his estate. His San Leonardo* vino da tavola *is a Cabernet and Merlot blend, and is regarded as one of the most elegant wines in northern Italy.*

Alto Adige

The sub-region of Alto Adige – known to the ancients as Retia – was making wine during the Iron Age and had a flourishing viticulture in place when the Romans arrived. Pliny noted how the wines were stored and matured not in amphorae, the Roman vessels, but in wooden containers held together by metal rings – prototype barrels.

In the early Middle Ages, winegrowing by Benedictine and Dominican monks fuelled the economic revival of the region, as the convents and bishoprics in southern Germany discovered the wines of southern Tyrol. In about AD800 the Alto Adige boasted a staggering 10,000 hectares of vineyards, approximately twice its current quota.

Today, this is one of the most interesting wine regions in Italy, and not just to the Italians. Most Alto Adige wines are exported to Austria and Germany – obvious markets, considering that both countries share a common language with the Alto Adige, where most people speak German.

The need for increased efficiency has prompted the formation of many small and medium-sized cooperative wineries – which have a good track record in excellent wines – besides some impressive private producers.

Wines and winemaking

The smallish DOC area of Alto Adige/Südtirol includes the valleys of the Adige and Isarco rivers, and oversees the production of approximately 80 per cent of the region's annual output of around 600,000 hectolitres.

This Italian/German-speaking region raises the need for bilingual denominations and labels. The Italian or French name of the grape variety is set beside the German name; thus Pinot Bianco translates to Weissburgunder, Pinot Grigio to Ruländer, Pinot Nero to Blauburgunder, Traminer Aromatico to Gewürztraminer and Lagrein Scuro to Lagrein Dunkel. The Cantina Cooperativa or Cantina Produttori (the cooperative winery) becomes Kellereigenossenschaft while the name of localities is also translated: Cornaiano is Girlan, Termeno is Tramin, Caldaro is Kaltern and Cortaccia is Kurtatsch.

The most common white wine is the Pinot Bianco/ Weissburgunder, followed by Riesling, Sauvignon, Pinot Grigio/Ruländer and Traminer Aromatico/Gewürztraminer. The most commonplace red is Schiava/Vernatsch, a delicious, light red wine which accounts for almost two-thirds of the region's production and is found everywhere. The Lago di Caldaro/Kaltarersee and Santa Maddalena are both 'noble' reds, made from Schiava grapes with the addition of a few other varieties – the latter is produced around Bolzano and both are Alto Adige/Südtirol DOC.

Lagrein is produced around the provincial capital, notably near the town of Gries. This red wine is similar to Trentino Teroldego and is made from grapes of the same name. The Riservas are interesting; among the most full-bodied and powerful in the region and very dark in colour.

Other important red wines are produced from international varieties, in particular Pinot Nero, Cabernet Sauvignon and Merlot. Alto Adige has a continental climate, which is ideal for the northern grape varieties. Besides Alto Adige/Südtirol DOC there are other areas which are sub-zones in their own right, such as Terlano/ Terlan, Valle Isarco/Eisacktaler and Valle Venosta. You will find their name next to that of the regional DOC when the wine comes from a specific region. The more famous regional wines include Sylvaner and Veltliner in Valle

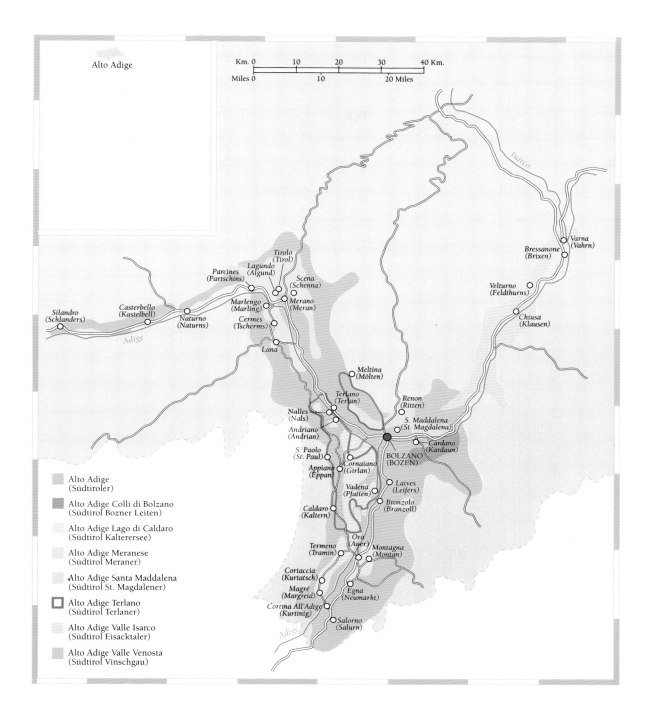

Alto Adige

Km. 0   10   20   30   40 Km.
Miles 0   10   20 Miles

Alto Adige
(Südtiroler)

Alto Adige Colli di Bolzano
(Südtirol Bozner Leiten)

Alto Adige Lago di Caldaro
(Südtirol Kalterersee)

Alto Adige Meranese
(Südtirol Meraner)

Alto Adige Santa Maddalena
(Südtirol St. Magdalener)

Alto Adige Terlano
(Südtirol Terlaner)

Alto Adige Valle Isarco
(Südtirol Eisacktaler)

Alto Adige Valle Venosta
(Südtirol Vinschgau)

Isarco, Pinot Bianco/Weissburgunder in the district of Terlano, and the magnificent Rheinriesling wines in the zone of Valle Venosta.

Soil, climate and viticulture

Winegrowing extends through the entire valley of the upper Adige river. Elsewhere, cultivation of vines and the production of wine is almost impossible, due to the high mountains and the increasingly alpine continental climate.

The soils are mostly sand and gravel, the respective percentages of which – along with the vineyard's exposure – can determine the suitability of a zone for a particular grape: the colder, more gravelly zones are perfect for most white varieties, while the likes of Cabernet Sauvignon and Lagrein thrive in sandy areas with a sunny exposure.

The main vine-training system in use is the Trentino pergola, which is smaller in Alto Adige and often densely planted in rows, but the classic Guyot training system is gradually taking precedence.

above *Autumnal vines above Lago di Caldaro, Alto Adige. This region is also known as the South Tyrol among the German-speaking natives, and many Austrian winegrowing methods remain.*

Notable producers

Cantina Produttori San Michele Appiano, Appiano/Eppan (BZ) The range of wines produced by the expert *kellermeister* Hans Terzer are made mainly from white grape varieties. There is an excellent – almost explosive – Sauvignon called St Valentin, which is characterised by a rich bouquet of varietal fragrances and boasts extraordinary balance and energy. There is a Chardonnay, refined in barriques but not dominated by wood, and a stylish Riesling Montiggl. The Pinot Bianco and Pinot Grigio are excellent choices, too.

Abtei Muri Gries, Bolzano/Bozen The Abtei (abbey) Muri Gries is an exceptional interpreter of the native variety, Lagrein. It offers a range of great reds, including the Lagrein Riserva, which is outstanding. This is a dense, powerful wine with a slightly bitter aftertaste and an intense fragrance of blueberries and blackcurrants.

Cantina di Gries, Bolzano/Bozen This winery has restored confidence in the Lagrein variety, with its favourable terroir and first-class cultivation methods. The two leading labels are Lagrein Prestige, which is matured in small wooden barrels, and Lagrein Collection.

Cantina Produttori di Santa Maddalena, Bolzano/Bozen The fame of this winery has traditionally been linked to the red Santa Maddalena, as is to be expected. But in recent years the winery has come up with another outstanding wine, a Cabernet: the region may be ideal for the variety, but the Mumelterhof is a genuine wonder. The various labels of Santa Maddalena (a basic version and the two *crus,* Stieler and Huck am Bach) are all delicious and very pleasant to drink. The two Lagreins, Taberhof and Perlhof, are matured in barriques and are also excellent.

Cantina Produttori di Caldaro, Caldar/Kaltern (BZ) Created in 1986 through the merger of three wineries, this cantina has quickly climbed the ladder in the Alto Adige. Besides its range of basic wines, it offers high quality Cabernet Sauvignon Riserva, Cabernet Sauvignon Campaner Riserva, Gewürztraminer Campaner and Chardonnay Wadleith.

Cantina Produttori Prima & Nuova/Erste & Neue, Caldar/Kaltern (BZ) This winery offers a vast selection of Alto Adige wines. The Puntay label is marvellous and the Gewürztraminer particularly successful.

Cantina Produttori Colterenzio/ Schreckbichl, Cornaiano/Girlan (BZ) Louis Raifer, the "professor" of Alto Adige oenology, has been running this winery for many years and it is considered the best cooperative in the region. The Cabernet Sauvignon and Sauvignon from the Lafoa estate are magnificent, while the red Cornelius, a blend of Cabernet and Merlot, is equally splendid.

Cantina Produttori Cornaiano/Girlan, Cornaiano/Girlan (BZ) One of the more traditional wineries in the district, notable chiefly for a Schiava made with grapes from the Gschleier vineyard – unanimously regarded as number one in the area.

Cantina Produttori Cortaccia, Cortaccia/Kurtatsch (BZ) The finest selections from this modern and functional cooperative winery are Cabernet Freienfeld and Merlot Brenntal. These are very modern wines, matured in small barrels and blessed with incredible elegance.

Tiefenbrunner, Cortaccia/Kurtatsch (BZ) In recent years this very traditional winery has specialised in refined, aromatic white wines. The best of the range, Feldmarschall, has Müller-Thurgau grapes as its main component: these come from a vineyard almost 1,000 metres above sea level.

Alois Lageder, Magré/Margraid (BZ) Alois Lageder runs the family wine estate, founded in 1855, with intelligence and passion. The leading wines are made from grapes cultivated in the holdings of Löwengang, Maso Römigberg and Lindemburg. All the *crus* are outstanding, from Terlaner Sauvignon Lehenhof to

Chardonnay and Cabernet di Löwengang, and Pinot Bianco Haberlerhof. Lageder has even transformed undervalued wines such as Lago di Caldaro into real winners.

Franz Haas, Montagna/Montan (BZ) This historic estate was founded in the 19th century and has ten hectares of vineyards, planted with grape varieties ranging from Chardonnay to Pinot Bianco, Riesling to Gewürztraminer, Lagrein to Pinot Nero. The Moscato Rosa, deliciously harmonious, is one of Haas's most successful wines, closely followed by the Gewürztraminer, which is distinguished more for its great aromatic refinement and delicate taste than for concentrated strength.

Castello Schwanburg, Nalles/Nals (BZ) A very traditional winery, owned by Dieter Rudolph Carli, a member of an old and noble family in the region. He produces a wide range of wines, but his trademark is the Castel Schwanburg, a Cabernet Riserva with mellow, velvety tones. This is arguably the region's only important red wine that can boast a long(ish) history.

Tenuta Falkenstein, Naturno/Naturns (BZ) An emerging winery at over 600 metres altitude, in the district of Val Venosta, in the region's northwest. It produces two excellent white wines: the Riesling is making ground on its German mentors and closing in on Italy's top white wines, while the fascinating Pinot Bianco is also near the top of its tree.

Cantina di Terlano, Terlano/Terlan (BZ) The most important winegrowing estate in the sub-zone of Terlano, and especially famous for white wines with great ageing potential. The richly aromatic Pinot Bianco deserves its recent plaudits, while the rich, intense Lagrein and the highly aromatic Gewürztraminer are worthy stablemates.

Cantina Produttori di Termeno, Termeno/Tramin (BZ) The Gewürztraminer Nussbaumerhof and Cabernet Terminum are real beauties. This is perhaps the most prominent winery in the south of the region, and its quality is increasing all the time.

Poderi Castel Ringberg e Kastelaz di Elena Walch, Termeno/Tramin (BZ) Elena Walch is a young woman who has made headlines in the Italian and German wine press in recent years and her wines are among the best in the region. The range is headlined by a splendid Gewürztraminer Kastelaz, made from grapes grown on near-vertical hillsides and offering a very elegant, aromatic bouquet. There is also an excellent Cabernet Sauvignon Riserva, which is not backward in coming forward, and in good years has an unusual structure for a red wine produced in the far north.

Hofstätter, Termeno/Tramin (BZ) Pinot Nero is a not a variety that fits easily into Italian oenology. However, there is one exception to this rule in Alto Adige. Martin Foradori, the energetic owner of the Hofstätter winery, produces Pinot Nero Sant'Urbano, the best Pinot Nero ever made from Italian vines. (No doubt a revamped cellar has helped.) There is also an excellent Gewürztraminer, Kolbenhof, which is one of the most interesting in the region.

Istituto Sperimentale Laimburg, Vadena/Pfatten (BZ) The Istituto Sperimentale di Laimburg has been training skilled oenologists for decades, and attached to the school is an excellent winery. Besides a range of superb white wines – including an outstanding aromatic Gewürztraminer and a stylish Riesling – it also produces some very pleasant reds. Lago di Caldaro Auslese Oelleitenhof has great strength and is very easy to drink, while the Cabernet is a fair, correct interpretation.

Abbazia di Novacella, Varna/Vahrn (BZ) The most northerly vineyards in Italy are those surrounding the ancient abbey of Novacella, where the Augustinian monks have been making wine for 800 years. Grapes grown include Sylvaner, Müller-Thurgau and Grüner Veltliner, producing aromatic, aristocratic white wines such as Sylvaner – very much at home in the Valle Isarco. The winery also uses vineyards further south to produce a splendid Sauvignon and an aromatic Moscato Rosa.

below *Alois Lageder at his influential winery in the Alto Adige. Lageder produces a DOC Chardonnay and Cabernet, and a raft of single-vineyard selections.*

Friuli-Venezia Giulia

The Eneti, an ancient Italic people, were probably the first to cultivate vines in the region, between the 13th and 12th century BC, and when the Venetic and Celtic tribes arrived in the 6th century BC they found a flourishing viticulture. The name Friuli is derived from Forum Julii, the ancient name of Cividale. Positioned at the crossroads of northern and southern Europe, of the Latin countries and the Slavonic world, it was subject to diverse influences, invasions and depredations. Its inhabitants produced excellent wines in the surrounding plains, and when they were forced in the 5th century AD to abandon Aquileia and flee from the marauding Huns, they founded the formidable commercial centre of Venice.

At the time, Pucinum's Carso wine, (probably the Prosecco of today) was famous throughout the empire. (From the Goths to the Byzantines and Lombards, all the invaders who crossed the region through the centuries praised the great quality of its wines.) There were mixed, wooded vineyards, where the vines were cultivated in the Etruscan manner and trained on "live" supports, usually elms. It was the monks in the Middle Ages who introduced the specialised vineyard, while the mixed system, although retained in a few places, was gradually abandoned.

Friuli was part of the Venetian Republic which strongly encouraged winemaking, although later it became part of the Austro-Hungarian Empire, until 1918. All these influences are reflected in the great richness of its oenological heritage.

Wines and winemaking

Friuli might produce over one million hectolitres annually, but it is also one of Italy's most prestigious wine regions, and has a modern outlook – especially with white wines.

The most important sub-region stretches along the border with Slovenia. This comprises two DOC areas, Collio Goriziano to the south, and Colli Orientali del Friuli, in the province of Udine. The boundary is the river Iudrio which, until the end of 1918, was also that which divided the Kingdom of Italy and the Austro-Hungarian Empire. The two regions are very similar: the predominantly hilly terrain alternates between chalky marl and sandstone, both perfectly drained soils.

In the central part of the region is the great irrigation plain of the Grave, created by thousands of years of alluvium, which is carried downstream by the Isonzo and Tagliamento rivers. This represents the DOC of Friuli Grave, and is the theoretical continuation of the Veneto regions of Piave and Lison-Pramaggiore.

The Grave and hilly regions are separated by a flat plain, where the clay soil favours red grape varieties. This is the Isonzo DOC, which is currently making the most of its exalted status. To the east of this area, between Gorizia and Trieste, is the tiny, hilly DOC region of Carso, while to the south are the regions of Friuli Aquileia, Friuli Latisana, and the recently created Friuli Annia.

One of the peculiarities of Friuli DOCs is that within the context of a fairly simple division of the various territories, each bears the Friuli prefix, to enhance the regional profile – although each of the eight DOCs is clearly distinguishable from the others.

Soil, climate and viticulture

The Friuli mountain system is made up of the Carnic and Julian Alps, forming a chain to the north and east. At the centre is a flat area of highly permeable alluvium. To the north, the fragmentation of rock masses has deposited

below *These vineyards near San Floriano lie close to the northern boundary of Collio, just across the border from Slovenia.*

gravel and pebbles: typical characteristics of the Grave del Friuli. The soil in the hilly areas of Colli Orientali and the Collio consists of sandstone, marl, clay and marine deposits – when perfectly drained, this proves ideal for vines. In the lowland regions of Latisana, Annia, Aquileia and the Friuli part of the Lison-Pramaggiore DOC,

cultivation is reminiscent of the Veneto; the vines are not planted too densely, though they are trained using the Sylvoz method, which gives fairly high yields. Planting is dense in the Colli Orientali, and the vines are usually low-yielding, with the Guyot and modified Guyot systems – or "Cappuccina" – in place.

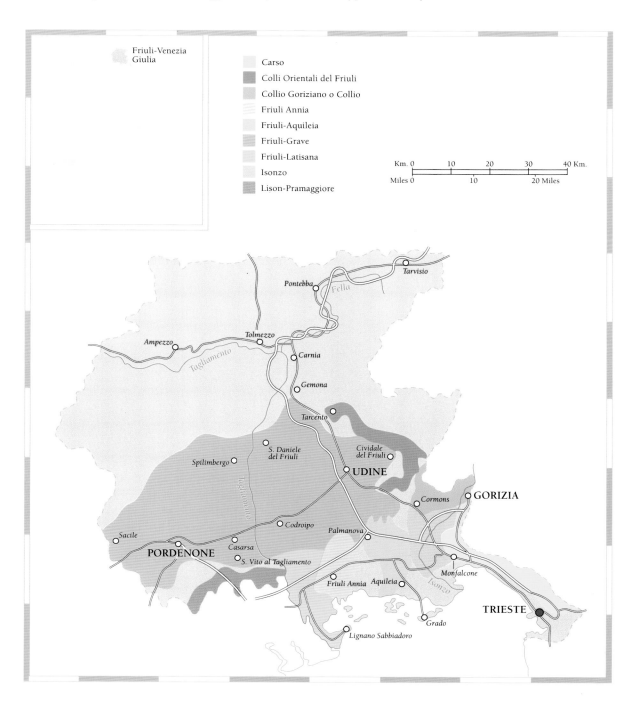

Friuli-Venezia Giulia

Carso
Colli Orientali del Friuli
Collio Goriziano o Collio
Friuli Annia
Friuli-Aquileia
Friuli-Grave
Friuli-Latisana
Isonzo
Lison-Pramaggiore

Km. 0   10   20   30   40 Km.
Miles 0   10   20 Miles

Il Collio Goriziano

This is arguably Italy's most celebrated white wine region, thanks to famous producers such as Mario Schiopetto, Silvio Jermann, Marco Felluga, Josko Gravner and Vittorio Puiatti, among others. It was also arguably the birthplace of modern Italian white wines at the end of the 1960s, when fermentation without contact between the must and grape skins resulted in a new, straw-coloured wine, rather than the orange hue typical of most Italian whites at that time.

Wines and wine regions

Collio Goriziano traces both the boundary with Slovenia – from Gorizia in the north to Dolegna del Collio – and the course of the Iudrio river, and basks in some of the continent's most enviable microclimates. The range of wines produced here is vast: white wines are invariably full-bodied and powerful – a far cry from light white apéritif wines – and the standard is set by the Tocai Friulano, which is particularly successful in areas such as San Floriano, Capriva and Cormons. (To clear up any potential confusion between the Tocai wines produced in both Friuli and the Tocai dell Collio – which are named after the Tokai grape – and those of the Hungarian locality of Tokaj – which are based around the Furmint grape – the International Court of Justice has ordered Italy to change the name of the Friuli Tocai wine before 2007.)

Other important wines produced in the region include Pinot Bianco, Sauvignon Blanc, Chardonnay, Pinot Grigio, Malvasia Istriana and Ribolla Gialla. These are beautifully structured whites, with the Ribolla proving the most characteristic and more acidic, while the Chardonnay is particularly full-bodied and intense.

Among the reds, Merlot and Cabernet Franc are exceptional. The former ages well, the latter does not, but both varieties are regarded as entirely local – anyone alluding to their French connections would be gently escorted off the premises. Ribolla, Malvasia and Tocai are used to make the occasional Collio Bianco, while Merlot and Cabernet Franc are used for Collio Rosso, a wine that appears with increasing regularity these days and which often outshines the straight Cabernet.

left *The efforts of wine producers in the Collio region are buoyed by a benevolent combination of Adriatic and alpine climates.*

Notable producers

Castello di Spessa, Capriva del Friuli (GO) This is a magnificent winery, set amidst an estate with 25 hectares of vineyards. Loretto Pali's excellent selection of Collio wines is spearheaded by the Pinot Bianco.

Russiz Superiore, Capriva del Friuli (GO) Previously owned by the counts of Orzoni, this is now the property of Marco Felluga and his daughter Patrizia. Among a range of excellent wines, Collio Rosso Riserva degli Orzoni is highly recommended.

Mario Schiopetto, Capriva del Friuli (GO) If there is one maestro of Friuli wine, it is undoubtedly Mario Schiopetto. The critical success of the great Friuli whites began here in the early 1970s with Schiopetto's first wines, innovative versions of Tocai and Malvasia Istriana. The maestro has overseen minor miracles in terms of winery technology, but few producers have emulated his ability to distil the personality of a region through its wines. His are generally matured in steel, although he has introduced new oak barriques with great success. The Tocai Friulano, made in the style of a Moselle Riesling, is intensely concentrated and stylistically of the greatest purity, while his Pinot Bianco is probably the finest in Italy. Not surprisingly, these are just a few of his many delightful selections – not bad for a man who came into winemaking by accident.

Villa Russiz, Capriva del Friuli (GO) Gianni Menotti, director and winemaker of this estate, has managed to capture the essential charm of Collio wines with a range of great whites: most notably the Sauvignon de La Tour, with its astonishing structure, and warm, intense reds such as the Merlot Graf de La Tour.

Ronco dei Tassi, Cormons (GO) Fabio Coser's prestigious selection of Collio wines ranges from Pinot Grigio to Collio Rosso Cjarandon. Pick of the bunch is the Collio Bianco Fosarin, an elegant wine matured in new wood.

Venica & Venica, Dolegna del Collio (GO) The Venicas have been excellent makers of Collio wines for many years. Their secret is vineyards with perfect (northwesterly) exposure and a meticulous approach to production. The Sauvignon Ronco delle Mele is stylish and aromatic, while the Pinot Bianco is elegant, with a complex palate.

Borgo Conventi, Farra D'Isonzo (GO) Gianni Vescovo owns vineyards and estates in various locations in Friuli, producing consistently good wines. Borgo Conventi is his top label, while the red Braida Nuova made from a Bordeaux-style blend is remarkable: a powerful combination of attractive fruit and robust tannins.

Vinnaioli Jermann, Farra D'Isonzo (GO) Silvio Jermann's Vintage Tunina has been one of the most wonderful and popular wines of recent decades. First produced 20 years ago, it continues to fascinate with a perfect balance of everything one could hope to find in a white Friuli. Jermann's masterstroke was to combine Chardonnay and Sauvignon with small proportions of Malvasia Istriana and Ribolla Gialla, as well as Tocai, Pinot Bianco and Picolit, and the floral, fruity aromas are unequalled. The longevity is amazing.

Jermann's exceptional wines are great whites, vinified in steel or in barriques of new oak and often with extraordinary names – Red Angel in the Moonlight, and Were Dreams, Now it is Just Wine.

Josko Gravner, Gorizia One of the region's most famous winemakers, and a passionate innovator, Gravner has been hit hard in recent years by bad weather, but is still a compelling fixture on the local scene. His revolution involved a move from steel to new wood, to terracotta amphorae – to revive a classic style – and then back to wooden butts.

La Castellada, Gorizia Giorgio and Nicolò Bensa buck the local trend with a shrewdly limited policy: only three labels are on offer, but each is of the highest calibre – Bianco della Castellada, Rosso della Castellada and Ribolla Gialla.

Conti Formentini, San Floriano del Collio (GO) Part of the Gruppo Italiano Vini, this offers a good range of typical Collio wines. The Chardonnay Torre di Tramontana is particularly commendable.

Livon, San Giovanni al Natisone (UD) The high-quality wines produced here by Tonino and Valneo Livon, in consultation with oenologist Rinaldo Stocco, result from years of research and experimentation. The excellent Sauvignon Valbuins is a fruity mouthful, while the white Braide Alte fully deserves its recent critical acclaim.

above *Collio Goriziano is best known for its refined and elegant white wines, made from – among others – Sauvignon Blanc, Tocai Friulano, Malvasia, Pinot Bianco and Pinot Grigio.*

Colli Orientali del Friuli

This may be a secondary region in importance, but it is first among equals for quality. The Colli Orientali del Friuli is home to the same varieties as the Collio Goriziano, and its calcareous-clay soil nurtures similar net results. However, the Colli Orientali comprises two official sub-regions, Cialla and Rosazzo, which preserve a few unique characteristics. Cialla is renowned for the Verduzzo, Picolit, Ribolla Gialla, Refosco and Schioppettino varieties; the first three are whites, the last two reds. The second sub-region is associated with Ribolla Gialla, which is thought to have originated in the vineyards of the Abbey of Rosazzo over a thousand years ago. Another sub-region to the north, Ramandolo, boasts a Verduzzo di Ramandolo, a famous sweet white wine.

The Picolit is one of the rarest and most famous sweet Italian white wines, and yet another legendary, ancient wine in this region. Count Asquini, an 18th-century nobleman with vast estates in the eastern part of Friuli, was one of the first to go on record about the riches of Picolit. He believed, with some partiality, that his own Piccolitto passito was the only local wine able to stand up to the Hungarian Tokaji.

In the 1970s there were only a few Picolit vines, cultivated in the vineyards of Rocca Bernarda. Villagers and producers had abandoned the variety, as it was too difficult to cultivate, the yields were too low, and above all it suffered from "floral abortion", a strange disease which drastically limited its production; a dose would prevent flowers from being fertilised and bunches would yield a paltry – if beautifully sweet – amount of grapes. Only the aristocratic Perusini family could continue to produce a wine from these cursed grapes.

Today, Picolit has returned to dominate the entire Colli Orientali del Friuli, so much so that, in 1979, it was finally rewarded with a DOC. Of course, the low yield and the different styles of vinification (some growers ferment the wine in small casks, while others prefer steel) make it impossible to identify a particular "type" of Picolit.

right *Looking towards Rosazzo, in the southern hills of Colli Orientali del Friuli. This region is home to Friuli's finest white wines and several improving reds.*

Notable producers

Girolamo Dorigo, Buttrio (UD) Girolamo Dorigo draws the best from the local terroir. His wines are impeccable, from the excellent Sauvignon Blanc to the outstanding Rosso Montsclapade.

Miani, Buttrio (UD) Enzo Pontoni embodies the romantic ideal of a winemaker, with stringent cultivation techniques that would drive his accountant to drink. His closely monitored, extremely low-yielding vines produce wines of extraordinary power and complexity, among the best Italian whites.

Paolo Rodaro, Cividale del Friuli (UD) Paolo Rodaro's wines are true to their terroir. His Tocai Friulano, Verduzzo and Sauvignon Blanc are superb.

Livio Felluga, Cormons (GO) Livio Felluga is a Friuli patriarch. He founded his own winery in 1956 and immediately bought vineyards with the best exposure in the Colli Orientali and the Collio. His winery has always been in step with the most modern technologies, while his philosophy is to develop each wine with a distinct personality – loyal to tradition and terroir, and technically flawless. His Tocai, Pinot Bianco and Pinot Grigio are always among the bestsellers, while every vintage of his Sauvignon Blanc is fascinating.

Livio has been the driving force behind Picolit's revival: his three hectares are planted in a splendid location, in the centre of his historic *cru* in Rosazzo. But one of his most fascinating wines is the Terre Alte, a skilful blend of Tocai, Sauvignon and Pinot Bianco, which perfectly embodies the spirit of the great whites of Friuli.

Walter Filiputti, Manzano (UD) Walter produces lovely table wines from the splendid vines of the Abbazia di Rosazzo. His red Pignolo and Ribolla Gialla are excellent, the latter a lesson in harmony.

Ronchi di Manzano, Manzano (UD) The success of Roberta Borghese's estate is due to years of hard work in the vineyards and winery. Merlot Ronc di Subule – intense and

concentrated with red fruit aromas and a warm, powerful palate – is one of the best Friuli reds of recent years.

Ronco dei Roseti – Zamò, Manzano (UD) The Zamòs have developed some of the best reds and whites in Friuli, such as Ronco dei Roseti, a Bordeaux-style vinification with the addition of local grape varieties, or Ronco delle Acacie, made from Chardonnay, Tocai and Pinot Bianco.

Ronco delle Betulle, Manzano (UD) Ivana Adami is blessed with some of the best vineyards in Rosazzo, the heart of the Colli Orientali, and produces distinguished wines such as the red Narciso.

Zamò & Zamò, Manzano (UD) The family winery of brothers Pierluigi and Silvano harvests some of the oldest vineyards in the region, often 50 years old. These ensure a high concentration, and extraordinary wines with great complexity – such as the Tocai and Merlot Vigne Cinquant'Anni.

Rocca Bernarda, Premariacco (UD) A Friuli institution. The 40 hectares of this estate, spread across hills basking in a superb exposure, are now the property of the Order of Malta. Director Marco Zuliani produces wines that improve year on year, and is putting great store in his Picolit.

La Viarte, Prepotto (UD) Franco Ceschin and his son Giulio bring a combination of knowledge and tenacity to their craft. They have also developed some of the most fascinating whites in the Colli Orientali, such as Bianco Liende: a legendary blend of Tocai, Pinot Bianco, Sauvignon Blanc, Riesling and Ribolla Gialla.

Ronco del Gnemiz, San Giovanni al Natisone (UD) Gabriele and Serena Palazzolo operate with the enthusiasm of wine-lovers, and their aim is absolute perfection. Excellent Chardonnay and Schioppettino, and an outstanding Rosso del Gnemiz – a Cabernet/Merlot – are the current benchmarks.

above *Livio Felluga in his cellar. Felluga founded his winery in 1956 and produces some of Friuli's finest wines. He was also the driving force behind the creation of the Rosazzo subzone.*

Isonzo, Grave, Latisana, Aquileia, Annia and Carso

right With cellars like this one at Beltrame – located in a restored farmhouse – Friuli is leading the way with modern white wines.

Isonzo is a fairly small area, which includes the communes of Mariano del Friuli, San Lorenzo Isontino and Gradisca d'Isonzo. A few producers have earned the region its "delightful" epithet, among them Pierpaolo Pecorari and Gianfranco Gallo at Vie di Romans. They produce some of the region's best Sauvignon and Chardonnay wines, as well as striking reds, based mainly on Merlot. Malvasia Istriana, Tocai Friulano and Pinot Bianco are more traditional wines: mellow, pleasant whites which make a perfect match for the risottos and brodetti of Grado's "lagoon" cuisine.

The DOCs from the lowlands – Friuli Grave, Friuli Latisana, Friuli Aquileia and Friuli Annia – are made from grape varieties similar to those outlined above, but the wines are less structured and have less body. However, some reds have sufficient class and concentration to compete with those from the hills: respectable Merlot, Cabernet and especially Refosco aren't uncommon, particularly when they're produced from densely planted vineyards and matured in small casks of French oak.

In Carso, the thirsty tourist would most likely be offered a glass of Terrano, a rough red much appreciated by the people of Trieste, where it enjoys a cult status. Made from Terrano grapes and closely related to Refosco, this is grown in very low-lying vineyards in the Carso dolines, an area extremely difficult to cultivate and almost impossible to harvest. Other noteworthy grapes include Malvasia Istriana, which is particularly distinguished in this region, and Vitovska, another white variety, widely regarded as Dalmatian in origin.

Notable producers

Tenuta Beltrame, Bagnària Arsa (UD)
Forty hectares, 25 of them planted with
vines, in the heart of the Aquileia
appellation. Renowned for its excellent Pinot
Bianco and Sauvignon.

Ca' Bolani, Cervignano del Friuli (UD)
Bought by the Zonin family in the 1970s,
this is now one of the most important
producers in the Aquileia DOC. Among the
many labels, all offering excellent value, the
fragrant Aquileia Sauvignon is particularly
impressive.

Borgo San Daniele, Cormons (GO) This
dynamic winery (which also owns vineyards
in Collio) is proof positive that Isonzo is a
rising star. The Isonzo Tocai Friulano is an
outstanding wine, mellow and structured
with a long finish.

Ronco del Gelso, Cormons (GO) A true
perfectionist, Giorgio Badin has been at the
cutting edge of Friuli wine for several years.
His Merlot and Tocai Friulano dell'Isonzo are
among the region's best varietal wines.

Edi Kante, Duino-Aurisina (TS) In a lost
corner of Carso, Edi Kante lovingly produces
little gems such as Terrano, and white wines
such as Sauvignon and Vitovska.

Vie di Romans, Mariano del Friuli (GO) A
name like Gallo can be a handicap when
you are involved in winemaking on an
international level. Gianfranco Gallo has
experienced this first-hand, having been
forced to rename the family estate Vie di
Romans following legal proceedings in the
United States with E&J Gallo, the Californian
mega-producers.

But Gianfranco Gallo's Isonzo wines have
a genuine international class and their
appearance in the 1980s heralded the
revival of the region. On this poor, stony,
calcareous soil Gianfranco grows some of
the most interesting Sauvignons in Italy,
such as Piere Sauvignon – with its goat's
cheese and elderberry – the Sauvignon
Vieris, and superb Chardonnay and Merlot.
Finally there is Flors di Uis, a fascinating

blend of Malvasia, Chardonnay and Riesling,
with extraordinary richness and structure
and a perfect Friuli style: the latest
masterpiece from a sublime talent.

**Tenuta di Blasig, Ronchi dei Legionari
(GO)** Elisabetta Bortolotto Sarcinelli's
Isonzo estate incorporates ten hectares of
prime terrain. The Chardonnay and
Falconetto, a blend of Chardonnay and
Malvasia, are of a high standard.

**Lis Neris – Pecorari, San Lorenzo
Isontino (GO)** The Pecorari family is a true
"voice" of the Isonzo terroir, and produces
some of the most interesting wines of the

region. The Isonzo Sauvignon Dom Picòl is a
an elegant, structured varietal wine.

**Pierpaolo Pecorari, San Lorenzo Isontino
(GO)** Isonzo is perfect for Sauvignon Blanc,
as the Sauvignon Kolàus testifies. Produced
by the venerable Pierpaolo Pecorari, this is
a concentrated, unctuous and
extraordinarily aromatic wine.

Castelvecchio, Sagrado (GO) Premier
wines from this beautiful, red-led estate
include the Carso Cabernet Sauvignon and
Carso Rosso Turmino, made from Terrano
and Cabernet grapes. Much of the success
is due to incredible cellar management.

left *The Borgo San Daniele estate covers
land in the Collio and Isonzo DOCs. Their
insatiable quest for innovation and
improvement has moved them towards
international styles.*

Adriatic Apennines

If the northeast is the antenna of central Italy, receptive to new and more cosmopolitan influences, then Emilia-Romagna, the Marches, Abruzzi and Molise could pass for a barometer of more "conservative" winemaking. But together, these regions are pivotal in terms of Italy's annual wine output: combined figures for the "aircraft carrier" Emilia-Romagna, the "battleship" Abruzzi, the "cruiser" the Marches and the "minesweeper" Molise accounted for over 20 per cent of national production in 1998 and 1999, the last in a series of weather-damaged harvests.

Tradition runs deep here, but the Adriatic Apennines are going through a period of reflection: producers are on a quest to unleash their quality wines. But with decades – if not centuries – of high yields and production systems geared mainly to achieving the best value-for-money ratio, the decision to concentrate on quality alone has not been an easy one. It has taken years to convert vineyards and wineries that were designed for large-scale production, and which had never seriously considered the idea of acquiring smaller vats for maturing wine. The aim of producing thousands of hectolitres of wine of an acceptable and uniform quality is entrenched in Emilia-Romagna, where giant cooperatives still churn out millions of bottles of wine a year. It is no coincidence that this sub-region produces the highest percentage of box-wine.

Yet Emilia-Romagna has also been keen to demonstrate its pedigree over the last few years. Emilia is the western part of the region, which specialises in sparkling wine and includes the fertile plains of Lambrusco, while Romagna, to the east, focuses on still wine. Lambrusco's leap in quality has been a clarion call for the region, but the revival began in the better-situated hilly regions, where the wineries were smaller and change was easier and quicker to absorb. Colli Piacentini and Colli Bolognesi are proof that traditional and international varieties can succeed side by side, and that great wines can be produced from local varieties such as Albana and Sangiovese. Other winegrowers have welcomed varieties such as Pinot Nero, Chardonnay and Cabernet, with brilliant results vindicating rigorous selection in the vineyards. Progress has also been made in large-scale production, with vineyards on the flat plains of the region proving amenable to mechanisation.

The Marches have always held a few trump cards. Verdicchio, for instance, is one of the most interesting white native varieties in the region, and the growing international success of producers who have followed a policy of lower yields has boosted these wines at the higher levels of classification. Their success is reminiscent of that enjoyed by the New Wave Friuli whites of the 1980s. The Marches – with the districts of Castelli di Jesi and di Matelica specialising in white wines, and Conero with its reds – has nothing to lose in comparison with its neighbours. Even the sleepy region of Piceno has woken from its atavistic torpor, and is striving to emulate the success of the great reds of Ancona.

Abruzzi has much to offer. Almost all its wines are produced from two varieties, the red Montepulciano and the white Trebbiano. This is the land of the large cooperatives, but one of the few places where a good red wine costs very little and the only region in Italy (perhaps the world) to have produced a great wine from Trebbiano grapes. The prestige of Abruzzi rests with a couple of excellent producers, who are closely followed by a small group of disciples. There is a vast gulf between the leaders and most of the chasing pack, but many experts rate the Abruzzi as the region with the greatest potential for quality.

There is little to say about Molise, a wonderful area which has remained untouched by economic and commercial interests. Of its two denominations, Pentro really exists only on the map, as its wine is sold almost exclusively in bulk. Biferno has one excellent producer, which is little return for a whole region, however small, but recent signs are promising.

right *The stunning hilltop town of San Biagio, in the Marches. This tranquil slice of the Apennines has been lifted by the success of its Verdicchio wines.*

Emilia-Romagna

In ancient times Emilia-Romagna was inhabited by the Italici people, but it was the Etruscans who introduced and cultivated *Vitis labrusca*, from which all Lambrusco varieties are derived, in the 7th century. Their system of growing vines with living supports, and the "promiscuous culture" of vines growing alongside other plants, survives today. In the Western district, on the other hand, Greek winemaking persists, in specialised vineyards, in the same grapes varieties as those grown in much of the rest of the Mediterranean – notably Malvasia and Moscato – and in the classic Greek training and pruning system.

One of the most important and ubiquitous native Italian grapes, Sangiovese, appears to have originated here, on the lower slopes of Monte Giove, near Sant'

Arcangelo di Romagna. Several new plantings of this variety have been carried out recently in Tuscany, with some of the best clones of the Sangiovese Romagnolo.

Wines and wine zones

Emilia-Romagna was created in 1860, from the duchies of Parma, Piacenza, Modena, Reggio and Ferrara, and the northern territories of the Papal States. Viticulturally, it reflects all these ancient divisions and acts as a bridge between the tradition of the northern regions – Lombardy, Piedmont and Veneto – and central Italy, particularly the Marches and Tuscany. The zones of Emilia-Romagna present markedly different styles, vineyards and

right *A vineyard overlooking the medieval town of Castell'Arquato. Vines are still trained and pruned in the classic Greek style in this western part of Emilia-Romagna.*

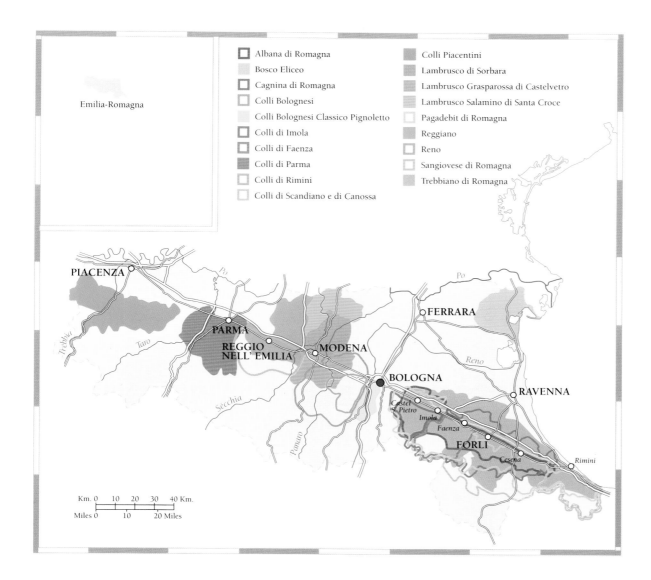

Emilia-Romagna

Albana di Romagna
Bosco Eliceo
Cagnina di Romagna
Colli Bolognesi
Colli Bolognesi Classico Pignoletto
Colli di Imola
Colli di Faenza
Colli di Parma
Colli di Rimini
Colli di Scandiano e di Canossa

Colli Piacentini
Lambrusco di Sorbara
Lambrusco Grasparossa di Castelvetro
Lambrusco Salamino di Santa Croce
Pagadebit di Romagna
Reggiano
Reno
Sangiovese di Romagna
Trebbiano di Romagna

traditions. Today, it is one of the largest wine regions in Italy in terms of production: the average is about 7 million hectolitres a year, of which 12 per cent is DOC or DOCG.

Colli Piacentini is the northwestern region, epitomised by Gutturnio, a Barbera and Croatina blend. This is a full-bodied, concentrated red wine that can be aged for at least five or six years. A supporting cast of at least a dozen other wines is led by Ortrugo, a light, often semi-sparkling white wine; Monterosso Val d'Arda, a white from Malvasia di Candia, Moscato, Trebbiano Romagnolo and Ortrugo; and Trebbianino Val Trebbia, a white wine predominantly from Ortrugo grapes. Chardonnay, Pinot Grigio and Sauvignon Blanc also have a part to play in the region. Meanwhile,

red varieties include Croatina (also known as Bonarda), Barbera and international varieties such as Pinot Nero and Cabernet Sauvignon. Colli di Parma is less well known but produces a similar range of wines: Rosso has similar ingredients to Gutturnio; Malvasia, often sparkling, is similar to Monterosso Val d'Arda; but Sauvignon Blanc is the area's key white wine.

The provinces of Reggio Emilia and Modena are notable for their sparkling wines, which have evolved largely because the region's rich cuisine calls for light white wines able to cut through oil. The DOC Colli di Scandiano e di Canossa includes a Bianco which is often semi-sparkling and sometimes sparkling, made

above *The leaning tower of Bologna. Between this academic city and the Adriatic lies a huge Sangiovese production zone, the wine beloved of the Bolognesi.*

Lambruscos hail from Modena: probably the most famous is the di Sorbara, but the most full-bodied, purple versions are Salamino di Santa Croce and the Grasparossa di Castelvetro. These are simple but fascinating wines, respected despite the fact that they are not great red wines for laying down. The Bosco Eliceo DOC, situated between Ferrara and Ravenna, produces mainly semi-sparkling wines, from a Bianco mixing Trebbiano and Sauvignon Blanc, to Sauvignon Blanc, the Fortana reds and a still Merlot. The Reno DOC straddles the provinces of Bologna and Modena and specialises in semi-sparkling wines, Bianco is a regional white blend and the traditional Montuni is made from Montù.

Colli Bolognesi is an interesting DOC region, distinct from all its neighbours. Its significant wine is Pignoletto: a light, fragrant white, frequently semi-sparkling and made from the Pignoletto grape. Cabernet Sauvignon is excellent in these parts, and there are also versions of Merlot, Chardonnay, Sauvignon Blanc, Riesling Italico, Pinot Bianco and Barbera.

Sangiovese, Trebbiano and Albana characterise Romagna, an area with no vinous similarity to Emilia: indeed, the former's grape varieties and cultivation methods tend instead to be replicated throughout central Italy. Romagna's most famous red wine is the Sangiovese di Romagna, which may also be a superiore when the alcohol exceeds 12 per cent, and riserva, when it is aged for at least two years. The best examples are excellently structured, with good concentration and emerge from hilly regions south of the via Emilia. The second red produced here is sweet and rare: Cagnina di Romagna is a close relative of Terrano del Carso, and the perfect accompaniment to roast chestnuts.

The predominant white wine is Trebbiano di Romagna, a classic for visitors to the Rimini riviera, and ideal with the local seafood. Less familiar is Pagadebit di Romagna: a grape that produces good wine even in difficult years, hence its name –*pagare i debiti*, "pay the debts". Albana di Romagna was the first Italian white wine to gain DOCG status and comes in several styles: there is an Amabile and a Dolce; the dominant Secco is a meaty white, and the Passita is arguably one of the finest Italian passitos.

Three recent DOCs in the region are Colli di Imola, Colli di Faenza and Colli di Rimini, all in the hilly regions of the Romagna Pre-Apennines. Besides red and white blends, varietals include Colli di Imola Barbera, Colli di Faenza Pinot Bianco and Colli di Rimini Cabernet

predominantly from Sauvignon Blanc, Malvasia and Trebbiano; a Sauvignon Blanc also grown as a sweet passito, and many other white varietals, from Pinot Grigio to Chardonnay and Malvasia Frizzante. The reds are mostly sparkling, with the exception of the Cabernet Sauvignon. There are two Lambruscos to choose from, Grasparossa and Montericco; a fragrant sweet red wine, Marzemino; and a red from the Malbo Gentile variety, which is unique to the region.

The classic heartland of Lambrusco starts a little further north, between Montecchio, Gualtieri and Cavriago. There – and in the communes surrounding Reggio Emilia – Reggiano (formerly Lambrusco Reggiano) is made, the lightest and easiest-drinking Lambrusco which is also available as a Bianco or Rosato. The other

Sauvignon, with some regulations proving flexible with regard to the woods used and the length of ageing. Styles range from semi-sparkling fruity whites to powerful "international" reds, reflecting a rebellion by winemakers against the limitations of more traditional local wines.

Soil, climate and viticulture

Almost 50 per cent of the land consists of fertile plains bordered by the River Po; 25 per cent is mountainous (the Tosco-Romagnolo Apennines) and 25 per cent is covered by hills. Emilia is largely defined by the provinces of

Piacenza, Parma, Reggio Emilia, Modena and parts of Bologna and Ferrara. The region's hills are rich in clay, marl and lime and along with the high plain – with its stony, sandy, well-drained soils – provide prime wine conditions. The fertile plains of the Po, on the other hand, are the home of Lambrusco and the lighter semi-sparkling wines, which benefit from a continental climate.

Romagna is the southeastern quadrant of the region; defined by Rimini, Forli, Ravenna and parts of Bologna and Ferrara. Its rocky, lime-rich chalk soil and a climate tempered by the Adriatic Sea – bringing cooler summers and a wide temperature range – encourage quality wines.

left *The town of Dozza is the seat of Emilia-Romagna's wine cellar, or* enoteca, *which is situated in a 15th-century castle.*

Notable producers

Celli, Bertinoro (FO) Produces a whole range of regional DOC wines, widely admired for their clean, modern style. The Sangiovese di Romagna Superiore Le Grillaie Riserva is a fine example.

Fattoria Paradiso, Bertinoro (FO) An historic name in Romagna, with large vineyards and managed by the Pezzi family. Sangiovese di Romagna Superiore Vigna delle Lepri is a standard-bearer in the region, and one of the first Italian wines to mention the vineyard on its label.

Francesco Bellei, Bomporto (MO) Besides an excellent Lambrusco, the Bellei family uses the *metodo classico* to produce a range of remarkable sparkling wines, including elegant cuvées of Chardonnay and Pinot Nero. The Vintage Cuvée Speciale is excellent.

Umberto Cesari, Castel San Pietro (BO) A large and very modern winery benefiting from the return of Vito Piffer. He oversees production of some of the best Romagna wines, most notably Albana di Romagna Passito Colle del Re and Sangiovese di Romagna Riserva. This winery is also home

to some innovative styles – Liano is a successful blend of Sangiovese and Cabernet Sauvignon, matured in French oak barriques and flaunting aromatic spices.

Vallona, Castello di Serravalle (BO) Maurizio Vallona is one of the most dynamic and innovative winemakers in the region. His excellent grapes produce quality Cabernet Sauvignon, Chardonnay Selezione and Sauvignon Blanc.

Cantine Cooperative Riunite, Reggio Emilia One of the most widely drunk Italian wine names in the world, having sold over a

below *High trained vines in Castelvetro, south of Modena. The rich clay and marl soils are a sound base for quality wines.*

million cases of Lambrusco in the US alone. Boasts a wide range, competitive prices and reliable quality.

Fattoria Zerbina, Faenza (RA) Cristina Geminiani studied oenology in Bordeaux, and now produces some of the best wines, in the region in collaboration with Vittorio Fiore, her technical consultant. Her finest is the Marzieno, from Cabernet Sauvignon and Sangiovese, an imposing, well structured wine with good concentration. Albana di Romagna Passito Scacco Matto is probably the best sweet Albana.

Tenuta La Palazza, Forlì Claudio Drei Donà produces thrilling wines in collaboration with Franco Bernabei. Magnificat is one of Italy's best Cabernets, while Chardonnay Il Tornese is exemplary, with balance and a rich bouquet.

Tre Monti, Imola (BO) With his sons David and Vittorio, Sergio Navacchia brings out the terroir of the Romagna hills near Imola, in wines such as Colli d'Imola Boldo – a Sangiovese and Cabernet Sauvignon

packing impressive elegance and power, and an equally outstanding Cabernet Sauvignon Turico. His research goes on...

Castelluccio, Modigliana (FO) This winery offers some of the most interesting versions of Sangiovese di Romagna, such as Ronco dei Ciliegi, Ronco della Simia and Ronco delle Ginestre, all from a single vineyard.

Tenuta Bonzara, Monte San Pietro (BO) Francesco Lambertini's great estate is a quality feather in the cap of the Colli Bolognesi. Its Bonzarone and Rocca di Bonacciara, both DOC, can rival the best Italian Cabernets and Merlots respectively.

San Patrignano-Terre del Cedro, Ospedaletto di Coriano (RN) In the forefront of Romagna winemaking, with spectacular Sangiovese di Romagna, such as Zarricante and Riserva Avi – extremely concentrated wines, with remarkable persistence.

La Stoppa, Rivergaro (PC) One of the first wineries in Piacenza to produce important

international-style wines, such as Pinot Nero and Cabernet Sauvignon. The *cru* Stoppa is a Cabernet of great elegance and harmony, a perfect synthesis of new wood flavours.

Cavicchioli, San Prospero (MO) Combines large production with high quality: Lambrusco di Sorbara Vigna del Cristo is a classic, as is Grasparossa di Castelvetro Col Sassoso.

La Tosa, Vigolzone (PC) The Pizzamiglio brothers present some of the best wines in Colli Piacentini, including Cabernet Sauvignon Luna Selvatica, Gutturnio Vignamorello and the delicate Malvasia Sorriso di Cielo.

Vigneto delle Terre Rosse, Zola Predosa (BO) Enrico Vallania was the father of the current owners, and a local wine pioneer. His densely planted, low yielding vines marked a turning point in Colli Bolognesi, and flourish today in wine such as the Rosso di Enrico Vallania Cuvée (Cabernet) and Riesling Malagò Vendemmia Tardiva.

The Marches

About AD1600, the rulers of the Papal States succeeded in unifying the whole of the Marches, as it is known today. But as this smallish region had previously been at the mercy of the Greeks, the Romans, the Goths, the Gallic Senones, the Byzantines and the Lombards, many vinous traditions developed, and the wines of the Marches still vary widely among the numerous specific districts.

Wines and winemaking

An annual production of almost two million hectolitres, over 15 per cent of which is DOC, makes the Marches one of Italy's most important wine regions.

From the north, the first DOC district is Colli Pesaresi, whose Sangiovese and Trebbiano wines encompass the Focara Rosso and Roncaglia Bianco, wines that reflect the influence of neighbouring Romagna. In Fano, Bianchello del Metauro grapes are used in an eponymous traditional and delicate white wine, while Ancona signals the start of the region's most important district, the vast Verdicchio, which contains two DOCs – Castelli di Jesi is the more prominent, while Matelica straddles the provinces of Ancona and Macerata. Both wines are full-bodied and made from the white Verdicchio grape, one of Italy's best native varieties. The Castelli di Jesi is more rounded and mellow, while Matelica is often sharper and benefits greatly from a couple of years' ageing. Both are classy wines whose quality has much improved in recent years.

Esino is a new DOC which produces a Verdicchio Bianco, and a Rosso from Sangiovese and Montepulciano. Two other new DOC red wines are produced in Ancona: Lacrima di Morro d'Alba (no relation to the Piedmontese Alba – Morro d'Alba is a locality in the hinterland of Senigallia) is made from the Lacrima grape variety and has medium body, while the rosso, from Montepulciano and Sangiovese, is the best red of this sub-region.

Macerata is home to the highly unusual Vernaccia di Serrapetrona: a sparkling red which is often sweet or semi-sweet and made from red Vernaccia grapes dried on mats – an unsophisticated but fascinating wine. Along the coast, the Colli Maceratesi DOC produces a light and pleasant white wine from Maceratino grapes.

Further south, in Ascoli, the Falerio dei Colli Ascolani is another white wine from Trebbiano with additions of Verdicchio and Pecorino, and the Rosso Piceno is a blend of Sangiovese and Montepulciano. The Rosso Piceno Superiore is found in the area between Ripatransone, San Benedetto del Tronto, Offida and ten other neighbouring communes throughout the province of Ascoli. The alcohol content must be over 12 per cent and the wine must be aged for at least a year. This is a full-bodied and concentrated red wine which can be kept in the cellar for at least another four or five years.

Soil, climate and viticulture

The Marches is like a long comb turned towards the Adriatic, with the largest valleys – of the rivers Foglia, Metauro and Cesano – at right angles to the coast, ideal for growing vines. The only valley running parallel to the coast is Matelica, inland of the central zone. Here, vines are grown from sea level to a height of 500 metres.

The region is vulnerable to cold northeasterly winds from the Balkans, hence the striking predominance of white grapes and wines. Vines are almost always trained on the Guyot system or the Tuscan *capovolto* (upside down), although a few vineyards use the *alberello* (sapling) method, "buttressed" wires or mixed cultivation.

below *The domed skyline of Loreto, in the Rosso Cònero district. Many of the vineyards in this vicinity fall within the suburbs of Ancona, a city described by ancient Greeks as the "elbow" of the coastline.*

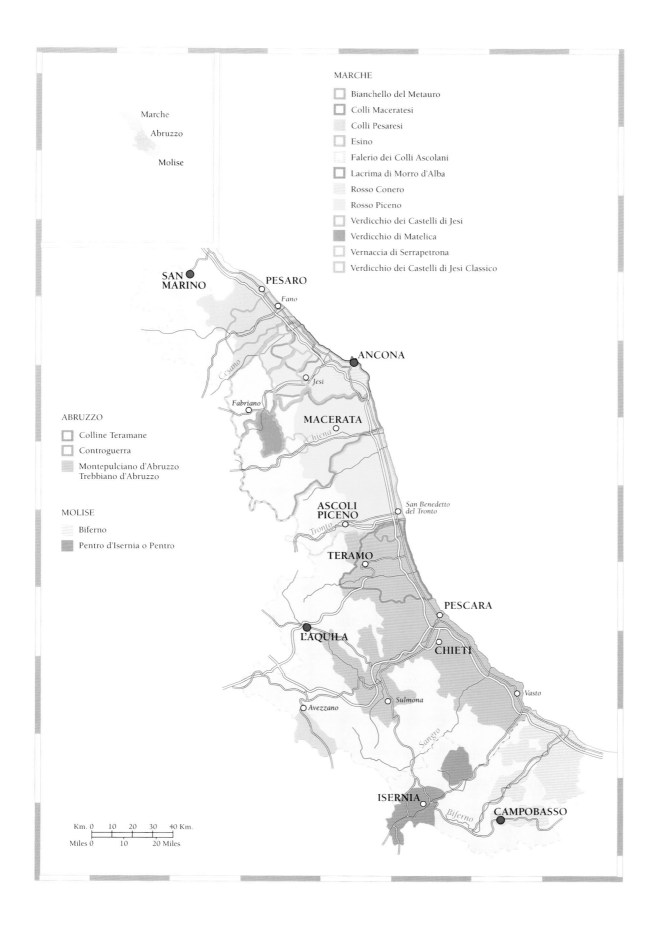

MARCHE

☐ Bianchello del Metauro
☐ Colli Maceratesi
▨ Colli Pesaresi
☐ Esino
☐ Falerio dei Colli Ascolani
☐ Lacrima di Morro d'Alba
▨ Rosso Conero
▨ Rosso Piceno
☐ Verdicchio dei Castelli di Jesi
▨ Verdicchio di Matelica
☐ Vernaccia di Serrapetrona
☐ Verdicchio dei Castelli di Jesi Classico

Marche
Abruzzo
Molise

ABRUZZO

☐ Colline Teramane
☐ Controguerra
▨ Montepulciano d'Abruzzo
   Trebbiano d'Abruzzo

MOLISE

☐ Biferno
▨ Pentro d'Isernia o Pentro

SAN MARINO

PESARO
Fano

ANCONA

Jesi

Fabriano

MACERATA

Cesano

Chienti

ASCOLI PICENO
San Benedetto del Tronto

Tronto

TERAMO

PESCARA

L'AQUILA

CHIETI

Vasto

Avezzano
Sulmona

Sangro

ISERNIA
Biferno
CAMPOBASSO

Km. 0   10   20   30   40 Km.

Miles 0   10   20 Miles

Verdicchio dei Castelli di Jesi

above *Late evening sunlight falls on vineyards at Montecarotto, one of the most significant wine towns in the Castelli di Jesi.*

use the geographical denomination "Classico", but this is always a white wine that can be aged for several years – a rare phenomenon among Italian whites. Its organoleptic profile is closer to that of the whites from northeast Italy than to the more Mediterranean and southern styles.

Verdicchio dei Castelli di Jesi is a typical partner for fish but also works well with the white meats central to the traditional local cuisine. It makes a pleasant apéritif and its excellent value marks it out as a popular "house white".

Verdicchio di Matelica

This is the most inaccessible yet exposed part of Verdicchio. Unlike Castelli di Jesi, there is no sea behind the hills; the climate is more continental and, uniquely for the Marches, its valley runs from north to south instead of east to west.

Matelica is small and landlocked and encompasses the provinces of Ancona and Macerata. It may demand a sense of adventure on the part of visitors, as it is far from main roads, but this is a region dedicated to winegrowing. The presence of Verdicchio has been recorded here since the 16th century, although it could go back even further: this would put the Verdicchio grape in that small group of varieties which are almost certainly of Italian origin.

The improvement in recent years among producers of Verdicchio di Matelica has been a symbolic victory for Italian winemakers – signifying the recovery of wine production using a native grape variety and on its home turf. This has been a part of the backlash, long brewing among Italian winemakers, against the global dominance of Chardonnay and Cabernet in high-quality wines. In other words, Matelica could soon become – and in part has already become – a totem for the preservation of Italy's viticultural heritage.

Verdicchio di Matelica is definitely not Jesi's little brother. It is a fresher and more direct counterpart: fragrant, harmonious and delicate. But it is also capable of flexing its muscles, acquiring an unsuspected complexity when aged for several years, as a result of its excellent initial structure. It displays balance and versatility (the native grape can accommodate the addition of small amounts of Malvasia or Trebbiano) and, like its "cousin" from Jesi, can also be produced in a spumante version.

Finally, Verdicchio di Matelica makes a perfect accompaniment to seafood hors-d'œuvres, white meat casseroles and traditional regional fish dishes. It is also used in sauces for "noble" fish.

Historically, Verdicchio is the most important grape variety in the Marches, as well as the best known. The most important winegrowing area is the Castelli di Jesi, in the province of Ancona, which is defined by the valley of the Esino river. The landscape here is dominated by a number of small towns, most notably Montecarotto, Staffolo, Castelbellino, Castelplanio, and Cupramontana, almost all of them medieval fortified villages around Jesi, hence the name Castelli di Jesi.

Verdicchio dei Castelli di Jesi combines delicate aromas with fragrances of fresh fruit, a dry taste and typical bitter aftertaste. The most prestigious sub-zone can

Notable producers

Verdicchio dei Castelli di Jesi

Santa Barbara, Barbara (AN) In the last ten years Stefano Antonucci has completely renovated his winery, concentrating on high-quality wines. His range now includes three selections of Verdicchio dei Castelli di Jesi Classico: Le Vaglie, Stefano Antonucci and the basic version.

Fazi Battaglia, Castelplanio (AN) The biggest, most famous winery of the district. Owner Maria Luisa Sparaco and consultant oenologist Franco Bernabei produce very good wines. Top of the list are Verdicchio dei Castelli di Jesi Classico San Sisto, matured in small oak barrels; the Verdicchio dei Castelli di Jesi Classico Le Moie; and the Rosso Cònero Riserva Passo del Lupo.

Tavignano, Cingoli (MC) Produces very respectable Verdicchio, including Misco, Tenuta di Travignano and Sante Lancerio.

Vallerosa Bonci, Cupramontana (AN) A prestigious winery, with quality selections, including Le Case, Barré, Focus and the San Michele – one of the best Italian whites.

Colonnara, Cupramontana (AN) A large, well-known cooperative, whose famous wine is Cuprese, a good Verdicchio dei Castelli di Jesi Classico.

Brunori, Jesi (AN) Some of the best Verdicchio dei Castelli di Jesi, nost notably the reasonably priced selezione San Nicolò.

Garofoli, Loreto (AN) One of the Marches' best ranges of Verdicchio and Rosso. The Verdicchio dei Castelli di Jesi Classico

left *Many vineyards in the Matelica DOC are well off the beaten track, such as these at Castel Santa Maria.*

Podium and Serra Fiorese – both matured in wood – and the Rosso Cònero Riserva Grosso Agontano are top of their category.

Monte Schiavo, Maiolati Spontini (AN) Verdicchio dei Castelli di Jesi Classico Palio di San Floriano has an enviable quality/price ratio. It is made from late-harvested grapes and matured in steel vats and barrels.

Terre Cortesi Moncaro, Montecarotto (AN) One of the most important wineries in the Verdicchio district. Passito Tordiruta, Verde di Ca' Ruptae, Vigna Novali, Le Vele, and even the organic version – of which the winery is rightly proud – are all excellent and reliable wines.

Umani Ronchi, Osimo (AN) Massimo Bernetti has produced some very successful wines in recent years, in collaboration with Giacomo Tachis. Pélago, a Cabernet, Merlot and Montepulciano blend, has been popular worldwide, while Verdicchio dei Castelli di Jesi Classico, Plenio Riserva and Casal di Serra are more recent assets.

Bucci, Ostra Vetere (AN) Ampelio Bucci has been producing two splendid Verdicchio wines for many years – the basic version is complemented by the magnificent Villa Bucci. Both are mellow and age well.

Sartarelli, Poggio San Marcello (AN) Donatella Sartarelli and husband Patrizio Chiacchierini's basic Verdicchio dei Castelli di Jesi Classico Superiore is fresh, with an excellent consistency and definition. Tralivio is more concentrated, but the most original wine is Verdicchio Contrada Balciana, made from late-harvested grapes. This has extraordinary body, is well-balanced and very creamy. One of the best Italian whites.

Casalfarneto, Serra de' Conti (AN) One of the most successful innovations of recent years. The two selections of Verdicchio dei

Castelli di Jesi Classico – Fontevecchia and, in particular, Gran Casale – combine high quality with very reasonable prices.

Fattoria Coroncino, Staffolo (AN) Gaiospino and Il Coroncino are the two *crus* of Verdicchio dei Castelli di Jesi Classico, and boost a cantina which has become one of the great local estates, under owners Lucio and Fiorella Canestrari.

Verdicchio di Matelica producers

La Monacesca, Civitanova Marche (MC) Has over 20 hectares of vines, mostly Verdicchio, the rest planted to Chardonnay, Sauvignon, Sangiovese and Merlot. The two Verdicchios are the "basic", and the beautiful *cru* La Monacesca, while Mirum is a superb white wine from late-harvested grapes.

Enzo Mecella, Fabriano (AN) Founded over 50 years ago, but run since 1977 by Enzo Mecella. He has two versions of Verdicchio di Matelica: Pagliano and Casa Fosca, the house symbol. Antico di Casa Fosca is an IGT wine made from a special cuvée of Verdicchio grapes, aged in barriques and produced only in the best years.

Belisario, Matelica (MC) The premier producer of Matelica DOC, with five versions and selected house *crus*, such as the Riserva Cambrugiano. Also offers two passitos: Carpe Diem (a Verdicchio) and Serrae Rubrae (from Vernaccia Cerretana).

Bisci, Matelica (MC) The Bisci brothers' estate produces two versions of Verdicchio di Matelica, the normal one and Riserva Villa Fogliano. There are also two reds: Fogliano is made from Cabernet Franc, Barbera, Merlot and Montepulciano grapes, and Villa Castiglioni from Sangiovese and Cabernet Sauvignon.

San Biagio, Matelica (MC) Sabina and Maya Girotti's San Biagio is one of the two remarkable *crus* of Verdicchio di Matelica; the other, a Riserva, is Vigneto di Braccano. There are also two IGT reds: Braguolo, from Sangiovese and Ciliegiolo grapes, and Grottagrifone, a Cabernet Sauvignon varietal.

Rosso Cònero & Rosso Piceno

The DOC of Rosso Cònero covers a fairly small area on the slopes of Monte Cònero, with little spurs extending into the communes of Ancona, Camerano, Offagna, Sirolo, Numana, Osimo and Castelfidardo. This is a dramatic region with breathtaking landscapes and hills rising steeply above the sea.

Rosso Cònero is made predominantly from Montepulciano with a 15 per cent addition of Sangiovese, but not all producers abide by this. The maximum yield is still fixed at 14,000 kg per hectare, but the shrewd producers have reduced this quantity drastically and produce some very fine wines. Among the most eminent is the magnificent Rosso Cònero Dorico di Alessandro Moroder, which has entered the Italian vinous aristocracy.

At its best Rosso Cònero is a wine of great firmness, with concentrated colour and an intense, long-lasting bouquet of wild black cherries and Mediterranean herbs. Producers have been striving to maximise the quality and harmony of Rosso Cònero's aroma, while on the palate it's a full, clean and powerful wine, perhaps comparable to the best Brunello and Tuscan Vino Nobile.

Rosso Piceno wines are grown in the largest region in the Marches. This includes most of the hilly strip which is ideally suited to winegrowing, but excludes the two rather smaller zones of Rosso Cònero and Lacrima di Morro d'Alba. Rosso Piceno is made from a minimum 60 per cent Sangiovese with a balance of Montepulciano and small amounts of Trebbiano and Passerina. If the alcohol content exceeds 11.5 per cent then the Superiore classification applies. This is a wine for drinking with the family, and the ideal accompaniment to well-seasoned dishes, roasts and the traditional regional dish of *bolliti* (boiled meats).

below *The brilliant blue seas of the Cònero promontory. This small corner of the Marches is blessed with beautiful landscapes.*

Notable producers

Moroder, Ancona The successful relaunch of Rosso Cònero is largely attributable to Alessandro and Serenella Moroder, a husband-and-wife team. Some ten years ago – in collaboration with consultant oenologist Franco Bernabei – they started producing Dorico, a fine, powerful Rosso Cònero selection. The basic Rosso Cònero is also a good, well-made wine.

Velenosi, Ascoli Piceno Ercole Velenosi is undoubtedly the best interpreter of Rosso Piceno in the region. Roggio del Filare and Brecciarolo are two of the more notable selections on offer. In addition, Velenosi produces a range of white wines in the southern region of the Marches, under the DOC Falerio Colli Ascolani. Of these, the best is the Vigna Solaria.

Boccadigabbia, Civitanova Marche (MC) One of the best wineries in the Marches. It produces a good, typical Rosso Piceno, but the outstanding wine is Akronte, a garnet-coloured wine made entirely from Cabernet Sauvignon.

Conte Leopardi, Numana (AN) The descendants of the great poet Giacomo Leopardi, Count Piervittorio Leopardi produce high-quality wines in the small district of Numana. Their Rosso Pigmento and Vigneti del Coppo selections are both full of character. Romeo Taraborelli is employed in the winery and helps ensure consistent results, even in lesser vintages.

Fattoria Le Terrazze, Numana (AN) This is a new name in the district of Cònero. The owners, Antonio and Giorgina Terni, produce a great and brilliantly named non-DOC red called Chaos, a blend of Montepulciano, Syrah and Merlot grapes. But the estate's premier wine is a Rosso Cònero: the Sassi Neri has wonderful aromas and remarkable concentration.

above *Alessandro and Serenella Moroder have been credited with the resurgence of top-notch Rosso Conerò.*

left *With its complexity and aroma, Rosso Conerò is well suited to barrel ageing. Its only drawback is a shortage in volume.*

Abruzzi and Molise

Winegrowing was introduced to the Abruzzi and Molise by the trusty Etruscans around the 7th-6th century BC, although the *apianae* grapes – very sweet and probably similar to modern Moscato – were widely cultivated in the territory as early as the 4th century BC. Local *apianae* wines were often praised by Roman and Greek scholars, most notably Ovid in the 7th century, who was a native of the Abruzzese city of Sulmona.

However, these ancient landmarks have been slowly disappearing since the Middle Ages, due to a gradual depopulation of rural and mountainous areas in this part of Italy that has gone unchecked for centuries. The revival in Abruzzi winemaking has thus been even more dramatic than in many other Italian regions, but has only arisen during the last 20 years, largely through the efforts of the numerous cooperative wineries that proliferate in the

below *A vineyard near Chieti, in the Montepulciano d'Abruzzo DOC. Not to be confused with the Tuscan town, the Montepulciano d'Abruzzo grape is the major red variety in the Abruzzi region.*

province of Chieti, in the central-eastern part of Abruzzi.

The situation in Molise remains doggedly antiquated: the sporadic vineyards often favour methods of cultivation more suited to Roman or Etruscan times. Visitors to this region should not be surprised to encounter rows of vines grown on a maple or mulberry tree for support.

Wines and winemaking

Abruzzi remains a major contributor to the Italian wine fountain, with an annual output of approximately four million hectolitres, 12 per cent of it DOC. However, its wine is often marketed in bulk and its pedigree has gone largely unrecognised – a fate shared by many regions in southern Italy. Now, perceptions are gradually changing and Abruzzi is leading the campaign for recognition for those regions which can muster only one or two DOCs.

Of the region's few DOC wines, the blue-riband is the Montepulciano d'Abruzzo. This red wine – unrelated to the Tuscan town of Montepulciano, though perhaps sharing an ancient connection – has excellent body and in the hands of producers such as Edoardo Valentini and Gianni Masciarelli merits a place in the top rank of Italian reds. (There is also a rosé version, known as Cerasuolo.) The only white is Trebbiano d'Abruzzo, one of the best wines produced mostly from Trebbiano, a much-maligned variety that gains concentration and body in this terroir.

Important sub-zones in the district include Colline Teramane and Controguerra. The latter has an autonomous DOC and produces Bianco, Rosso and a series of DOC wines from international varieties.

Molise is one of the most mountainous regions of the country and produces barely 400,000 hectolitres of wine a year – only two per cent of it DOC. The two *denominazioni*, Pentro d'Isernia and Biferno, are largely ignored by the few producers in the region. Pentro d'Isernia exists in a Rosso and a Rosato version, both from Montepulciano and Sangiovese, and a Bianco is made from Trebbiano and Bombino. The vineyards are situated in two different areas: Isernia is in northern Sannio, and Agnone is beyond the Mainarde, near the boundary with Sangro.

Biferno's eponymous wines follow the same path as Isernia's, although the Rosso contains some Aglianico and Tentiglia as well as Montepulciano. The differences lie in production, and as Biferno is in the Campobasso province – where the mountains give way to high plains sloping down to the sea – its wines have more body and less acidity.

Soil, climate and viticulture

The Apennine range peaks in the Abruzzi, with the Gran Sasso d'Italia soaring to 3,000 metres above sea level. The situation changes in Molise, though not substantially: the mountains yield to a high plain, surrounded by the Matese and Mainarde ranges, which descend to the Adriatic.

The soil is calcareous and morainic almost everywhere. Cultivation of vines is possible only in the gorges and wide valleys, cut by rivers running at right angles towards the coast, on the coastal plains, rich in clay, and in the lower valleys and high plains. Vine training is usually on the classic Abruzzese *tendone* system.

The climate here is very distinctive. In San Martino sulla Marrucina and Guardiagrele, in the province of Chieti, it is possible within a radius of 30 kilometres to go skiing during the day on the slopes of the Majella, and dine out that evening by the sea. There are also great

below *Trebbiano grapes being unloaded at the Cantina Sociale in Ortona. Trebbiano is the dominant white grape in Abruzzi.*

climatic differences between winter and summer, and at harvest-time significant temperature differences between night and day. In September, for instance, the daytime high can reach 30° C (86° F), and drop as low as 10° C (50° F) during the night. There is very little rain between June and October, when drought is often a problem.

In Molise, climatic extremes are possibly even more pronounced, except in coastal regions such as Campomarino, which has a uniformly Mediterranean aspect.

Montepulciano d'Abruzzo

This is the most important Abruzzese DOC and is constantly increasing its share of international markets, due largely to the excellent value of its wines – a moderate rise in prices is a fair levy for a big increase in DOC output. The trend now is towards a modest reduction of yields and the use of wood for the traditional range of wines – and the results speak for themselves, although there is still scope for improvement.

In a good year the grapes reach levels that justify making the Abruzzi Cerasuolo, a fruity rosé that is a local speciality, ready to drink young. Montepulciano grapes are vinified for a short time in their skins, producing a wine which probably has few rivals in its category in Italy.

Trebbiano d'Abruzzo

Trebbiano is following in the wake of Montepulciano in Abruzzo, but still awaits similar recognition. A traditional weakness for enormous yields made Abruzzi a "tank" region of Italy, while advanced technology and vinification methods have been slow in coming.

Winegrowers in the Abruzzo region have now taken up the challenge and introduced a new, modern oenological approach. Valentini and Masciarelli have shown that great white wines can be produced from Trebbiano grapes, wines capable of ageing if matured or vinified in wood. And there are other promising signs: besides the use of international grape varieties introduced in recent years – Chardonnay, Sauvignon, Pinot and Riesling – native varieties such as Passerina, Pecorino, Cococciola, Montico and Moscati have resurfaced, with some encouraging results.

Notable producers

Zaccagnini, Bolognano (PE)

Montepulciano d'Abruzzo Abbazia di San Clemente is a speciality of this cantina. It's a great red wine with a very concentrated colour and a delicate, velvety taste. The rest of the range is also very good, in particular the Montepulciano d'Abruzzo Castello di Salle and the pleasant Myosotis rosé.

Di Majo Norante, Campomarino (CB)

The best and most famous cantina in Molise is located in Campomarino – not far from the Adriatic coast. Alessio Di Majo has enlisted the help of famous Umbrian oenologist Riccardo Cotarella, and in the past few years the duo have transformed the style and range of the wines on offer. Besides the classic Biferno Rosso Ramitello and Molì, there is a series of well-made white wines from Greco and Fiano grapes.

Illuminati, Controguerra (TE)

Lumen, Zanna Vecchio and the pleasant Riparosso are three Montepulciano d'Abruzzo wines from Dino Illuminati, one of the best producers of this variety. Also worth trying is the surprising Spumante Brut Metodo Classico, a unique wine in this region.

Valentini, Loreto Aprutino (PE)

Edoardo Valentini has been the uncontested champion of Abruzzese winemaking for several years. His Trebbiano and Montepulciano d'Abruzzo are legendary, with wine critics full of praise: the Trebbiano has been described as the best in the world, while the Montepulciano is wonderfully rich, spicy and intense.

Valentini has been working with his son Francesco for several years. The secret of his success lies in the excellence of his vineyards, Camposacro, Colle Cavaliere and Castelluccio, all in the countryside around Loreto Aprutino, where the family has been growing vines since 1560. Strict selection of grapes ensures top fruit, which is vinified

right The town of Loreto Aprutino, near Pescara. The white building in the centre is the home of Edoardo Valentini.

in wooden vats. The Trebbiano, with its rich and opulent aromas, can easily age for ten years, while the Montepulciano is incredibly concentrated and also ages well. Montepulciano Cerasuolo is a powerful wine with a high alcohol content, reminiscent of the great rosé wines of Bandol, in Provence.

Cataldi Madonna, Ofena (AQ)

One of the very few good wineries in the province of L'Aquila, in the central region of the Abruzzi. The region is mountainous and cultivation of vines is possible only in valleys protected from the extreme cold. Luigi Cataldi and his oenologist Giovanni Ballo make an excellent Montepulciano d'Abruzzo called Tonì, and their Montepulciano Cerasuolo Pié delle Vigne is one of the region's finest.

Orlandi Contucci Ponno, Roseto degli Abruzzi (TE)

One of the rising stars in Abruzzese. Marina Orlandi Contucci and oenologist Donato Lanati produce modern wines from international varieties: Cabernet Sauvignon is vinified on its own to produce Liburnio, or blended with other varieties in Colle Funaro, two excellent reds. Tradition is upheld by the concentrated and powerful Montepulciano d'Abruzzo La Regia Specula.

Masciarelli, San Martino sulla Marrucina (CH)

Gianni Masciarelli and his wife Marina Cvetic are among the most famous producers of Trebbiano and Montepulciano d'Abruzzo. Their best selection is the Villa Gemma, made from grapes grown on their estate. This is a red wine with substantial body and an alcohol content of 14%. Decisive character and amazing structure earmark this as an outstanding wine. The Trebbiano d'Abruzzo and the Chardonnay, which Masciarelli has dedicated to his wife, are also impressive.

Cantina Tollo, Tollo (CH)

A large co-operative winery and arguably the flagship of Abruzzese winemaking. Produces very well made wines, particularly reds – all Montepulciano d'Abruzzo, in various selections. These wines offer better value for money than most in Italy. The finest are Montepulciano d'Abruzzo, Montepulciano d'Abruzzo Cerasuolo and a Trebbiano d'Abruzzo in three versions: Colle Secco, Rocca Ventosa and Valle d'Oro.

The Central Tyrrhenian

The heart of Italian wine may encompass Tuscany, Umbria and Latium, but Tuscany alone was the cradle of Italy's vinous renaissance. It was here in the 1960s that a select group of producers, led by Antinori, revitalised Chianti and set the new standards for Italian wine. And while the venerable *vecchio Piemonte* ("old Piedmont") was beset by a staid image from the 1970s until the mid-1980s, Tuscany came to epitomise the perfect synthesis of tradition and the new international style, its wines made from a combination of local varieties. "Noble", "voluptuous" and "pleasant" were the buzzwords, but the region's grape varieties also demonstrated great potential for ageing.

An urgent need to restyle Chianti led to the formation of its DOCG in 1984, which virtually abolished the use of white grapes and instead welcomed the international – or "improving" – varieties. This was also the dawn of the Super-Tuscans, the ambitious but controversial new wines with noble ancestors such as Sassicaia by Incisa della Rocchetta, and Tignanello by Antinori (both from the expert hand of Giacomo Tachis). Supported by the excellent harvests of the decade and produced in barriques, soon to become the most popular method of vinification, the Super-Tuscans were an international sensation. New technologies were in vogue and oenologists became "winemakers", stars capable of creating new cantinas and great wines in the course of just a few harvests.

Winegrowers also became aware of the need to restructure their vineyards and select the best clones of Sangiovese, the Tuscan grape variety par excellence. By the end of the 1980s Bolgheri had become a little Mediterranean Bordeaux and Chianti Classico an experimental laboratory. With new plantings of Sangiovese and the improvement of vinification in the 1990s, quality began to climb.

Two famous names explored new directions: Montepulciano, with its Vino Nobile, and Montalcino with its Brunello – the latter albeit with extreme caution. San Gimignano and its white Vernaccia were rejuvenated and Sangiovese emerged as a varietal wine, but above all Tuscany began to produce great Merlot, excellent Syrah and Pinot Nero wines in the more inland districts. The only risk in this new development was that focusing on the production of super table wines might "impoverish" the historical *denominazioni,* such as Chianti Classico, and even the DOC and DOCG wines.

Today, though, every available square inch of land in the more aristocratic DOC and DOCG regions is planted with vines, and it falls to the province of Grosseto to bear the brunt of new denominations, new cantinas and new wines – all created to quench the growing thirst for Tuscany. But satisfying this demand appears to be a difficult task: the region's recent harvests are still far from reaching the level of three million hectolitres, less than five per cent of Italy's national production.

Tuscan dynamism has affected neighbouring Umbria, which is now a quasi-extension of Tuscany towards the interior – it's the only Italian wine region not bordered by the sea. Umbria has experienced an amazing revival in recent years: Montefalco, Orvieto and Colli del Trasimeno are the most lively and promising areas, and while Torgiano appears to be in a period of reflection after the death of Giorgio Lungarotti, it is bubbling with talent and enthusiasm. The most striking aspect of the region's production is the growing success of its red wines, even in white strongholds such as Orvieto.

In average years Latium has a production of over three million hectolitres (six per cent of Italian production). Quality is improving and while the reputations of Frascati, Marino and other traditional white wines from the classic Castelli Romani are safe, the coastal zones in the centre, southern parts of the region and Montefiascone have real potential. Yet again, the future is red: Merlot, Syrah and Cabernet Sauvignon are shaping up nicely.

Tuscany

above *A winding road lined with cypress trees, near Montepulciano. Classic Tuscan landscapes are often the first images to spring to mind with foreign tourists, and its wine enjoys a similar prominence.*

Tuscan wines can be traced back to the period between the 8th and 5th century BC, when Tuscany was part of Etruria, a vast area which also included Umbria, northern Latium and parts of Emilia and the Marches. Although traits of the Etruscan legacy were still evident in the 1950s, such as "mixed cultivation" – vines supported by apple, mulberry or olive trees – theirs was a culture of local produce for local consumption. Today's large-scale, specialised viticulture only evolved in the 1960s.

Although Vernaccia from San Gimignano and red wine from Montepulciano were being quaffed before the Renaissance, it was only in the 19th century that modern Tuscany took shape. Chianti overtook Vermiglio in central Tuscany, and Brunello di Montalcino made its debut with the Biondi Santi vintage of 1888. This was also the dawn of Carmignano, Rufina and commercialised Chianti.

Wines and winemaking

Only three million hectolitres of wine are produced in Tuscany, but 45 per cent of this is DOC or DOCG standard, establishing Tuscany at the summit of Italy's quality wine range. Its six DOCGs comprise: Brunello di Montalcino, Carmignano, Chianti, Chianti Classico, Vernaccia di San Gimignano and Vino Nobile di Montepulciano. The numerous DOCs range from Bolgheri, Montecarlo and Morellino di Scansano, to Pomino, Rosso di Montalcino and Rosso di Montepulciano – and these are just a selection of the more famous names.

A generation of skilled and enterprising winemakers has brought Tuscany within spitting distance of Bordeaux, Burgundy and California. Grabbing most of the headlines are the "Super-Tuscans", the experimental high quality red wines produced here from the late 1960s to the late 1980s. While these have been extremely competitive at an international level, they represent a diversion from the traditional regional styles.

For many years – and, in some cases, even today – the SuperTuscans were refused the honour of a DOC, and relegated to the rank of *vino da tavola*, with a regional label. Although these inventions are standard-bearers for Tuscany, they did not adhere to production regulations established by law – often, for example, the blends were "unlawful". This has banished such distinguished wines as Tignanello by Antinori, Cabreo by Ruffino, Vigorello by San Felice, and Fontalloro by the Fattoria di Felsina to a second division, at least from a legislative viewpoint.

(Sassicaia was once similarly dismissed, but now has a DOC in the form of Bolgheri Sassicaia). But the market reacted quite differently, especially overseas, and the Super-Tuscans soon enjoyed a status and value far in excess of DOC or DOCG wines from the same region.

Among the grape varieties, Cabernet Sauvignon and Merlot are increasingly popular in the vineyards of Chianti and Montalcino, where they are used alongside Sangiovese, or vinified alone to produce highly prized varietals matured in French oak barriques.

Soil, climate and viticulture

Tuscany boasts a tremendous variety of microclimates: the coastal region, the area of Bolgheri and a large part of Maremma di Grosseto have a Mediterranean climate. The soil is varied but sandy and clay soils are common, especially beside rivers or the sea. Winemaking here is highly innovative, particularly in the north of the region, and vineyards are densely planted with international varieties and native Sangiovese and Vermentino. More traditional methods and homespun varieties predominate to the south, with the likes of Morellino – a sub-variety of Sangiovese – Alicante (similar to Grenache) and, among white varieties, the classic Tuscan Trebbiano and Malvasia.

Central Tuscany is the quality lynchpin. The district of Montalcino, in the most southern part of Siena, has a chalky clay soil that is especially amenable to Sangiovese. The Mediterranean climate includes a few continental microclimates, with winters colder and summers often hotter than those on the coast. And at important times of the season, the proximity of Mount Amiata tempers an excessively intense heat. Montepulciano's climate is more continental, because its altitude and inland location can lead to severe winters.

Growing conditions are varied in the vast region of the Chianti Classico, with clay soils featuring to the south and chalkier soils to the north. The climate is a mixture of Mediterranean and continental, with dry summers and often bitterly cold winters. Sangiovese is the key grape variety in all these regions, and is cultivated in vineyards with a planting density of between 3,000 and 4,000 vine stocks per hectare.

The situation is similar in the more northern areas, especially Carmignano and Rufina, although these are fringe districts, restricted by the altitude of their vineyards and the proximity of the Apennines.

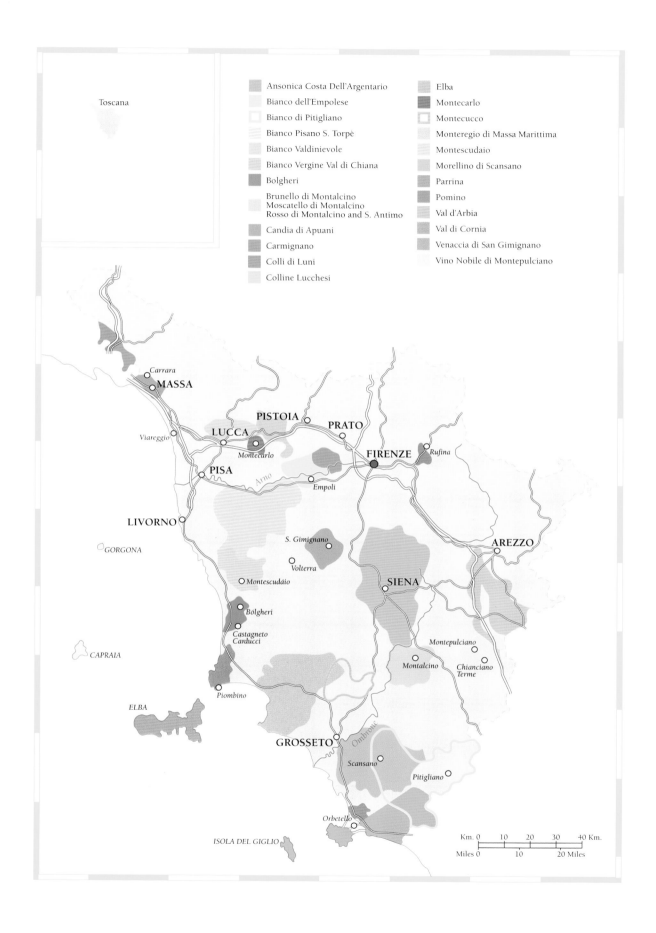

Toscana

Ansonica Costa Dell'Argentario
Bianco dell'Empolese
Bianco di Pitigliano
Bianco Pisano S. Torpè
Bianco Valdinievole
Bianco Vergine Val di Chiana
Bolgheri
Brunello di Montalcino
Moscatello di Montalcino
Rosso di Montalcino and S. Antimo
Candia di Apuani
Carmignano
Colli di Luni
Colline Lucchesi

Elba
Montecarlo
Montecucco
Monteregio di Massa Marittima
Montescudaio
Morellino di Scansano
Parrina
Pomino
Val d'Arbia
Val di Cornia
Venaccia di San Gimignano
Vino Nobile di Montepulciano

Carrara
MASSA

PISTOIA
PRATO
LUCCA
Viareggio
Montecarlo
FIRENZE
Rufina
PISA
Arno
Empoli

LIVORNO

GORGONA

S. Gimignano
Volterra
Montescudàio

AREZZO

Bólgheri
Castagneto
Carducci

SIENA

CAPRAIA

Montepulciano
Montalcino
Chianciano
Terme

Piombino

ELBA

GROSSETO
Ombrone
Scansano
Pitigliano

Orbetello

ISOLA DEL GIGLIO

Km. 0   10   20   30   40 Km.

Miles 0   10   20 Miles

Chianti

The vast winegrowing region of central Tuscany – in which Chianti DOCG and all its sub-denominations are produced – stretches into the provinces of Prato, Florence, Arezzo, Pistoia, Pisa and Siena. This ocean of vineyards yields more than 750,000 hectolitres of wine each year, the highest of any Italian DOC. This is despite the fact that, in 1996, Chianti Classico was awarded its own DOCG, so it no longer counts as a sub-denomination of Chianti. DOCG status has also been conferred on other sub-districts: Colli Fiorentini, Colli Aretini, Colline Pisane, Colli Senesi, Montalbano, Rufina and the very recent Superiore (which was approved in 1997), which is applicable only in areas of the Florence and Siena provinces that are not covered by the Chianti Classico DOCG.

In recent years Chianti has experienced a small-scale revolution in its wine laws, which has contributed to a remarkable improvement in quality and an increase in prices. This unashamed upward mobility has allowed the region to jettison that insipid image of straw-coloured bottles of Chianti in tourist trattorias. Much of its progress is due to the virtual elimination of white grapes (mostly those usual suspects, Trebbiano and Malvasia) from blends. Until 1984, when the DOCG came into force, the wine laws allowed blends to contain as much as 20 per cent white varieties, as well as Sangiovese and Canaiolo. Now, the maximum permitted is six per cent, though in

below *The Campo and Torre del Mangia in Siena. The city stages the famous Palio horse race, and is the hub of the Colli Senesi.*

practice a large number of producers use almost 100 per cent Sangiovese, especially in the Riserva and Superiore categories, and in the prestigious sub-denominations – in particular Rufina and Colli Senesi.

Chianti dei Colli Aretini

This fairly large zone has an annual production of around 35,000 hectolitres. Its wines are mostly sold within the province or region and lack a convincing image. Obvious characteristics include a rather light body, noticeable acidity and a bouquet which is simpler and less complex than wines from other Chianti regions.

Chianti dei Colli Fiorentini

This sub-zone lies between Florence and the northern boundary of the vast area of Chianti Classico, and includes such mini wine capitals as Impruneta and Montespertoli. Wines from Chianti dei Colli Fiorentini are often similar to the Chianti Classico of the more northern zones of the DOCG, though perhaps a little fresher and with a slightly less complex bouquet.

Chianti dei Colli Senesi

This is the largest and most important sub-denomination, including a huge chunk of Siena province. There are many excellent producers and interesting wines, with Sangiovese frequently excelling – and comparable to selections in the more prestigious Chianti Classico.

Chianti Montalbano

In the province of Prato, northwest of Florence, Chianti Montalbano is among the less well-known sub-zones. Its light, pleasant red is one of the most short-lived Chiantis and should be drunk young, ideally with Tuscan food.

Chianti Rufina

This tiny district, northeast of Florence, has a continental climate and vineyards planted over 400 metres above sea level. Its fragrant wines lack the body or power of Chianti Classico or Colli Senesi, but can age – especially Montesodi and Nipozzano dei Marchesi Frescobaldi, and Bucerchiale di Selvapiana – all DOCG, and all typical local Sangiovese.

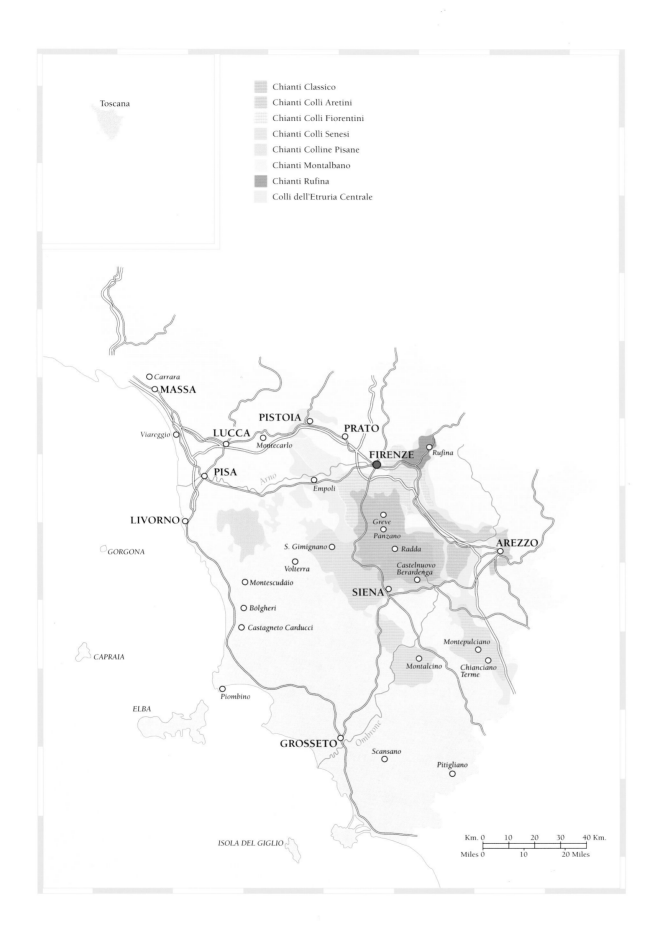

Toscana

Chianti Classico
Chianti Colli Aretini
Chianti Colli Fiorentini
Chianti Colli Senesi
Chianti Colline Pisane
Chianti Montalbano
Chianti Rufina
Colli dell'Etruria Centrale

Carrara
MASSA
PISTOIA
PRATO
Viareggio   LUCCA
Montecarlo   FIRENZE   Rufina
PISA
Arno   Empoli
LIVORNO
GORGONA   Greve
                                               Panzano
              S. Gimignano   Radda
              Volterra   Castelnuovo
                                        Berardenga
              Montescudáio   SIENA   AREZZO
              Bólgheri
              Castagneto Carducci
                                           Montepulciano
CAPRAIA   Montalcino   Chianciano
                                                   Terme
              Piombino
ELBA

                              GROSSETO   Ombrone
                                        Scansano
                                               Pitigliano

ISOLA DEL GIGLIO   Km. 0   10   20   30   40 Km.
                         Miles 0   10   20 Miles

Notable producers

Chianti

San Fabiano Borghini Baldovinetti, Arezzo An historic estate of great size – over 650 hectares – making a pleasant, fresh Chianti and Armaiolo, a great Super-Tuscan and a wine to remember.

Villa La Selva, Bucine (AR) Chianti Evento is one of the best Chiantis, but this winery is famous largely for its two Super-Tuscans: Felciaia is made from Sangiovese, and Selvamaggio is a blend of Cabernet Sauvignon and Sangiovese. These are two great Tuscan red wines.

Chigi Saracini, Castelnuovo Berardenga (SI) The owners of this splendid estate could be described as "specialists in Chianti Superiore" and produce attractive DOCG Chianti Colli Senesi.

Tenuta di Ghizzano, Ghizzano di Peccioli (PI) One of the rare serious wineries in Chianti Colli Pisani, though it prefers the simple denomination "Chianti". The estate produces well-made, good-value wines. Veneroso is a Super-Tuscan from Sangiovese and Cabernet, while Nambrot is a Merlot. Both are excellent.

Fattoria di Petrolo, Mercatale Valdarno (AR) Lucia Sanjust is one of the best growers in Arezzo, and has teamed up with Giulio Gambelli, one of the most talented Tuscan winemakers. Lucia produces a good Chianti Riserva but her great wines are something else: Torrione – a Sangiovese varietal – and Galatrona, from Merlot, are vinous wonders.

Donatella Cinelli Colombini Fattoria del Casato, Montalcino (SI) This excellent producer of Brunello also makes a very good Chianti Superiore, a wine of which Donatella is very proud – with good reason.

left *Tuscan wine became big business in the 1960s, but there are remnants of the ancient art of "mixed cultivation": here, olives grow out among the vineyards.*

Colli Aretini

Villa Cilnia, Pieve al Bagnoro (AR) By far the best winery in this sub-zone, producing excellent red wines since 1974. The Chianti Colli Aretini (also in a Riserva version) and Vocato, a Super-Tuscan from Sangiovese and Cabernet, are very good.

Colli Fiorentini

Podere Lanciola II, Impruneta (FI) The best winery in Impruneta and breathtakingly beautiful. Produces a pleasant Chianti dei Colli Fiorentini (also in a Riserva), and Terricci, a delicious Super-Tuscan blend of Sangiovese and Cabernet Sauvignon.

Le Calvane, Montagnana Val di Pesa (FI) A little-known but extremely reliable winery, producing a good Chianti dei Colli Fiorentini: Quercione is well-balanced and highly drinkable. The Borro del Boscone is even better, an outstanding Cabernet Sauvignon which — though not very full-bodied — has great elegance and harmony.

Castello di Poppiano, Montespertoli (FI) This famous winery and estate has been owned by the Guicciardini princes since the end of the 12th century. It includes over 120 hectares of vineyards and produces probably the most impressive Chianti dei Colli Fiorentini Riserva: a mellow, elegant red wine that's surprisingly concentrated. The Tricorno is equally attractive: a very unusual red blend of Sangiovese, Nebbiolo, Barbera, Cabernet Sauvignon and Merlot, all of them cultivated in the heart of Tuscany.

Colli Senesi

Chigi Saracini, Castelnuovo Berardenga (SI) Chigi Saracini produces several Chianti Colli Senesi wines, including a young, easy-to-drink version at a very reasonable price.

Ficomontanino, Chiusi (SI) Home to Tutulus, one of the most famous wines of Chianti Colli Senesi. This estate also makes an excellent Super-Tuscan from Cabernet

right *Mechanisation is widespread in Tuscan vineyards, where huge harvests fuel the largest wine output of any Italian DOC.*

Sauvignon – Lucumone, whose name comes from ancient Etruscan lords. (Chiusi was a major Etruscan city in Tuscany.)

Castello di Farnetella, Sinalunga (SI) Run by Giuseppe Mazzocolin (the "soul" of Fattoria di Felsina, one of the great marques of Chianti Classico) and expert oenologist Franco Bernabei. Their Chianti Colli Senesi is excellent. Note, too, the outstanding Poggio Granoni, a fine Super-Tuscan red; the Pinot Nero di Nubi; and a surprising and successful Sauvignon.

Montalbano

Enrico Pierrazzuoli, Capraia e Limite (PO) The best Chianti Montalbano, from one of the new-wave Tuscan winemakers. The Riserva version is a mellow, pleasant red wine with a slight aroma of wood. The normal version has the typical fragrance of the area's Sangiovese, along with velvety texture and a fullness on the palate.

Rufina

Marchesi de' Frescobaldi, Florence One of the most famous names in the world of wine and one of the largest estates in Tuscany, with almost 1,000 hectares of vineyards. Typical wines include the Chianti Rufina Riserva Montesodi, Chianti Rufina Nipozzano, and Mormoreto, a Super-Tuscan Cabernet Sauvignon. From the Pomino DOC come the Pomino Bianco Il Benefizio, a Chardonnay and Pinot Bianco blend, and Pomino Rosso, a Sangiovese topped up with a sprinkling of Cabernet.

Tenuta di Bossi, Pontassieve (FI) The Marquesses Bonaccorso and Bernardo Gondi, in collaboration with oenologist Carlo Corino, make the best red wines in Rufina district. The Chianti Rufina Riserva is very good and typical of its kind, while the Mazzaferrata – a Cabernet Sauvignon – is a powerful red, concentrated and with excellent ageing potential.

Fattoria Selvapiana, Pontassieve (FI) The Chianti Rufina Riserva Bucerchiale is a classic of the region. It is produced by Marchese Francesco Giuntini with the assistance of oenologist Franco Bernabei, and is one of the most balanced and long-lasting wines in Tuscany. This superb selection is largely responsible for the promotion of this historic estate to the aristocracy of regional winemaking.

Fattoria di Basciano, Rufina (FI) Reliable value for money – an increasingly prized commodity in Tuscany – is one of the key attractions of this winery, which is still relatively unknown internationally. Paolo Masi produces a good Chianti Rufina, which is pleasant, fruity and simple, and a remarkable Chianti Rufina Riserva. But two superb reds distinguish this cantina: I Pini is an elegant Super-Tuscan (50/50 Sangiovese and Cabernet Sauvignon), while Il Corto is a lovely Sangiovese with a Cabernet top-up.

Chianti Classico

Chianti Classico may be a byword for Italian wine, but few are aware that this is also one of the most beautiful landscapes in the world, excepting perhaps the British literati. Chianti is a lightly-wooded countryside speckled with vineyards, olive groves and cypress trees. It's situated at the heart of Tuscany, a region as rich in history and culture as any in Italy. Vineyards clinging to the hills of Chianti Classico were once the setting for battles and wars, but the castles and fortified abbeys have been transformed into magnificent country houses.

Legend has it that at the start of the 13th century, the burghers of Florence and Siena decided to put an end to their incessant wars, by defining their respective areas of influence. It was decided that two riders would set out at cock-crow, one each from Florence and Siena, and the place where they met would form the boundary between the two states. Apparently, the Florentines starved their black cockerel so that, driven by hunger, it started crowing very early. The Florentine riders left the city well before dawn and met their Sienese rivals at Fonterutoli, only 15 kilometres from the walls of Siena.

Thus, a large part of Chianti passed over to the Florentine Republic. And it was an important region to control, both from a strategic and economic point of view. The castles of Brolio, Cacchiano and Badia a Coltibuono were situated in the district of Gaiole, in the heart of

below This vineyard near Panzano, at the centre of the historic Chianti Classico area, belongs to Tenuta Fontodi.

Chianti, a countryside already covered with vineyards and olive groves. Here, wine production benefited from extremely favourable microclimates: besides an almost perfect symbiosis between Chianti's stony, dry soil and its vines, there is a unique light reflected by the limestone rocks, which warms the countryside – creating spectacular light contrasts and rainbows. The Chianti hills sweep in from the sea, bringing warm, humid winds, while the mountains separating this region from Valdarno usher in the cold air. Autumn rains presage the cold winter winds and are vital in determining the time of harvest. If the good weather lasts until the middle of October the wines will be excellent, the sunshine encouraging wine with harmony and warmth. But if the harvest takes place in rainy weather, the wine will almost invariably be acidic and sharper, colder and paler. Still, these are fascinating wines in their own right – more like the reds of the north, such as Burgundy.

When Cosimo III issued an edict defining the production zone of Chianti in 1716, it became a DOC long before its time. The grand duke's vision would protect the name of the wine, which has since become the most famous in Italy. Perhaps more importantly, it also protected the name of Chianti Classico. This is one of the most famous and celebrated Italian reds, produced in a vast region that straddles the provinces of Florence and Siena. The wines have been made to stringent regulations since 1984, when the DOCG was introduced. Upgrading from DOC to DOCG has necessitated a reduction in the permitted yields per hectare from 11,000 to only 7,500 kilograms, a unique case in Italy. DOCG rules have also eliminated the use of almost all white grape varieties (notably Trebbiano and Malvasia), which reduce the wine's longevity, in favour of Sangiovese. The latter has long been the region's pre-eminent grape variety and can now constitute 85-100 per cent of the grapes used in Chianti Classico DOCG.

Thus Chianti Classico has been reborn, and can now be described as the epitome of Italian wine. Vintages such as 1985, 1988, 1990 and 1997 show a refinement and harmony that few other Italian reds can emulate.

right An olive grove in San Régolo, to the south of Chianti Classico. Superb single estate olive oils are often produced by leading Chianti wine houses.

Notable producers

Casa Emma, Barberino Val d'Elsa (FI)
One of the most innovative wineries in the region. It produces excellent Chianti Classico, including a Riserva, and Soloio, a red IGT wine from Merlot. These are powerful, mellow, concentrated wines matured in small casks of French oak.

Isole e Olena, Barberino Val d'Elsa (FI)
Owned and established by Paolo De Marchi, Isole e Olena is one of Chianti's leading lights and improving by the year. His Chianti Classico is among the best and most reliable, even in unremarkable years, while his "innovative" wines are outstanding. The Cabernet Sauvignon is among the top five in Italy, and both Cepparello, a varietal Sangiovese, and Eremo, a Syrah, should follow in its footsteps.

Monsanto, Barberino Val d'Elsa (FI)
Famous worldwide for its Chianti Classico Riserva, and some of Tuscany's proudest wines of recent times. It also offers a pleasant, mellow Chardonnay matured in barriques. The Nemo, made from Cabernet Sauvignon, and Il Poggio Riserva, produced from Sangiovese, are worth a try.

Castellare, Castellina in Chianti (SI)
This estate's Chianti Classico is easy to drink and attractive – a wine which fascinates at the first sip. I Sodi di San Niccolò – a red wine made from Sangiovese and Malvasia Nera matured in small casks – and Coniale, a Cabernet Sauvignon, display the smooth texture of Chianti.

Castello di Fonterutoli, Castellina in Chianti (SI)
Fonterutoli, owned by the Mazzei family, is undoubtedly one of the most improved Chianti wineries of recent years, and has streamlined its list. The eponymous Chianti Classico Riserva is a great Chianti red; with a deep ruby colour in good vintages, rich bouquet and great refinement. The winery also produces Siepi, from Sangiovese and Merlot, and a delicious Chianti Classico "annata".

Castello di Lilliano, Castellina in Chianti (SI)
Giulio Ruspoli Berlingieri has recently turned Lilliano into a great estate. From Chianti Classico, both riserva and vintage, to Anagallis, made from 85 per cent Sangiovese and 15 per cent Canaiolo, these are reliable, good value wines.

Cecchi – Villa Cerna, Castellina in Chianti (SI)
This famous large winery produces a few million bottles of wine each year, always distinguished by reliability and consistency. The most prestigious in the range are Spargolo – a table wine from Sangiovese – Chianti Classico, Villa Cerna Riserva, Chianti Classico Messer Piero di Teuzzo and Chianti Classico Riserva.

Nittardi, Castellina in Chianti (SI)
A new name in high quality Chianti. In the best years the Chianti Classico Riserva has a concentrated ruby colour, with a vanilla fragrance and a pleasant, toasty aroma – a mellow and fine wine, with a powerful, supple structure.

Rocca delle Macìe, Castellina in Chianti (SI)
The standard-bearer of a traditional and much-prized style of wine. Home to voluptuous reds with a pleasant bouquet, which combine ease of drinking with a rounded taste.

San Fabiano Calcinaia, Castellina in Chianti (SI)
Guido Serio, a Milan-based Florentine financier and owner of this magnificent estate, offers a range of well-made Chianti Classicos. Riserva wines are made with grapes from the Cellole vineyards, while Cerviolo is a knockout red made from Sangiovese, with 30 per cent Cabernet Sauvignon.

Felsina, Castelnuovo Berardenga (SI)
A winery which has astonished everyone over the last few years with its progress, and now ranks as one of Tuscany's premier producers. Everything from the basic wine to the more select Riservas is extremely high quality, even in unexceptional vintages. Chianti Classico Riserva del Vigneto Rancia and Fontalloro, a Sangiovese varietal, are matured in small casks of French oak.

San Felice, Castelnuovo Berardenga (SI)
One of the largest and best estates in Chianti, Castelnuovo Berardenga offers a wide range of predominantly red wines, from Sangiovese, including a couple of real gems: Vigorello, from Sangiovese and Cabernet Sauvignon, and Chianti Classico Poggio Rosso Riserva.

Marchesi Antinori, Firenze
This winery is the achievement of one of the "noble fathers" of Italian wine, Marchese Piero Antinori, probably the best winemaker in Tuscany. His flagship is Tignanello, made from Sangiovese (80 per cent) and Cabernet Sauvignon (20 per cent), which is to Tuscany what Château Mouton-Rothschild is to Bordeaux. The most 'representative' wine in the range is Solaia (80 per cent Cabernet Sauvignon and 20 per cent Sangiovese), one of the greatest Italian reds. He also produces Chianti Classico Riserva, Badia a Passignano, Tenute del Marchese and Villa Antinori.

Agricoltori del Chianti, Geografico Gaiole in Chianti (SI)
This winery is a cooperative noted for excellent, consistently reliable wines. Vittorio Fiore, a highly skilled oenologist with that rare gift of common sense, has overseen a dramatic rise in quality.

below Marchese Piero Antinori, one of the "noble fathers" of Italian wine, with his daughters Albiera and Allegra.

Badia a Coltibuono, Gaiole in Chianti (SI) Reliability and good value are the watchwords at this famous estate, owned by the Stucchi family. Under oenologist Maurizio Castelli, its wines are well structured and extremely drinkable, including a typical red Chianti which is particularly food-friendly.

Castello di Ama, Gaiole in Chianti (SI) This estate resembles a Bordeaux château. The house is surrounded by vineyards planted with the likes of Merlot, Pinot Noir, Chardonnay and Sauvignon, as well as traditional Sangiovese, Trebbiano and Malvasia. Maturation involves traditional French casks and results in great wines of an international class. Among the most representative are Chianti Classico Bellavista, and La Casuccia and Vigna l'Apparita from Merlot.

Castello di Brolio - Ricasoli, Gaiole in Chianti (SI) Brolio has reappeared on the scene determined to regain a leading role

which had been theirs for centuries. This revival has been prompted by Francesco Ricasoli, who helped the estate through countless controversies and is already offering exceptional wines. Casalferro, a red wine produced from Sangiovese and Merlot, and Chianti Classico Castello di Brolio are both outstanding.

Castello di Cacchiano, Gaiole in Chianti (SI) The Ricasoli Firidolfi family's estate is a historic name in Chianti and one of the very few with several centuries' experience. Production has been entrusted to Giovanni Ricasoli, a highly skilled young winemaker whose leading wines are Chianti Classico Millennio Riserva and RF Castello di Cacchiano, a red wine from Sangiovese and Canaiolo, matured in barriques.

Riecine, Gaiole in Chianti (SI) A small winery now in the hands of Carlo Ferrini and Sean O'Callaghan, it has produced some of the best wines in the region for at least two decades. Both Chianti Classico Riserva and

La Gioia, a red wine made entirely from Sangiovese, are masterpieces.

Rocca di Montegrossi, Gaiole in Chianti (SI) Marco Ricasoli's range includes very modern Chianti Classico and Geremia, an intensely fruity Sangiovese.

Castello di Verrazzano, Greve in Chianti (FI) This winery has certainly fulfilled its potential in recent years. Its Chianti Classico Riserva is always magnificent, as is Sassello – yet another dazzling Sangiovese varietal.

Nozzole, Greve in Chianti (FI) The estate is owned by the Folonari family, which owns Ruffino. Pareto, a wine made from Cabernet Sauvignon, is one of the best "innovative" wines in the region, a worthy rival to the best of its ilk in Tuscany, California and Bordeaux. The Chianti Classico La Forra Riserva is equally outstanding.

Vignamaggio, Greve in Chianti (FI) Legend has it that Leonardo da Vinci

above This vineyard in Radda is owned by Castello di Albola, an historic estate with a stunning location and now owned by Zonin.

ago, by Prince Alceo di Napoli, one of the most far-sighted winemakers in the region. Now in the hands of Luca and Maurizia di Napoli, the most representative wines are both reliant on Cabernet Sauvignon: Vigna di Alceo has a small amount of Petit Verdot, while Sammarco is topped up with Sangiovese. The Chianti Classico Riserva is also excellent.

La Massa, Panzano in Chianti (FI)
The tale of a minor miracle. Giampaolo Motta is a young Neapolitan who first worked at the Castello dei Rampolla winery, then set up on his own; investing everything he had in an estate, also in Panzano, and producing his own wine. His Chianti Classico Giorgio Primo is outstanding and the basic Chianti Classico is among the best in its category.

Tenuta Fontodi, Panzano in Chianti (FI)
Chianti Classico Vigna del Sorbo Riserva is a great wine with a concentrated dark ruby colour, a complex bouquet with the noblest perfume of Sangiovese, and vague hints of Cabernet Sauvignon: in short, it's a masterpiece. Also interesting are Flaccianello della Pieve, made entirely from Sangiovese, and Pinot Nero Case Via. Dynamic owner Giovanni Manetti continues to work wonders.

Vecchie Terre di Montefili, Panzano in Chianti (FI)
This winery's best red wine is Anfiteatro. It was once a Chianti Classico Riserva, but was moved some years ago to the category of vino da tavola. This decision by Roccaldo Acuti, Vecchie Terre di Montefili's charismatic and highly skilled winemaker, certainly goes against the current trend.

Villa Cafaggio, Panzano in Chianti (FI)
A reliable cantina, producing wines of a consistently high quality. The Chianti Classico Riservas are powerful and complex, while the Chianti Classico is elegant and easy to drink. There is also a range of Super-Tuscans made entirely from Sangiovese or with the addition of Cabernet Sauvignon: Cortaccio, San Martino and Solatio Basilica.

above Grapes drying out on straw mats for *vin santo* ("holy wine"), produced throughout Tuscany. Some of the finest hail from the central Chianti region.

painted the Mona Lisa in one of the rooms of the villa di Vignamaggio. Modern works of art include the Chianti Classico Monna Lisa and Gherardino, made entirely from Sangiovese: peerless wines, that regularly scoop awards for this category.

Querciabella, Greve in Chianti (FI)
Querciabella is slowly becoming a leading estate in Chianti Classico, with an unmistakable style of wine. Success is based on first-class raw materials and the use of barriques, which give the wines their appealing vanilla notes.

Carpineto, Greve in Chianti (FI) Carpineto
is exemplary in many respects, not least for its excellent record in value-for-money wines. Besides an excellent range of Chianti Classico, in both "ordinary" and Riserva versions, it also offers a classic Cabernet Sauvignon matured in small casks.

Castello di Querceto, Greve in Chianti (FI)
This producer's best red is Cignale, made from Cabernet Sauvignon with small additions of Merlot. It's a magnificent wine; concentrated, mellow and elegant. The Chianti Classico wines are very good too, especially the Riserva.

Castello dei Rampolla, Panzano in Chianti (FI) The historic estate of Panzano
was founded in its present location 30 years

Melini, Poggibonsi (SI) A standard-bearer of Chianti Classico, this famous estate exports wine all over the world. Its hallmark is consistent quality throughout the range as well as offering good value-for-money. Chianti Classico I Sassi costs little yet is absolutely delicious in all its versions: pleasant, soft and not too demanding. Chianti Classico Riserva, La Selvanella and Laborel can be exceptional.

Ruffino, Pontassieve (FI) One of the leading estates in Italy, owned by the Folonari family for 70 years. Over the last decade the estate has been transformed into an ultra-commercial, very modern winery, capable of producing a wide range of high quality wines. So, as well as the admirable Chianti Classico and Libaio, a delicious white wine made from Chardonnay and Pinot Grigio, there is the distinguished Cabreo La Pietra, a Chardonnay matured in barriques, and a powerful Cabreo Il Borgo, made from Sangiovese and Cabernet Sauvignon. Two other recommended reds are produced in the tenuta di Santedame: Chianti Classico Santedame and Romitorio, a red made from Colorino and Prugnolo.

Castello di Albola, Radda in Chianti (SI) Tempted partly by the incomparably beautiful location, Gianni Zonin bought this estate a few years ago and has restored it to its ancient splendour. He also built a modern winery and acquired Franco Giacosa, so classy wines are now in full swing. The best is Acciaiolo, a Sangiovese, but the Chianti Classico Riserva and the Le Fagge Chardonnay are also good.

Castello di Volpaia, Radda in Chianti (SI) The wines of Castello di Volpaia have always had a unique style, partly because the vineyards are at a very high altitude, thus producing fragrant reds with good body. Typical of the range are Chianti Classico Riserva, Coltassala, a Sangiovese, and Balifico, a Cabernet Sauvignon.

Montevertine, Radda in Chianti (SI) Sergio Manetti, the owner, does not produce any Chianti Classico DOCG, because he disagrees with DOCG regulations. However,

he offers Sangiovese wines of some quality, even in lesser years. The best is Le Pergole Torte, which has attractive refinement and balance, though its complexity may vary. Montevertine Riserva and Il Sodaccio come a close joint-second, with forward bouquets.

Poggerino, Radda in Chianti (SI) This small winery is owned by Piero Lanza Ginori, a highly skilled young winemaker. His Chianti Classico Riserva Vigna di Bugialla is a dream; resulting from meticulous cultivation of the vines, bordering on perfection, and the intelligent use of barriques. The one drawback is that production is limited to a few thousand bottles. His basic Chianti Classico is always among the best wines, year after year.

Antica Fattoria Machiavelli, San Casciano Val di Pesa (FI) We have the greatest admiration for Nunzio Capurso, one of the "founding fathers" of Chianti Classico and the technical director of Melini and Machiavelli, the two Chianti-based stars in

the Gruppo Italiano Vini galaxy. The best wines produced by Machiavelli are Solatio del Tani – a Cabernet Sauvignon – Il Principe – a Pinot Nero – and Chianti Classico Fontalle Riserva.

Le Corti, San Casciano Val di Pesa (FI) One of the most beautiful villas in Chianti Classico, and owned by the Corsini princes. The wines are entrusted to the young winemaker Duccio Corsini, whose best wines are Chianti Classico Don Tommaso and Cortevecchia, the latter a Riserva. A good range, promising a few surprises.

La Sala, San Casciano Val di Pesa (FI) Laura Basonti, owner of La Sala, is making great progress. Her star wine is the Campo all'Albero, an intense Sangiovese with a touch of Cabernet Sauvignon. The Chianti Classico Riserva may lack concentration now, but San Casciano is renowned for producing the most mellow, ready-to-drink reds in Chianti Classico and this wine will be at its best within a couple of years.

above Chianti Classico's two most important products, wine and oil, are advertised on this roadside sign in the Chianti hills. Wine estates often produce the two.

Montalcino

above *Sign of the times, past and present. Biondi Santi has been at the forefront of Montalcino wine since the end of Garibaldi's campaigns.*

right *Montalcino has produced wine since the Middle Ages. Then, wines from different estates were often blended, but now the focus is on individual marques.*

Montalcino is a small commune in the province of Siena which has been known for its wine since the Middle Ages, especially Moscadello – a delicate sweet white. Several other white grape varieties were cultivated here besides the ubiquitous Sangiovese, the main grape of Chianti, but the phylloxera epidemic destroyed huge tracts of vineyards. The district produces four DOC wines.

Brunello di Montalcino

Some of the great Italian wines of today, such as Chianti and Barolo, forged their definitive personality at the time the modern Italian state was born, in the 1860s. Brunello di Montalcino is part of the great inheritance from the period of the Risorgimento (the unification of Italy), but a wine which was known only to a select number of wine-lovers until a few decades ago.

Its origins date to around 1870 when Ferruccio Biondi – a young veteran of Garibaldi's campaigns – returned home to look after the family estate, the Fattoria del Greppo, and to carry on the work of his grandfather, a pharmacist and passionate oenologist called Clemente Santi. As Santi had already discovered, the Sangiovese of Montalcino had special characteristics that distinguished it from the Chianti version. Biondi replanted the vineyards destroyed by phylloxera with a clone of Sangiovese Grosso, but his great breakthrough was in vinifying these grapes on their own, contrary to the procedure in other districts of Tuscany – where red and white grape varieties were blended. His aim was to produce an outstanding red wine with great ageing potential, like the great French and Piedmontese reds. So, instead of the customary "Tuscan treatment" of a second fermentation, which added fruity notes and liveliness, Biondi's wine was matured for a long period, first in barrel and then in bottle.

The great vintage of 1888 bore the legend Biondi-Santi – a few bottles still remain, in perfect condition – and it signified the birth of Brunello di Montalcino. Until the

1970s Brunello remained a little-known wine, but in recent years many local estates have been bought by "foreign" businessmen from other Italian regions, and they have begun to produce this fascinating red in larger quantities. Montalcino now has over 1,200 hectares of vineyards and produces over two million bottles of Brunello each year.

The wine regulations have changed several times. At present, the rules require at least four years' ageing (five for the Riserva), of which at least two must be in wood. Since 1980, Brunello has been a DOCG and can only be produced in the commune of Montalcino.

Moscadello di Montalcino

This very small production zone was recently awarded DOC status. The Moscadello grape variety is of historical importance in Montalcino, although in recent years it has been popular with only a few growers. Today, Moscadello may be produced in the traditional version or as passito, where it reveals an unexpected potential for ageing.

Rosso di Montalcino

This red has enjoyed a certain prominence and, similar to Brunello, is produced from Sangiovese Grosso grapes – albeit from the region's more recently planted vineyards. This is a less weighty wine than Brunello: aged in barrels for only one year, it should be drunk within four or five years of the vintage.

Rosso di Montalcino has built up a keen following at home and abroad, but it would be a mistake to talk it up as a "young Brunello". This is to all intents and purposes a wine in the best Tuscan tradition, a drinkable, full-bodied red rather than a wine with great ageing potential. Reds for laying down are still the exception here.

Sant'Antimo

This was the last denomination to be created in the district, in 1996, and takes its name from the Sant'Antimo abbey. The DOC provides a wide range of red and white wines, including a Bianco made from Trebbiano, Malvasia and Chardonnay varieties, and a Rosso, from Sangiovese, Malvasia Nera and Cabernet Sauvignon. Other prominent grape varieties include Cabernet Sauvignon, Merlot, Pinot Nero, Pinot Grigio, Sauvignon and Chardonnay. There is also a Vin Santo.

above *Brunello vineyards at Montalcino. Brunello is a latter-day derivative of Sangiovese and is often sensitive to its terroir.*

Notable producers

Altesino, Montalcino (SI) One of the most important wineries in the north of the district. Produces Brunello and Rosso di Montalcino, as well as two excellent Super-Tuscans, Alte d'Altesi and Palazzo d'Altesi. In the best years it also produces the selection Montosoli di Brunello, which is named after a famous sub-zone.

Argiano, Montalcino (SI) Owned by Noemi Cinzano, who works in collaboration with Giacomo Tachis, one of the greatest Italian oenologists. Cinzano produces Brunello, Rosso and an excellent Super-Tuscan – Solengo is a blend of Cabernet Sauvignon, Sangiovese, Syrah and Merlot.

Castello Banfi, Montalcino (SI) An estate stretching over 800 hectares of vineyards and owned by the Mariani family, famous for exporting Italian wines to the United States. The entire production is of a high standard: the Brunello is very reliable, the Rosso di Montalcino is extremely pleasant, and the two Super-Tuscans outstanding. Excelsus is a blend of Cabernet and Merlot, while Summus is made from Sangiovese, Syrah and Cabernet. In the best years the estate produces Brunello Riserva Poggio all'Oro. Other wines worth keeping tabs on are Sant'Antimo Centine, Moscadello Passito "B", Chardonnay Fontanelle, Merlot Mandrielle and Cabernet Tavernelle.

Fattoria dei Barbi, Montalcino (SI) Stefano Cinelli runs this important winery in Montalcino. His Brunello is famous and the Rosso is very pleasant. In the best years he turns out the selections Brunello Vigna del Fiore and Brigante dei Barbi, both from Sangiovese and Merlot grapes.

Biondi-Santi Il Greppo, Montalcino (SI) This estate was the birthplace of Brunello. It is now owned by Franco Biondi-Santi, who produces the classic Brunello Riserva, Brunello Annata and Rosso di Montalcino. The style is traditional and the ageing potential of the wines is excellent – the 1955 Riserva is still perfectly drinkable, while the 1964 is a mere stripling.

(Not surprisingly, the prices are correspondingly high.) In recent years, Franco's son Jacopo has been producing and marketing new-style Tuscan wines, including Sassoalloro, from Sangiovese grapes; Rivolo, from Sauvignon; Lavischio, from Merlot; and Schidione, from Sangiovese and Cabernet Sauvignon. The estate also owns Cantina Montepo, which produces wines in the Maremma.

Campogiovanni, Montalcino (SI) Belongs to the Ras group, which also owns the San Felice winery in Chianti Classico. Its finest wine is Brunello Riserva Vigna del Quercione, which in good years is among the very best wines of the region.

Capanna, Montalcino (SI) Owned by Patrizio Cencioni, who has been a reliable source of excellent and traditional Brunello di Montalcino for years. Recently his red wines have become more modern in style, though they retain their excellent potential for ageing. The Moscadello di Montalcino, which also comes in a Vendemmia Tardiva (late harvest) version, is worth a mention.

Tenuta Caparzo, Montalcino (SI) Another very famous name in the region, Tenuta Caparzo was founded in 1968 and is now run by Nuccio Turone, in collaboration with oenologist Vittorio Fiore. The winery offers well-made Brunello and Rosso and in the best years a selection of Brunello – always particularly well-balanced – made from grapes harvested at the La Casa vineyard. The white Sant'Antimo Le Grance, made from Sauvignon and Traminer, is also good.

Casanova di Neri, Montalcino (SI) Giacomo Neri is one of the new generation of Brunello producers. With the assistance of oenologist Carlo Ferrini he produces a well-made modern Brunello and, in exceptional years, the Cerretalto selection – one of the best Brunellos in the region.

Fattoria del Casato, Montalcino (SI) Donatella Cinelli Colombini, former co-owner of the Fattoria dei Barbi and president of the Movimento per il Turismo del Vino (Movement for Wine Tourism), now

has her own winery. She offers a good Brunello and a selection produced by a small group of consultants, all of the fairer sex – hence the Brunello Prime Donne.

Castelgiocondo, Montalcino (SI) A large estate, owned by the Marchesi de Frescobaldi. Produces a vintage Brunello and Riserva, Rosso di Montalcino and Lamaione, a Sant'Antimo DOC Merlot.

Cerbaiona, Montalcino (SI) Here Diego Molinari, known as "the commander" because of his aviation escapades, produces a traditional and slightly rustic Brunello. It's a fascinating wine made with technical ingenuity, and stands out like a slight squint in a beautiful woman.

Col d'Orcia, Montalcino (SI) A classic name in Montalcino winemaking, producing a very reliable Brunello, an extremely powerful Brunello Riserva made from grapes grown in the Poggio al Vento vineyard, and a good Rosso di Montalcino. There is also an excellent fragrant Moscadello, a remarkable IGT Toscana Cabernet Sauvignon and Olmaia – an amazing red wine.

Costanti, Montalcino (SI) Andrea Costanti is an intelligent young Brunello producer. From vineyards situated in Colle al Matrichese, in the central-eastern zone of the district, he produces elegant and pleasant Brunello and Rosso wines.

Fanti San Filippo, Montalcino (SI) This well-run cantina specialises in Brunello and also produces one of the best Rosso di Montalcinos in the entire district.

Tenuta Friggiali, Montalcino (SI) The Brunello and Rosso produced here are from the *cru* Pietrafocaia – not far from Santa Restituta – and are excellent.

Eredi Fuligni, Montalcino (SI) Excellent Brunello and Brunello Riserva wines, from top vineyards. The winery is owned by Roberto Guerrini, a university professor, who specialises in the fruity, vegetal Rosso di Montalcino Ginestreto. Guerrini has no equals in this category.

Greppone Mazzi Tenimenti Ruffino, Montalcino (SI) Run by the Folonari family from their stylish villa, and part of the huge Tenimenti Ruffino. The vineyards are close to those of Biondi-Santi, the exposure is favourable and the stony soils are ideal. Produces Brunellos that are always correct and traditional in style.

Lisini, Montalcino (SI) Nearly 83 years old, Elina Lisini is the lively owner of this historic cantina at Sant'Angelo in Colle. He produces Brunello, Rosso and a Brunello selection, Ugolaia, which is absolutely wonderful in the best years.

Luce della Vite, Montalcino (SI) Formed as a joint venture by the Frescobaldi family and the Mondavis of California, this winery produces Luce – a red Super-Tuscan made from Sangiovese and Merlot grapes. The Lucente is from similar varieties but, like the Danzante range, is less interesting. Has no track record with Brunello.

Il Marroneto, Montalcino (SI) With the help of oenologist Paolo Vagaggini, Alessandro and Antonello Mori produce a very pleasant and elegant Brunello from a vineyard of barely 1.5 hectares.

Mastrojanni, Montalcini (SI) One of the best wineries in Montalcino, located near Castelnuovo dell'Abate, a fashionable area. Run by Antonio Mastrojanni, in collaboration with oenologist Maurizio Castelli and expert winegrower Andrea Machetti, the winery boasts a sumptuous Brunello Schiena d'Asino, a San Pio (Sangiovese and Cabernet Sauvignon) and a good Rosso, besides the "normal" Brunello.

Nardi, Montalcino (SI) Since the early 1990s the young owner, Emilia Nardi, has revived the fortunes of an historic wine estate that had fallen on hard times. Today, the Brunello and Rosso are well-made and

clearly improving, while recently planted vineyards promise more progress.

Siro Pacenti, Montalcino (SI) Giancarlo Pacenti is one of the "infant prodigies" of Brunello and Rosso, and has a fastidious, uncompromising approach. His wines are rich, mellow and full of character.

Pieve di Santa Restituta, Montalcino (SI) Owned by Angelo Gaja, who produces a Brunello di Montalcino Rennina that has proved promising since the '95 vintage.

Il Poggione, Montalcino (SI) An historic name in Brunello, owned by the Franceschi family and run until recently by the late

Pierluigi Talenti, who will be hard to replace. Still, his successor Fabrizio Bindocci is a prodigy of Talenti and his wines have not deviated from type: the Brunello and Rosso are reliable and well-made.

Salvioni La Cerbaiola, Montalcino (SI) A leading light of Brunello, cherished by oenophiles at home and abroad. Giulio and Mirella Salvioni do not compromise: their production is small and notable for its mellow and elegant qualities.

Talenti Pian di Conte, Montalcino (SI) A well-known and reliable cantina, offering vintage Brunello, Brunello Riserva and Rosso di Montalcino – good, honest wines.

Val di Suga dei Tenimenti Angelini, Montalcino (SI) Owns excellent vineyards in the celebrated zone of Montalcino. The best vineyard, Spuntali, is wonderful, with very densely planted vines, more than 50 years old, and excellent exposure. These grapes are used to make an excellent Brunello, which has great ageing potential. Brunello Vigna del Lago is made from another of the establishment's vineyards and boasts impressive depth and complexity. The fruit isn't shy either – the good blackberries and cherry come through nicely. The Brunello Riserva and Brunello "annata" are reminiscent of the other two outstanding wines, but in a lower key. The Rosso is good and easy to drink.

right *The Tuscan tradition of secondary fermentation gave way at the end of the 19th century to greater barrel ageing.*

Montepulciano

Vino Nobile di Montepulciano

Modern Vino Nobile di Montepulciano began to take shape in the 1920s, under the guidance of a small group of winegrowers led by Adamo Fanetti, owner of the eponymous cantina. As with the Brunello variety, Sangiovese in Montepulciano had unique characteristics, thereby earning itself a new identity – as Prugnolo Gentile. This clone is the main element of Vino Nobile di Montepulciano, but accommodates additions of other local varieties such as Canaiolo, Mammolo, further red grape varieties authorised in the Siena province and small (optional) amounts of white grapes.

Awarded a DOC in 1966, Vino Nobile di Montepulciano was a key part of the great Italian revival and – after an unglamorous period – recovered its prestigious status in the 1980s. The award of a DOCG in 1980 and a series of exceptional harvests have consolidated its reputation.

Rosso di Montepulciano

The Rosso is a medium-bodied red, easy to drink and suitable for keeping for a short time. Rosso here is much the same as in Montalcino, but with regional differences in style making this a fresher, more direct alternative to Vino Nobile di Montepulciano. It is produced in the same area as its older brother, from the same grapes: Prugnolo Gentile is the mainstay, with additions of Canaiolo Nero and other red varieties – to a maximum 20 per cent.

Vin Santo di Montepulciano

Vin Santo is a special wine in Tuscany: every producer has his own way of making it, using different percentages of grape varieties and drying them for varying lengths of time. These grapes are then pressed to obtain a wine whose fermentation ceases naturally. It is then left to mature in 250-litre casks, for various lengths of time and without being touched.

The only constant factors are the basic grape varieties: Malvasia and Trebbiano, or Sangiovese and Malvasia Nera in the Occhio di Pernice – oeil de perdrix or partridge's eye, the rosé version. There are Vin Santo DOCs in various Italian zones: most important are Pomino, which is also offered in a red version, Carmignano, Bolgheri, Elba and recently Chianti Classico and Montepulciano. The latter is almost always sweeter and has more body than the others.

above *Vines tied up before the castle at Montepulciano. The town has a fine artistic heritage and, in Vino Nobile, a pillar of the Italian wine renaissance of the 1960s.*

Montepulciano is a splendid medieval hill town located between the Val d'Orcia and Valdichiana. As well as being one of the great art centres of Tuscany, it is home to one of Italy's most famous red wines, Vino Nobile. This ancient town, once called Mons Politianus, has yielded archaeological finds which date the local wine culture back to the Etruscans – Montepulciano was already renowned for excellent red wines in the 8th century BC.

The town's wine peaked in the 15th century, when Poliziano – the great humanist and poet, who was born in Montepulciano – took up residence at the court of Lorenzo dei Medici. No doubt partly on his recommendation, this magnificently structured wine became a firm favourite of the Medicis and other Tuscan aristocrats, and acquired the designation *nobile* – referring to the properties of the wine and its privileged consumers. The poem *Bacco in Toscana* (Bacchus in Tuscany), written by Francesco Redi at the end of the 17th century, describes Vino Nobile as "the king of all wines". The poem tempted King William III of England to send a delegation to Tuscany to buy Vino Nobile and the celebrated Moscadello di Montalcino.

Notable producers

Avignonesi, Montepulciano (SI) Vino Nobile's status as one of Italy's greatest red wines is largely due to Alberto and Ettore Falvo, who relaunched it in the early 1980s. Their Vino Nobile vintage and Riserva Grandi Annata are excellent and very reliable. Their other wines include the Super-Tuscans Grifi (a blend of Sangiovese and Cabernet); Desiderio (from Merlot and Cabernet); Il Marzocco (Chardonnay); and Il Vignola (Sauvignon). Spectacular Vin Santos come in basic and Occhio di Pernice versions; both are wonderful and rare wines.

Boscarelli, Montepulciano (SI) The De Ferrari family has owned this historic estate for many years. The Vino Nobile Riserva del Nocio is one of the region's most impressive wines, while the basic Vino Nobile and red Super-Tuscan Boscarelli are also excellent.

La Braccesca, Montepulciano (SI) Owned by the Marchesi Antinori, this estate produces an excellent Vino Nobile Riserva and a very interesting Merlot.

La Calonica, Valiano di Montepulciano (SI) A cantina whose wines are constantly improving in quality. Owner Federico Cattani produces a range of very good wines: his finest are the Vino Nobile, the Rosso di Montepulciano and the Girifalco, a Super-Tuscan Sangiovese.

Fattoria del Cerro, Montepulciano (SI) A very modern winery owned by Saiagricola, the winegrowing branch of SAI, one of the largest Italian insurance companies. It makes an excellent Vino Nobile Antica Chiusina, while the basic Vino Nobile and Rosso di Montepulciano are interesting.

Contucci, Montepulciano (SI) Alamanno Contucci's ancestors were already making wine in this region at the end of the Renaissance. His building housing the winery is the monumental Palazzo Contucci, with subterranean rooms dating back to the 13th century. His Nobile and Rosso di Montepulciano reds are fine examples. The Sansovino, also from Prugnolo Gentile

grapes, is equally characteristic, and the Vin Santo – with its full taste and good balance – is an excellent wine.

Fassati, Montepulciano (SI) This well-known estate is owned by Fazi Battaglia and produces Salarco, a very distinguished Vino Nobile, and a good Rosso di Montepulciano.

Il Macchione, Montepulciano (SI) A new name in the district. Owner Robert Kengelbacher offers a selection of Vino Nobile Riserva from grapes grown in Le Caggiole, one of the regions's top vineyards.

Lodola Nuova Tenimenti Ruffino, Valiano di Montepulciano (SI) One of the finest cantinas for Rosso di Montepulciano, and the Vino Nobile is also impressive.

Poliziano, Montepulciano Stazione (SI) Federico Carletti is one of the leading producers of Vino Nobile. His selection Vigna dell'Asinone is an aristocrat, only produced in the best years. The basic Vino Nobile is excellent and the Rosso di Montepulciano and Chianti are good – and reasonably priced. Le Stanze, a Cabernet Sauvignon Super-Tuscan, is sensational.

Redi, Montepulciano (SI) From this historic winery comes a range of wines produced by the Vecchia Cantina, one of the largest cooperatives in Siena. Valerio Coltellini has 1,000ha of vines to work with and makes a superb Vino Nobile selection, Briareo, and a terrific Vino Nobile Riserva.

Salcheto, Montepulciano (SI) One of the most interesting new estates in the region. The Vino Nobile Riserva is delicious, and the Vino Nobile and Rosso are very good.

Trerose Tenimenti Angelini, Montepulciano (SI) A reliable cantina. Vino Nobile Simposio is a concentrated, mellow wine with a long aftertaste. The Vin Santo compares favourably with the best in the district and the basic Vino Nobile is always very good.

left Pruning vines at the Fattoria del Cerro. The estate is so large (over 150 hectares) that the oldest vines can be "retired" each year and new ones phased in.

below A hands-off approach is required when cellaring Vin Santo, Montepulciano's often exquisite dessert wine.

Carmignano

Carmignano is one of the most famous Tuscan red wines, as well as one of the most historic wine zones in Tuscany. Located in a region to the west of Florence that also includes the communes of Carmignano and Poggio a Caiano, Carmignano was rewarded with DOCG status in 1990. This classification is applicable to, among others, Carmignano's high-quality Riserva wines, which must be aged until the 29th of September of the third year after the harvest – a date that is also given over to celebrate the feast of Saint Michael, the patron saint of Carmignano. The wine is a complex affair: 45 per cent is Sangiovese, with the remainder comprising a blend of Canaiolo Nero, Cabernet Franc, Cabernet Sauvignon and sometimes up to ten per cent Trebbiano Toscano,

right *The vineyards of Tenuta di Capezzana, owned by the Contini Bonacossi family – custodians of the finest Carmignano.*

Malvasia Bianca and Canaiolo Bianco. Carmignano is a full-bodied red wine, which is initially extremely tannic but matures beautifully. For wine and food match-makers and trainspotters, Carmignano is perfect with roasted and grilled meat and should be served at 18°C in large balloon glasses.

A new face in the Carmignano pantheon is a young red wine a little more than 20 years old. This is the Barco Reale, a lighter and less intense wine but one possessing good body. It is produced from the region's favourite grapes, Sangiovese, Canaiolo and Cabernet Sauvignon, but the last must not exceed 15 per cent of the vinification. The DOC also includes Rosato and a wonderful Vin Santo.

Notable producers

Tenuta Cantagallo, Capraia e Limite (PO)
Enrico Pierazzuoli may be a young winemaker and a new name in the region, but he has been producing well-made, reliable and stylistically innovative wines for some time. His best is the Carmignano Le Farnete, both the normal and riserva. His Carleto is an intriguing varietal from Riesling Renano.

Fattoria Ambra, Carmignano (PO)
Fattoria Ambra and its owner Beppe Rigoli are famous characters in Carmignano. For several years Rigoli has produced a range of reliable wines occasionally distinguished by a few gems. His range of Carmignano is certainly impressive and includes Elzana Riserva, Le Vigne Alte Riserva and Vigna Santa Cristina in Pilli, produced from three different vineyards on the estate. The range is completed by a Barco Reale, which is lighter and deliciously easy to drink.

Capezzana, Carmignano (PO)
The Capezzana cantina and the Contini Bonacossi have both played a prominent role in local history, and the wines produced by this historic estate have always been renowned for quality – at the reliable end of the scale. The selections are authentic, traditional and occasionally outstanding. Top of the range are two Carmignanos: Villa di Capezzana Riserva, the more rigorously traditional wine, and Villa di Trefiano. The Barco Reale is also excellent, and the Ghiaie della Furba, a blend of Cabernet Sauvignon, Cabernet Franc and Merlot, is worth its place in this durable line-up.

above *Carmignano differs from other great Tuscan reds in allowing space for Cabernet Sauvignon alongside the core Sangiovese.*

above left *The riserva wines must be aged until September 29th of the third year after harvest, the feast of Saint Michael.*

San Gimignano

Vernaccia di San Gimignano has as rich a history as any wine in Italy. Its name is thought to derive from the Latin *vernaculum*, meaning "of the place", which would explain why different varieties were given this name in various Italian regions. The Marches, the Alto Adige and Vernazza in Liguria all lay claim to the original Vernaccia, but what isn't in doubt is that around AD1000 Vernaccia di San Gimignano was already prominent among Tuscan wines. At a time when white wine was far more popular than red, only Vernaccia could compete on a popular level with the famous "Greek" wines of the south.

Vernaccia di San Gimignano has always been a much-loved wine. At the end of the 13th century, Pope Martin IV was said to be fond of eel cooked in Vernaccia, a weakness that inspired Dante Alighieri to cast him among the gluttons of purgatory in his *Divina Commedia*. Florentine and Venetian merchants sold Vernaccia as far afield as northern Europe, and in the 14th century an early Irish enthusiast emerged in the form of the Benedictine monk Godfrey of Waterford, who claimed it was healthier than the wines of Cyprus and Greece and could be drunk in large quantities: "Its strength is moderate, it develops gently in the mouth, caressing the nostrils, and comforts the brain, it is mellow on the palate and yet powerful…" In 1685 Francesco Redi cursed those who spoke ill of Vernaccia in his celebrated eulogy *Bacco in Toscana*.

Vernaccia was the first wine to be awarded a DOC in 1966, and earned the DOCG appellation in 1993. It is among the most charismatic Italian white wines and is associated with the remarks of Cecco Angiolieri, who in the 13th century declared: "it would not be interesting if it was Greek and not Vernaccia…"

It is expected that Vernaccia di San Gimignano will soon be joined by a Rosso di San Gimignano – made mostly from Sangiovese – once the latter's production regulations are approved.

Notable producers

Melini, Poggibonsi (SI) This great house of Chianti offers an absorbing Vernaccia di San Gimignano known as Le Grillaie. It's a full-bodied white wine with bags of character, and matures for a short time in small barrels of French oak.

Baroncini, San Gimignano (SI) An historic name in these parts, Baroncini produces Dometaia, a top-quality Riserva; Poggio ai Cannicci, a conventional Vernaccia; and an outstanding Vernaccia Brut, made by the Charmat method. The range is rounded off by an attractive Chianti Colli Senesi.

Guicciardini Strozzi, San Gimignano (SI) The history of the Fattoria Cusona is closely interwoven with that of Vernaccia. The Guicciardini Strozzi family owns 60 hectares of vineyards with a large but reliable production, but their Vernaccia di San Gimignano Perlato is a pearl of a wine.

La Lastra, San Gimignano (SI) Nadia Betti and Renato Spanu are the skilled duo at the helm of this relative newcomer, and their Vernaccia Riserva has deservedly won them a place in the San Gimignano "Who's Who". They also make a remarkable Chianti Colli Senesi while the red Rovaio, made from Sangiovese, Cabernet Sauvignon and Merlot, is worth a try.

Mormoraia, San Gimignano (SI) Ostrea, a white made from Vernaccia and Chardonnay grapes and matured in barriques, is one of the most interesting wines produced in San Gimignano. It is an innovative, irreverent wine and perhaps even better than the superb Vernaccia di San Gimignano.

Giovanni Panizzi, San Gimignano (SI) Giovanni Panizzi revels in his role as the king of Vernaccia di San Gimignano, a regal status currently conferred by his Riserva. This is a dream wine, perhaps the best in the entire district and a fitting tribute to skilled cultivation and refined winemaking. The Chianti Colli Senesi is also impressive.

Ponte a Rondolino, San Gimignano (SI) Enrico Teruzzi is the man who revived Vernaccia di San Gimignano when it was stumbling towards oblivion at the end of the 1970s. He is still the driving force behind Vernaccia and always produces wines whose high quality match his reputation. Vernaccia Vigna a Rondolino is excellent, as is Terre di Tufi – also made from Vernaccia grapes. Carmen is a great white wine made from Sangiovese (fermented as a white, of course), with the blend of Trebbiano, Vernaccia and Vermentino ensuring a great structure.

San Donato, San Gimignano (SI) Umberto Fenzi and the young oenologist Paolo Salvi work in tandem to produce San Donato's Vernaccia di San Gimignano. The straw-coloured Selezione is excellent, the Riserva outstanding and the standard version pretty palatable. All reflect the expert production methods in the winery.

Signano, San Gimignano (SI) The Vernaccia wines of Manrico and Ascanio Biagini have always been noted for their innovative style, especially since technical consultancy was entrusted to the young oenologist Paolo Salvi. The use of small wooden casks (*barriques d'Allier*) enhances the taste and increases the complexity on the nose. In fact, all their wines are among the best in the region.

Fratelli Vagnoni, San Gimignano (SI) Gigi Vagnoni is the new name on local lips in San Gimignano. His Mocali Vernaccia from the Il Mulino vineyard is consistently among the best in the region. It's powerful, with good structure and ages well. The basic Vernaccia also ranks among the best of its class – a perfect example of reliability and excellent value for money, too.

below *Vernaccia was Italy's first DOC wine. Its image was boosted in 1993 when new DOCG status curtailed grape yields.*

Bolgheri and Northern Maremma

Bolgheri was one of the *agents provocateurs* in the great revival of Tuscan wines in the late 1960s. It was here in 1968, in this halfway-house between Grosseto and Livorno, that Sassicaia was born, a Cabernet Sauvignon that swiftly revolutionised Italian wine. The brains behind Sassicaia were the Marchese Mario Incisa della Rocchetta and the oenologist Giacomo Tachis. For the first time in Italy, and in a region lacking a serious wine legacy, an incredible red wine was hatched from French vines planted close to the Tyrrhenian sea. With a colour far more intense than any Sangiovese, Sassicaia was matured in small French oak barriques of 225 litres and the first batch of three thousand was bottled without filtration. And it became the stuff of legend.

below *Cabernet Sauvignon grapes heading for the Sassicaia winery. This seminal Italian red was the first single estate wine to gain DOC recognition.*

When Sassicaia was conceived, there were no DOCs in the region. Bolgheri produced only *vini da tavola*, under a geographical name. Whites could be made with Trebbiano and Malvasia, and the reds and rosés with Sangiovese, but Cabernet Sauvignon was not even a recommended variety. Yet Bolgheri's transformation galvanised the whole of Tuscany: the region now resembles an oenological Eldorado, with the most up-to-date wineries using the most advanced equipment.

Besides Sassicaia, which revels in a specific DOC, Bolgheri now has Bolgheri Rosso and Rosato – both from Cabernet, Merlot and Sangiovese – and Bolgheri Bianco, from Sauvignon Blanc and Trebbiano or Vermentino. There is also a Bolgheri Sauvignon and Bolgheri Vermentino, both top-of-the-range white wines.

Located to the north and deep into the province of Pisa, behind hills visible from the sea, is the DOC of Montescudaio, a region very similar to Bolgheri but which has yet to follow in the footsteps of its neighbour. Its white wine is a classic but old-fashioned blend of Trebbiano and Malvasia, while its red is a Sangiovese topped up with white grapes, in the old-fashioned Chianti tradition.

Thirty kilometres south of Bolgheri, around Suvereto, is the new DOC of Val di Cornia. A few years ago this wine region was virtually unknown, but a few experimental wines made from Merlot, Cabernet Sauvignon and Sangiovese have captured worldwide interest: the Val di Cornia Bianco (Trebbiano and Vermentino) and Val di Cornia Rosso (Sangiovese, Cabernet, Merlot and Canaiolo) have tapped the extraordinary potential of this region, whose sandy clays are ideal for great red grape varieties.

The Isle of Elba, Napoleon's former – enforced – residence, has a long history of wine-making. Its flagship wine is Aleatico, a sweet red made from the Aleatico grape which has been cultivated on the island for centuries. This is one of the few Italian sweet red wines to show a high alcohol content, and one of the very few wines which can be drunk with puddings based on chocolate – which is a notoriously difficult partner for wine.

Aleatico is not alone here. The Elba DOC also includes Bianco, made from Trebbiano grapes, and Rosso from Sangiovese. Finally, Ansonica – the local monicker for Inzolia, which also thrives in Sicily and along much of the Tuscan coast – provides the muscle for Ansonica dell'Elba, a well-structured white wine, which is slightly salty and ideally suited to the local dishes *alla marinara*. A Passito version is also produced.

Notable producers

Tenuta Belvedere, Bolgheri (LI) Owned by Marchesi Antinori, this cantina offers high-quality wines with an increasingly high profile. The most famous is Guado al Tasso, a Bolgheri Superiore made from Cabernet Sauvignon and Merlot. Bolgheri Vermentino and the Bolgheri Rosato Scalabrone are also serious contenders.

Le Macchiole, Bolgheri (LI) Eugenio Campolmi is the owner of this beautiful estate, which has recently benefited from new vineyards. His fruity, ruby-rich Bolgheri Rosso Superiore Paleo is one of the best wines in the region.

Tenuta dell'Ornellaia, Bolgheri (LI) A very modern winery owned by Marchese Lodovico Antinori, and one of the premier sites on this coast. He makes particularly fine wines including Masseto, from Merlot, and the well-known Ornellaia, from Cabernet and Merlot.

Tenuta San Guido, Bolgheri (LI) Many Bolgheri producers will have raised a glass to this estate and to its owners, the Incisa della Rocchetta family. It was Marchese Mario Incisa who discovered the great potential of this region with Sassicaia, which has boasted the specific Bolgheri Sassicaia DOC since 1994. Made predominantly from Cabernet Sauvignon, this occasionally adorns the summit of Italy's great innovative reds. The 1977, 1985, 1988, 1996, 1997 and 1998 vintages are top of the tree.

Grattamacco, Castagneto Carducci (LI) Piermario Meletti Cavallari is a pioneer of Bolgheri wines. He offers the traditional Grattamacco and the modern Bolgheri Rosso Superiore, one of the region's most famous wines. Recent vintages have tended to vary in quality.

Michele Satta, Castagneto Carducci (LI) Michele Satta is a winemaker of great sensibility and has now established a unique identity. His Bolgheri Rosso Piastraia and Vigna al Cavaliere are two of his finest reds.

Tenuta del Terriccio, Castellina Marittima (PI) In the province of Pisa, yet close to the Bolgheri region, the Tenuta del Terriccio run by Gian Annibale Rossi di Medelana makes a range of consistently outstanding wines, especially reds. The star of the region is the Lupicaia, one of the best Tuscan Cabernet Sauvignon and Merlot blends.

Sorbaiano, Montecatini Val di Cecina (PI) Montescudaio is one of the least-known but most interesting areas in Tuscany, and the Fattoria Sorbaiano is a winery noted for reliable and consistent quality: its Rosso delle Miniere is a fantastic Montescudaio Rosso, matured in small casks.

Poggio Gagliardo, Montescudaio (PI) The Montescudaio Bianco Vigna Lontana is a complex and mellow DOC white from the Poggio Gagliardo, proving that there is more to the region than red wines.

Acquabona, Portoferraio (LI) From one of the most famous cantinas on the Isle of Elba comes a delicious rare wine, the superb Aleatico dell'Elba, a sweet red, reminiscent of the French Banyuls.

Gualdo del Re, Suvereto (LI) The southern boundary of the province of Livorno is represented by the DOC region of Val di Cornia. The most famous cantina in the district is probably the Gualdo del Re winery, which offers a fine and reliable range of wines. Top choice is Val di Cornia Gualdo del Re Riserva, a concentrated wine with a good bouquet and finish.

Tua Rita, Suvereto (LI) Signora Rita Tua's tiny cantina has many supporters, and owes its lofty reputation to two exceptional wines: Redigaffi is a muscly Merlot with a beautiful structure, and Giusto di Notri is an earthy, robust blend of Cabernet Sauvignon and Merlot. These are two beauties of international repute.

right *A winemaker monitors the stainless steel fermentation tanks at the hi-tech Ornellaia winery, in Bolgheri.*

Southern Maremma

Tuscany's quality catchment area now encompasses the hills and lightly wooded countryside of the Maremma Grossetana. In the last few years several new DOC regions have evolved here, most recently the Monteregio di Massa Marittima: which comprises Massa Marittima itself as well as the districts of Gavorrano, Roccastrada and Rocca-tederighi on the Colline Metallifere. Also shaping up nicely are the DOC wines of Monteregio Vermentino and Monteregio Rosso (predominantly Sangiovese).

Further south, the large region of Morellino di Scansano gives its name to both a red grape (a variety of Sangiovese) and a wine in a distinctly modern, classy but easy-drinking style. This is a contemporary Morellino di Scansano and in its infancy, but Morellino previously flourished as a sweet wine, made from *appassito* (dried) grapes. Besides Sangiovese it also contained a high percentage of Alicante – a form of Grenache, or Cannonau, most probably imported from Spain. Indeed, the little Stato dei Presidi, consisting of the Monte Argentario and the districts of Orbetello and Talamone on the Grosseto coast, was under Spanish rule for centuries.

There are also two different white wines. Ansonica Costa dell'Argentario is made from grapes of that name, in vineyards bordering the well-known coastal resorts of Cala Galera and Porto Santo Stefano. This is an almost salty white wine, full-bodied and particularly well-suited to the region's highly seasoned *marinara* dishes, which are cooked in oil, garlic and white wine.

There is also Bianco di Pitigliano (Trebbiano and Malvasia), which has a distinctive sharpness and hails from an inland region known for centuries as a refuge for Jews fleeing the neighbouring Pontifical State. Even today, Pitigliano produces the best-known Italian kosher wine.

Finally, the three versions of Parrina – Bianco (Trebbiano, Ansonica and Chardonnay), Rosso and Rosato (both Sangiovese) – are fairly similar to the white wines outlined above, but are produced in the more southern districts of the Maremma.

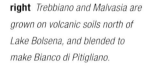

right *Trebbiano and Malvasia are grown on volcanic soils north of Lake Bolsena, and blended to make Bianco di Pitigliano.*

Notable producers

Le Pupille, Magliano in Toscana (GR)

A fine modern estate, owned by Elisabetta Geppetti – a young winemaker from Maremma – and husband Stefano, whose previous experience includes a stint as a wine merchant. Their best wine is Morellino di Scansano Poggio Valente, a full-bodied red matured in small casks and produced from a single vineyard. The Morellino di Scansano Riserva is also excellent.

La Stellata, Manciano (GR)

The seminal Bianco di Pitigliano is produced by Manlio Giorni and Clara Divizia, owners of La Stellata. Lunaia is made in the traditional manner, using only Trebbiano and Malvasia, and is named after the stream which flows past their little vineyard. It is a simple white wine, deliciously fruity, very pleasant and ripe for drinking young.

Massa Vecchia, Massa Marittima (GR)

This cantina's signature wine is La Fonte di Pietrarsa. It may not be a DOC wine, but this Cabernet Sauvignon is a great, generous red – neither heavy nor difficult to drink, but strong, mellow and typical of the terroir. Also makes a fair Terziere, from Alicante.

Moris Farms, Massa Marittima (GR)

Gualtierluigi Moris owns 400 hectares of land across two estates, and production is expected to rise in a few years' time. His best wine is Avvoltore, one of the greats of the Maremma: a fine red from Sangiovese and Cabernet Sauvignon. He also boasts a spectacular version of Morellino di Scansano Riserva, which is powerful, rounded and rich and typical of this very Mediterranean region.

Villa Patrizia, Roccalbegna (GR)

In a region that could stick up a 'take it as red' sign across most of its vineyards, it's good to see a white wine winning some headlines – even if Romeo Bruni's choice wines are non-DOC. Alteta is a white made from Chardonnay and a small amount of Sauvignon Blanc, matured in small casks and kept in bottle for ten months before sale, while Orto di Boccio is a promising red blend of Sangiovese, Cabernet Sauvignon and Merlot. Also offers a dependable Morellino and Rosso.

Meleta, Roccatederighi (GR)

Erika Suter is the owner and driving force of this striking, ultra-modern winery, a testament to the huge investment being poured into the Maremma. Erika produces fascinating wines and completely ignores the obsolete regulations pertaining to DOC. Her best wine is Rosso della Rocca, a ruby-red blend of mostly Cabernet Sauvignon grapes, with a lively nose, interesting touch of wood and such class and concentration that the absent DOC seems immaterial.

Erik Banti, Scansano (GR)

Erik Banti is a pioneer and standard-bearer of Morellino di Scansano, laying down his roots long before the Maremma was seduced by Mammon. His *cru* Ciabatta is a classic of the region, but his Aquilaia – made exclusively from the Alicante grape – is especially well-balanced and the Morellino di Scansano Riserva a powerful, mellow red. Both are hugely evocative of their terroir.

Elyane & Bruno Moos, Soiana (PI)

Fontestina and Soianello are two attractive red Sangiovese-based wines. They cannot boast a DOC, which is a pity, because they are undoubtedly among the top wines in the whole province. They are also produced from organic vines, proving – along with some esteemed counterparts in Burgundy – that environmentally sound wines can also become quality wines.

Lucca and Lucchesia

The independent-minded district of Lucca, in the northwestern corner of Tuscany, is celebrated for its refined, delicate extra-virgin olive oil. Its wines are less well-known, although there are two DOC wines worthy of note. The most famous is Montecarlo Bianco, which is made from an interesting blend of grape varieties, including Trebbiano Toscano, Sémillon, Pinot Grigio, Pinot Bianco, Sauvignon and Roussanne. This is a full-bodied and mellow wine which can be kept for several years, in other words, a typical Mediterranean wine, reminiscent of those of Provence or the southern Rhône – whose soil and climate are very similar to Lucca's.

Montecarlo Rosso is more traditional and at its best in *vini da tavola*, though it includes some exotic varieties. Besides Sangiovese, there is Ciliegiolo, Colorino, Malvasia Nera, Cabernet, Merlot and even Syrah, in small quantities. The rosso is a very well-structured red, with a typical, slightly bitter aftertaste. In this case, too, there are a few similarities with the wines of the Rhône Valley, in particular Châteauneuf-du-Pape, the famous red wine appellation of Avignon with which Montecarlo Rosso runs parallel. The production zones of both the bianco and rosso are found in the communes of Montecarlo, Altopascio, Capannori and Porcari, in the province of Lucca.

Finally, the DOC Colline Lucchesi – which includes only the municipal districts of Capannori and Porcari – also produces a rosso and bianco. The rosso is along the lines of Chianti and suitable for drinking young, although some vintages age well. The bianco, however, lacks the full body and ageing potential of its rival in Montecarlo.

above *The Palais Pfanner and* **(right)** *the San Frediano tower, which dominates Lucca's skyline.*

right *The* terroir *in Lucca shows similarities to the southern Rhône, while the Fattoria del Buonamico is widely regarded as the yardstick for local bianco and rosso.*

Notable producers

Fattoria del Buonamico, Montecarlo (LU)
The most famous estate in the district, with a reputation for consistent quality, and a virtual barometer of regional fortunes. In recent years the vineyards have been redeveloped and today the Montecarlo Rosso and Bianco and the famous Cercatoia Rosso, made from Merlot and Cabernet grapes, are among the best in the region. These are concentrated and mellow wines, typical of the modern oenological trend, but retaining excellent ageing potential.

Fuso Carmignani, Montecarlo (LU) The eponymous owner is a great character. "Fuso" is a nickname which roughly translates as "crazy", but make no mistake – he's an excellent wine producer, and passionate about jazz and blues. In fact, he has dedicated his best wine, For Duke – made from Sangiovese and Syrah grapes – to Duke Ellington, while his Montecarlo Bianco is called Stati d'Animo ("feelings"). Both hit the high notes. Carmignani also

produces Montecarlo Rosso Sassonero and a Vin Santo bearing the madcap name Le Notti Rosse di Capo Diavolo ("The Red Nights of the Devil's Head"). But there's no need for anxiety: Fuso Carmignani may be wildly unorthodox, but he's bang on form.

Fattoria di Montechiari, Montecarlo (LU)
A standard-bearer for the Lucca region, with over 20 years' experience and a hatful of commendations. The winery's Montecarlo Rosso is excellent and its Super-Tuscans are outstanding. It also produces a very good Cabernet, a Pinot Nero and a Chardonnay. These are all modern wines, the result of quality vine-growing combined with modern vinification techniques – a slightly unusual approach in a region known for highly traditional wines.

Fattoria del Teso, Montecarlo (LU)
Another historic name in the Lucchesia district, this is the largest estate in the Montecarlo zone and boasts fine facilities. Local grapes, grown on 30 hectares of vines, still take priority. The cantina's

headline wine is a Montecarlo Rosso with the colourful name of Anfiteatro di Lucca – a very traditional yet fascinating selection, intense and full of aromas.

Vigna del Greppo, Montecarlo (LU)
This famous winery embodies the finest viticultural traditions in the district. The flagship wine is Montecarlo Rosso Carlo IV Riserva, a powerful wine with excellent potential for ageing.

Wandanna, Montecarlo (LU) An estate worth watching, as the Fantozzi family are not inclined to let the grass grow under their feet. Terre dei Cascinieri is one of the best (maybe even *the* best) Montecarlo Rosso wines, while Montecarlo Bianco Terre della Gioiosa is very good and Virente, a Merlot and Cabernet Super-Tuscan, is excellent. This large estate also produces Montecarlo Rosso Terre della Gioiosa, a substantial "younger brother" of Terre dei Cascinieri, and the Labirinto – a white wine made from Sauvignon grapes, which has an exotic aroma and a pleasant, mellow charm.

Umbria

Numerous archeological finds in Umbria reveal a local wine culture that predates the Romans' arrival. Indeed, the Romans became fond of Umbrian wines; which were mostly white, with some reds and rosés, and produced from "promiscuously" cultivated vineyards – with the vines growing alongside other plants.

In the Middle Ages the sweet whites of Orvieto took a seat of honour at the papal table, while Sagrantino became cherished for its mellowness and robust fruit. However, compared with neighbouring Tuscany and Latium, Umbria remained isolated and "untouched" until recently; but modernised winemaking and a vast range of reasonably priced wines have roused the region from its slumber.

Winemaking and wine styles

Over 20 per cent of Umbria's output, of just under one million hectolitres a year, boasts a DOC or DOCG. This upswing is driven by two DOCGs, Torgiano Rosso Riserva and Sagrantino di Montefalco, and a growing league of excellent DOCs: some have the Umbria IGT, which is likely to become a DOC in the very near future and is Umbria's equivalent of the "SuperTuscans". (Cervaro della Sala is a brilliant example.)

The northern parts of this region are home to four DOCs covering a vast area. Most of the cooperatives which dominate the local wine scene have traditionally favoured pleasant, decent and good value wines, though they tend to lack concentration. Colli Altotiberini and Colli Perugini DOCs produce a Bianco, from Trebbiano, and a Rosso and Rosato from Sangiovese (with a little Merlot in Colli Altotiberini), while the recently created Assisi DOC makes a Grechetto varietal and a Novello.

Producers in Colli del Trasimeno have transfomed their denominazione, widening their range and allowing the more innovative table wines to claim a DOC label. So, in addition to Sangiovese, there is a Rosso with a large amount of Gamay Perugino, and additions of Ciliegiolo, Merlot and Cabernet. The Scelto (selected) version is made from a grape yield of no more than nine tonnes per hectare, while the Riserva is a rich, complex wine.

The Novello DOC blends a Vin Santo along Tuscan lines, with Trebbiano, Grechetto, Verdicchio and Verdello, with optional additions of Pinot Bianco and Grigio. The Bianco, also available as a Scelto, is 40 per cent Trebbiano, with Chardonnay, Pinot Bianco, Pinot Grigio and Grechetto. The latter is used alone in Colli del Trasimeno Grechetto.

Armed with this balance of native and international grape varieties, Umbrian producers are challenging the great Italian wine regions. They have also banished Trebbiano and other varieties with high yields but little character, grapes which for years had underpinned winemaking in central Italy. Twin spearheads of the Umbrian crusade are the zones of Torgiano, which produces many styles of whites and reds in a market dominated by the near-legendary estate of Lungarotti; and further south, near Foligno, the area of Montefalco.

Surrounding Montefalco is the DOC of Colli Martani, which is virtually synonymous with Grechetto, and the sub-zone of Grechetto di Todi. In addition to the latter's fairly full-bodied, bold wine, there is also Colli Martani Sangiovese and Colli Martani Trebbiano, which constitute the backbone of Torgiano's production.

In Terni the scene is dominated by Orvieto, a famous white defined as Classico in the most traditional zone, while two red DOCs have recently boosted the local range – Rosso Orvietano and Lago di Corbara. The last and most southern DOC zone is the Colli Amerini, which produces a Bianco from Trebbiano and Grechetto; a Rosso from Sangiovese; and a pleasant Malvasia dei Colli Amerini, whose style and taste are reminiscent of Latium wines.

Soil, viticulture and climate

Umbria is a region of mountains and hills, rivers and lakes, stretching away from the Tyrrhenian slopes of the Umbro-Marchigiano Apennines, parts of which are 1,500 metres high. To the north and east, the Apennine ridge forms a watershed where the Tiber has its source: the river crosses the entire region lengthways and, along with its various tributaries, ushers in atmospheric currents from the south and west. The mountains gradually become hills and upland plains marked by many rivers and lakes, the most important of which is Lake Trasimeno – the fourth largest in Italy. Plains make up only six per cent of the territory.

The nature of the soil is rather varied, consisting of rock formations dating from various periods. Winemaking flourishes on the hillsides where the weather is influenced by the more moderate Tyrrhenian maritime climate, while the many rivers and Lake Trasimeno ensure the right level of humidity. Mixed cultivation has now been abandoned throughout the region, and in recent years vineyards in the most important zones have adopted the Guyot system and spur cordon, thereby increasing the planting density.

above *Sunflowers in Umbria. The region revels in its unspoilt charm, but local wines are dragging Umbria into the limelight.*

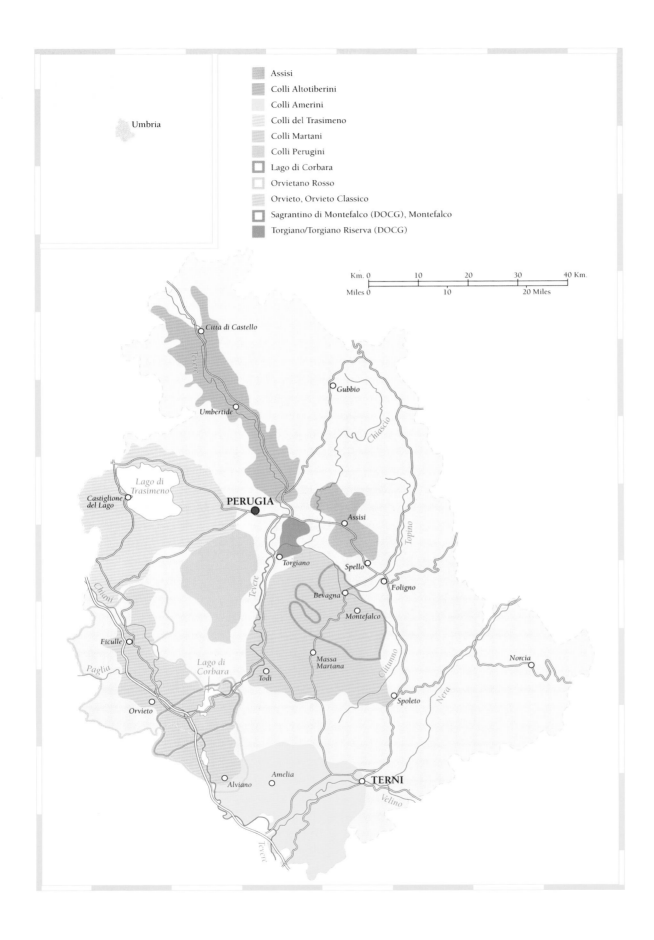

Umbria

	Assisi
	Colli Altotiberini
	Colli Amerini
	Colli del Trasimeno
	Colli Martani
	Colli Perugini
	Lago di Corbara
	Orvietano Rosso
	Orvieto, Orvieto Classico
	Sagrantino di Montefalco (DOCG), Montefalco
	Torgiano/Torgiano Riserva (DOCG)

Km. 0   10   20   30   40 Km.
Miles 0   10   20 Miles

Citta di Castello

Tevere

Gubbio

Umbertide

Chiascio

Lago di
Trasimeno

Castiglione
del Lago

PERUGIA

Assisi

Topino

Torgiano

Spello

Foligno

Bevagna

Chiani

Montefalco

Ficulle

Massa
Martana

Clitunno

Norcia

Paglia

Lago di
Corbara

Todi

Nera

Spoleto

Orvieto

Amelia

Alviano

TERNI

Velino

Tevere

Orvieto and Lago di Corbara

above *The ancient hilltop town of Orvieto. The town's eponymous white wine has been at the heart of Umbria's emergence, and has long been coveted in Chianti.*

Even the large establishments in Chianti were tempted to make Orvieto, in order to add a good-quality white to their range of reds. Now, after a relatively dormant period, many winemakers are again producing first-class Orvieto, from Trebbiano grapes (known locally as Procanico), Verdello, Grechetto, Drupeggio and/or Malvasia Toscana. It is a light white wine, rich in white fruit flavours and extraordinarily pleasant to drink. But, almost inevitably, Orvieto has been modified to reduce the percentage of Trebbiano and increase the proportion of "noble" varieties, such as Grechetto, international varieties and some recently identified Procanico clones.

A new Orvieto DOC is Orvietano Rosso (or Rosso Orvietano), an appellation whose emergence had been widely anticipated for some time: for many years, wine-makers have been demonstrating the region's potential to make great red wines with a strong sense of terroir. The Rosso is a rather "free" blend, made from a 70 per cent mix of Aleatico, Cabernet Franc, Cabernet Sauvignon, Canaiolo, Ciliegiolo, Merlot, Montepulciano, Pinot Nero, and Sangiovese; and up to 30 per cent Barbera, Cesanese, Colorino and even Piedmontese Dolcetto! But that is not quite the end of it: Orvietano Rosso may also be a varietal from any of the following – Aleatico, Cabernet Franc, Cabernet Sauvignon, Canaiolo, Ciliegiolo, Merlot, Pinot Nero or Sangiovese. The only boundary is the winemaker's imagination.

Within the Orvieto region is Lago di Corbara, an autonomous sub-zone with its own DOC, which includes the communes of Baschi and part of Orvieto. The soil, rich in red clay, tufa and small pebbles, is ideal for full-bodied red wines. The Rosso is made from a complex blend of grapes, similar to that of Orvietano Rosso, and here too it is possible to produce single variety wines from Cabernet Sauvignon, Merlot and Pinot Nero grapes.

But a survey of the region would not be complete without mention of one of Italy's greatest winemakers, Antinori, which has its own very large estate – Castello della Sala – in Ficulle. An impressive vinous "research laboratory", La Sala has developed some of the most interesting Italian wines of the last two decades. Best of all is its Cervaro, one of the greatest Italian whites, which can stand toe-to-toe with the great Burgundies and the muscular Chardonnays of California and Australia. Not surprisingly, the success of Antinori has been a spur to other producers in the area, and the upward trend is gathering momentum.

Orvieto is one of the most stunningly photogenic of the medieval Italian cities, and is situated in a region whose tufa soil, enriched by centuries of volcanic detritus, produces excellent wines. The greater Orvieto wine region is extensive and includes part of the province of Viterbo, in Latium. The wines produced in the area around Orvieto – which historically is the most celebrated sub-region – are entitled to use the coveted Classico term on the label. The most widespread is Orvieto Secco, but it's not uncommon in these quarters to find Abboccato (slightly sweet), Dolce and Amabile (semi-sweet).

In ancient times the region was famous throughout the Italian peninsula for its fine table wines, and for many years Orvieto was the flagship of Umbrian winemaking.

Notable producers

Cantina Sociale dei Colli Amerini, Amelia (TR) A very large estate, responsible for almost the entire production of the Colli Amerini DOC. Its white and red wines, with their distinctive clean style, have brought fame to this part of southern Umbria. The Rosso Superiore Carbio and Merlot Olmeto are excellent.

Barberani-Vallesanta, Baschi (TR) Produces its vast range of wines from grapes grown in the vineyards overlooking Lake Corbara. Wines range from Orvieto Classico to Orvieto Classico Superiore Calcaia, a delicious sweet botrytis wine. Also worth trying are the red Foresco, Pomaio, a good Sauvignon Blanc, and Moscato Passito Villa Monticelli.

Monrubio, Castel Viscardo (TR) This large wine cooperative, known until recently as Vi.C.Or, produces good white wines and a remarkable Olmaia – made from Merlot, Pinot Nero, Cabernet Sauvignon and Cabernet Franc.

Tenuta di Salviano, Civitella del Lago (TR) This beautiful estate belonging to the Corsini princes has 60 hectares of vineyards on the shores of Lake Corbara. Produces outstanding wines, from Orvieto Classico Salviano to Lago di Corbara Turlò, and an elegant Vin Santo.

Castello della Sala, Ficulle (TR) Piero Antinori's Castello wines rank among the finest in Italy, thanks to ongoing research and a very modern winery. The most famous is Cervaro, a Chardonnay with a small amount of Grechetto, an elegant, intense and concentrated style. Muffato is a delicate but extremely concentrated sweet wine from Sauvignon and Gewürztraminer grapes affected by noble rot.

Bigi, Orvieto (TR) Part of Gruppo Italiano Vini, and the largest winery in the Orvieto. Produces about three million bottles a year, including some excellent Orvieto, such as Vigneto Torricella, and interesting Grechetto and Sangiovese table wines.

Decugnano dei Barbi, Orvieto (TR) The Orvieto Classico wines produced here have always been noted for their discreet refinement. Beside traditional wines there is "IL": a modern red version, fermented and refined in barriques and notable for its startling depth. Also interesting is Pourriture Noble, an elegant sweet white wine and – for historians – the first Umbrian wine ever made from botrytised grapes.

Le Velette, Orvieto (TR) This beautiful estate is a few kilometres from Orvieto, and has 95 hectares of vineyards in a prime location. A leading name in the region, it is responsible for some of the best Orvieto whites and an outstanding red: Calanco is made from Sangiovese and Cabernet Sauvignon and is well structured, very subtle and elegant.

Palazzone, Orvieto (TR) Giovanni Dubini makes some of the best wines in the Orvieto, such as Campo del Guardiano and Terre Vineate. Also excellent is a rare Muffa Nobile, a complex Orvieto Vendemmia Tardiva (Late Harvest) and Armaleo, a fantastic Cabernet Sauvignon. Chardonnay and Grechetto are the pick of the whites.

La Palazzola, Stroncone (TR) Stefano Grilli, owner of this beautiful estate, has produced some of the most interesting Umbrian wines in recent years, both from traditional grapes such as Verdello, or introduced varieties such as Pinot Nero: the standard is consistently high. His range includes a *metodo classico* Spumante Brut, a fine Riesling, a fascinating Vendemmia Tardiva (Late Harvest) and a great Rubino.

right *The man behind so many wines: consultant oenologist Riccardo Cotarella is one of the most recognisable talents in Umbria, and elsewhere.*

Torgiano and Montefalco

Umbria's two DOCG wines are meaty, full-bodied reds suitable for long ageing and are produced in the hills at the centre of the region. One of these, Torgiano Rosso Riserva, was the first to be awarded the recognition of DOC and DOCG in 1990. It is made from Sangiovese grapes, with small additions of Canaiolo, from vineyards on the hills surrounding Torgiano. It must be aged in the barrel for at least three years and possess a minimum alcohol content of 12.5 per cent.

The few attempts by other wineries to produce DOC and DOCG wines in Torgiano have not been particularly successful. However, Torgiano Rosso Riserva della Vigna Monticchio has intense, well-developed aromas and great mellowness, resulting from years of refinement in bottle. It is a great partner for roasts and peerless as a match for black truffle dishes. Other DOC wines in Torgiano include the Torgiano Bianco, made mostly from Trebbiano and some Grechetto, which may be aged for several years in bottle – especially if it comes from good vineyards and is matured in small oak casks. Torgiano Rosso, made from Sangiovese and Canaiolo, is better known by the name of the winemaker, Rubesco. The same grape varieties are also used to produce a pleasant Rosato which, with those of Assisi and Bolgheri, is one of the best in central Italy.

Torgiano offers another range of wines which began as experiments, but now revel in DOC and Series A legal status. The Chardonnay is a fairly straightforward wine to drink young, and benefits from maturation in new wood. Pinot Grigio and Riesling Italico give the impression of originating far further north than Torgiano, a result of carefully developed vinification techniques, while the Cabernet Sauvignon and Pinot Nero reveal the region's red wine potential. The crowning glory is Lungarotti's San Giorgio – a superb blend of Cabernet Sauvignon, Canaiolo, and Sangiovese – and this producer also claims another winning blend, the Vessillo.

Finally, Torgiano is home to a palatable *metodo classico* Torgiano Spumante, from Chardonnay and Pinot Nero.

Montefalco

Montefalco Sagrantino is the second DOCG wine of the region, with a production zone some 20 kilometres from Torgiano. This great red has been made from Sagrantino grapes since the Middle Ages, in Montefalco's urban vineyards. These are surrounded by dry-stone walls and were once cultivated by the nuns of the convent to make sacramental wine, hence the name. At one time only sweet wine was produced, but now most styles are dry and capable of lengthy ageing. The maestro of this icon is the young and enterprising Marco Caprai, who has made some spectacular versions in recent years – through careful clonal selections and by replacing the traditional *palmetta* (fan-trained) system with the spur cordon in high density plantings. Marco has also dramatically reduced the yield per hectare through severe pruning, yielding a red wine with a high alcohol content, world-class concentration and a richness in polyphenols. A traditional version, the Passito, is increasingly rare and expensive.

Whether dry or sweet, Montefalco Sagrantino is matured for at least 30 months, of which 12 must be in wooden barrels. Its production zone includes the communes of Montefalco and parts of Bevagna, Castel Ritaldi and Giano nell'Umbria. The Montefalco DOC includes a superlative Rosso, made from Sangiovese and Sagrantino grapes, which may be labelled Riserva when aged for at least 30 months. The fresh, fragrant Bianco is made from Grechetto and Trebbiano.

below *The Monticchio vineyard belonging to the Lungarotti estate. Torgiano Rosso has been greatly influenced by this family.*

Notable producers

Cantine Lungarotti, Torgiano (PG)

Giorgio Lungarotti was the grand old man of Umbrian oenology, and though he has passed away his family's wines are among the most celebrated of all Italian wines. The company recently celebrated the 30th anniversary of its flagship wine Rubesco, a Torgiano Rosso, but the most prestigious wine is Torgiano Riserva Vigna Monticchio, a red left to mature for a long time in cask and in bottle before it is sold, ten years after the vintage. It has an elegant, ethereal bouquet, great body, finesse and great complexity. Teresa Serofini Lungarotti is now in charge at this famous estate.

Pieve del Vescovo, Corciano (PG)

The leading winery of Colli del Trasimeno. Iolanda Tinarelli produces outstanding wines which range from a fruity, young, fragrant Rosso to a champion Lucciaio – a great Sangiovese, Gamay and Canaiolo blend, with the body of a Super-Tuscan.

Arnaldo Caprai-Val di Maggio, Montefalco (PG)

A role model of reorganisation and modernisation. Arnaldo Caprai and son Marco – in tandem with wine maker Attilio Pagli – have reinvented Sagrantino di Montefalco after years of investment, research and experimentation, and launched this little-known wine onto the world stage. The flagship wine, Sagrantino, has a strong, fruity character and polyphenolic structure, epitomised by the exceptional 25 Anni selection – deep, balanced and a true Italian aristocrat. Rosso di Montefalco and Cabernet Sauvignon dell'Umbria are also excellent.

Antonelli-San Marco, Montefalco (PG)

Filippo Antonelli is one of the best "interpreters" of the terroir and grapes of Montefalco, driving his wines out of reach of some of his slightly pedestrian local rivals. The Sagrantino is full-bodied, rich and assertive, while his Sagrantino Passito is probably the finest in the region. The Rosso di Montefalco is equally outstanding.

above *The late Giorgio Lungarotti in his museum. Torgiano's statesman was a local and national icon.*

right *Harvesting Chardonnay in Torgiano. This global white grape enjoys moderate success here, mostly when oak-aged.*

Latium

above *Looking above the Eternal City, from the Spanish Steps. Rome is at the centre of more wine zones than any other city in the world.*

The wines of Latium had a high reputation in Roman times, with great wines such as Caere (today Cerveteri), Setinum (from Sezze, in Latina) and Albanum produced on the shores of Lake Albano. This renown continued undiminished throughout the Middle Ages and the Papacy into the modern era, with the best wines made from white grapes. While the movement towards high volume production of variable-quality wines has been a hallmark of the last few decades, this tendency is being reversed. There are encouraging signs in the wines emerging from Castelli Romani to the southeast of the capital; in Aprilia; Cerveteri; and as far as the border with Umbria.

The dry, perfectly drained volcanic terroir of the region's best areas is ideal for great reds. So far, the most interesting wines have been Cabernet Sauvignon, Merlot and Syrah, but the future may yield a few surprises.

Winemaking and wine styles

With an annual output of over three million hectolitres, about 16 per cent DOC, Latium is the sixth Italian wine region in order of importance. Yet the image of its wines, mainly white (the reds make up less than one-fifth of the total) is lower than that of other emerging regions.

Latium is known abroad for the dry white wine of Castelli Romani, the most important region in Latium. A general, basic DOC covers the entire region and provides Bianco, Rosso and Rosato. The first is from Trebbiano and Malvasia di Candia, and the second from Sangiovese, Cesanese, Montepulciano, Merlot and Nero Buono di Coro. Castelli Romani's one red wine is Velletri, available either as a robust Rosso – from Sangiovese, Cesanese, Montepulciano, Merlot and Ciliegiolo – and a Riserva.

However, the region's best-known wine is Frascati, one of the most famous and traditional Italian whites. Made from Malvasia di Candia, Trebbiano Toscano and Greco, it may also be produced in *amabile* and *cannellino* (sweet) versions, and *superiore* if the alcohol exceeds 11.5 per cent. There are many other DOC wines in the region, made more or less from the same grapes as Frascati and offering the same typical flavours, with small variations.

From the enormous Castellana region come Frascati and Marino-style whites with a slightly more acidic, fruity tone – Zagarolo, Genazzano and Cori Bianco use Malvasia and Trebbiano – while at Cori, a Rosso is produced from Nero Buono di Coro and Montepulciano. Further east, the vast region of Cesanese is divided into three DOCs:

Olevano Romano, Affile and Piglio. These offer red wines, often semi-sparkling and sometimes in *amabile* and sweet versions, essentially very traditional, even rustic. The dry and sweet styles are at their best with the local cuisine and traditional Christmas delicacies, including pangiallo.

Spreading out towards the sea is the Pontine plain, home of the Aprilia DOC, which specifies Trebbiano for whites, Sangiovese for rosés, and Merlot for reds. The varieties and flavours are reminiscent of Romagnolo and Veneto, from where the settlers who reclaimed the marshy areas of the plain during the 1930s and 1940s originated. Meanwhile, the Circeo DOC is in some respects an extension of Aprilia, and creates similar wines.

On the coast just north of Rome lie the Cerveteri and Tarquinia. In both areas Bianco wines are made from Trebbiano and Malvasia, and Rosso from Sangiovese, Montepulciano and Cesanese. Inland and slightly east of Lake Bracciano is Bianco Capena, where Malvasia and Trebbiano still hold sway, as they do further north in Vignanello, although Greco is also on form here. As well as Greco di Vignanello and Bianco, there are fruity Rosso and Rosato wines, made mainly from Sangiovese but with additions of Ciliegiolo, among others.

In the provinces of Rome, Rieti and Viterbo are Colli dalla Sabina and Colli Etruschi Viterbesi, with the usual Bianco and Rosso wines made from Trebbiano/Malvasia and Sangiovese/Montepulciano. The latter DOC is home to whites (Grechetto and Moscatello) and reds (Canaiolo, Merlot and Violone, the local Montepulciano). Finally, there is the well-known DOC wine of Lago di Bolsena – Aleatico di Gradoli is a rare sweet red also made in a *liquoroso* (fortified) form – and the legendary Est! Est!! Est!!! di Montefiascone.

Part of the Orvieto region is in Latium, but that wine is discussed in the Umbria chapter.

Soil, viticulture and climate

Latium has hills and plains, with the Tyrrhenian Sea on one side and the central mountainous region on the other. The region is crossed by four great volcanic systems ranged along the coast – some of the largest craters contain lakes – while the coastal plain of the Latium marshes continues the Tuscan plain, and ends with the hills of Tolfa at the level of Civitavecchia. All the hilly regions are ideal for viticulture, especially the volcanic terroirs with their lava and tufa, which is rich in potassium.

The key influence here is the sea, although there is greater rainfall further inland, towards the Apennines. Near the mountains themselves there is a much wider variation of temperature – even though these areas are protected by the Apennine relief from the much colder winds sweeping down from the northeast.

Latium has a heritage of indigenous vines which have fought back against Trebbiano and Malvasia di Candia, and after years of neglect and carelessness there are some very positive signs. Even the cooperative organisations, responsible for the greater part of the region's production, have made a decisive change of direction.

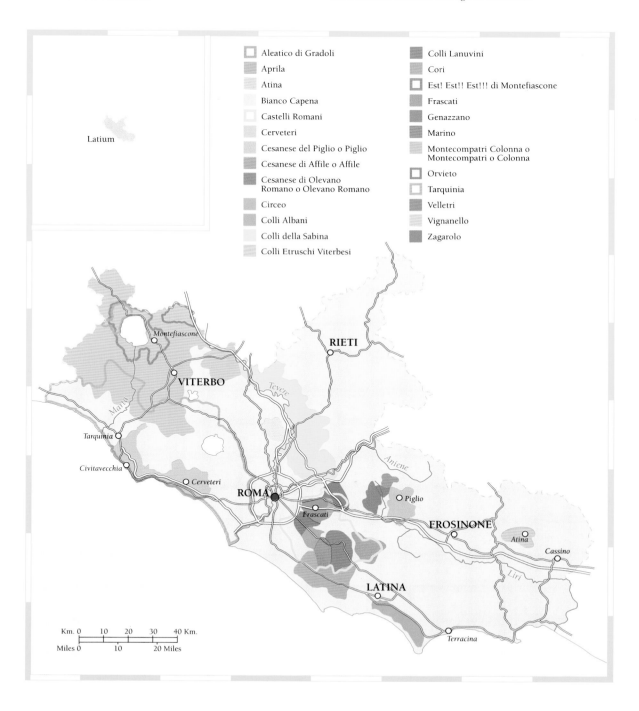

Latium

Aleatico di Gradoli
Aprila
Atina
Bianco Capena
Castelli Romani
Cerveteri
Cesanese del Piglio o Piglio
Cesanese di Affile o Affile
Cesanese di Olevano Romano o Olevano Romano
Circeo
Colli Albani
Colli della Sabina
Colli Etruschi Viterbesi
Colli Lanuvini
Cori
Est! Est!! Est!!! di Montefiascone
Frascati
Genazzano
Marino
Montecompatri Colonna o Montecompatri o Colonna
Orvieto
Tarquinia
Velletri
Vignanello
Zagarolo

Km. 0   10   20   30   40 Km.
Miles 0   10   20 Miles

Est! Est!! Est!!! di Montefiascone and Tuscia

Few wines tell such an intriguing story as Est! Est!! Est!!!, which hails from the pretty village of Montefiascone, in Viterbo. Around 1100AD a Flemish bishop, Giovanni Defuck, came to Italy in the retinue of the German emperor Henry V. A great lover of wine, Defuck sent his servant Martin to travel ahead of him by a couple of days, reserving rooms at inns serving good wine. To mark such a place, Martin would write the word "Est!"on the door of the inn, the Latin for "It is!", or in this case "It has good wine". At Montefiascone, on the shores of Lake Bolsena and a little way from the Pope's palace, Martin found a wine so good that he wrote "Est!" three times on the door. Instead of returning home, the bishop stopped at Montefiascone to enjoy the local wine and drank so much that he remained there for the rest of his life. For centuries, the custom was to pour a bottle of wine over his tomb on the anniversary of his death, until it was condemned in the 17th century by the puritanical Counter-Reformation. Goethe later made the acquaintance of this fine white wine from Latium on his journey through Italy.

After this colourful interlude, Est! Est!! Est!!! slipped into relative obscurity, but in Rome it is still consumed in large quantities. A handful of quality producers have successfully relaunched it: selecting the best terroirs, low yields, the best clones of Trebbiano, Malvasia and Rossetto (the local name of Trebbiano Giallo) and opting for modern technology. A delicate version of Passito, made from grapes affected by noble rot, has been well received.

On the shores of Lake Bolsena around Ciradoli there has been a slow revival of interest in Aleatico, among smaller winemakers. This was once widespread throughout the whole of central-southern Italy, and the new DOCs – such as Colli Etruschi Viterbesi, Sabina and Tarquinia – are allowed generous grape yields by the authorities. Typical quotas seldom fall below ten tonnes per hectare and sometimes reach fifteen, thereby

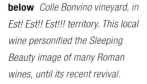

below *Colle Bonvino vineyard, in Est! Est!! Est!!! territory. This local wine personified the Sleeping Beauty image of many Roman wines, until its recent revival.*

producing honest, everyday wines rather than outstanding styles. Yet some of the region's most celebrated wines are made here, such as Montiano by Falesco, an excellent Merlot-based red. The reds of Cerveteri (and some whites) are proof that vineyard reorganisation, drastic lowering of yields and the adoption of modern winemaking techniques can deliver results that would have been unthinkable only ten years ago.

There are other suitable terroirs in these regions, waiting for worthy producers to unwrap their potential.

left *For tying up vines, vineyard workers favour the osier shoots from willow trees.*

Notable producers

Mazziotti, Bolsena (VT) Signora Flaminia Mazziotti, her husband Alessandro Laurenzi and oenologist Gaspare Buscemi offer two versions of Est! Est!! Est!!!: the annata has a fresh style and a rich, fruity bouquet; while Canuleio is an interesting selection matured for a long time in the cellar.

Cantina Cooperativa di Cerveteri, Cerveteri (RM) This cantina and its vineyards have been successfully renovated

by Riccardo Cotarella, one of Italy's most talented and energetic winemakers. At the top of an enormous range of wines are Cerveteri Bianco Vigna Grande, mostly from Malvasia and Trebbiano, and Cerveteri Rosso Vigna Grande, from Sangiovese, Montepulciano and Merlot.

Mottura, Civitella d'Agliano (VT) The Sergio Mottura estate is on the Latium slope of the Orvieto DOC, and makes a fascinating range of wines: notably Grechetto Latour a Civitella and Muffo, the latter from

botrytised grapes. Orvieto Vigna Tragugnano and Mottura Metodo Classico spumante are also interesting.

Falesco, Montefiascone (VT) Despite its tender age, Falesco is envied by some of the most celebrated names in Italian wine and already enjoys a worldwide reputation. Riccardo Cotarella's top wine here is Montiano, a Merlot with great qualities of softness and suppleness, produced in very few vintages. The whites are also good, among which the Est! Est!! Est!!!

Vendemmia Tardiva – made from grapes affected by noble rot and matured in French barrels – is a little wonder.

Cantina Oleificio Sociale di Gradoli, Gradoli (VT) One of the few producers of Aleatico, a delicate, sweet red which was once widespread, but is now in very limited production. There is a Liquoroso (fortified) version with additional distilled wine, which has an alcoholic strength of 17.5%. When aged for at least three years (two in bottle), it earns the denomination Riserva.

Frascati and Castelli Romani

An undoubted proximity to Rome and its hordes of tourists has exerted a strong populist pressure on the wines of these regions, with the anonymous Castellani whites finding an easy if unspectacular berth in traditional bottles in a trattoria of the capital. This is unfortunate for the area's winemakers, not least because the slopes of spent volcano craters which form the region of Castelli Romani are capable of producing excellent whites and reds. Here and there a flash of grandeur still appears, perhaps Prince Ludovisi Boncompagni's Fiorano Rosso, produced on the outskirts of Rome – a red which was in the front row of Italian wines during the tumultuous 1960s.

However, in the name of quantity, Malvasia di Candia and Trebbiano Toscano were widely planted during the 1950s and 1960s, and these vines still form the basis of almost all the DOC whites in the region. The authorities have in many cases permitted excessive yields of more than 16 tonnes of grapes per hectare, yields that can only be achieved by using growing methods which militate against a harvest of high-quality grapes. In spite of this, "big" wines such as Frascati and Marino have maintained a standard sufficient to merit global distribution.

The prince of Castelli Romani wine is Frascati, which is grown in vineyards situated in the communes of Frascati, Grottaferrata and Monteporzio Catone, and in a small enclave which is still part of the commune of Rome, in the outskirts of the locality of Colle Mattia. A real cult wine among the inhabitants of the region, Frascati is also the white wine best loved by the Romans and has long been celebrated by writers, poets and chefs; it is also an essential partner for many local traditional dishes, including globe artichokes and lamb.

Tradition requires that Frascati should be fermented "on its skins", which gives the wine a golden colour and a slightly rustic, astringent style. It is good with meat dishes, but does not like to travel and tends to fade away when summer comes. These features are the exact opposite of the wines still served in the inns of Castelli Romani, which are light, cool, colourless and slightly acidic whites, often produced and marketed by price-conscious cooperatives.

Fortunately a "new school" has arrived, intent on creating wines with a full flavour: powerful and alcoholic, with a high proportion of indigenous vines such as Malvasia del Lazio – also known as Malvasia Puntinata – Cacchione, Bellone, Bonvino, Greco and perhaps a small amount of Chardonnay or Sauvignon Blanc, but with very little Malvasia di Candia and Trebbiano Toscano. This style is best expressed by Vigna Adriana, the Frascati Superiore wine by Castel de Paolis, which often manages to reach an alcohol level of 14 per cent, and the Santa Teresa from Fontana Candida – the enterprise responsible for a spectacular increase in quality over the last ten years.

Change is certainly reverberating around the Castelli region, particularly in Frascati and Marino. In a few years' time, if this progress continues, these denominations will be associated with a range of powerful, full-bodied whites.

below *Looking toward the Piazza di Spagna. Its ambience, lovely villas and proximity to Rome have earned Frascati a capital following.*

left *Grotto, temple or cellar? One of the more unusual ways of storing wine, at the estate of Sotteranea in Frascati.*

One of the groundbreaking establishments in Marino is Di Mauro-Colle Picchioni, which seems well on track. Year after year its whites are more carefully tended, although its lower altitude and exposure cannot guarantee the fruity aromas typical of Frascati. Still, it is no accident that one of the greatest reds of the region, Vigna del Vassallo – an admirable Bordeaux style – is produced from grapes grown in these vineyards.

In Latium, renewal lies in recovering the many traditional indigenous varieties, both red and white. At the end of the last century the pungent Verdicchio, also called Trebbiano Verde, was native to these vineyards. So too was Greco – probably today's Grechetto di Todi – and various kinds of Trebbiano, as well as Bellone, Malvasia del Lazio, Moscati, Passerina, and Pecorino. Basic red varieties included the Cesanese Comune and Cesanese di Affile, Greco Nero and Aleatico, plus a range of minor varieties such as Abbuoto and Nero Buono di Cori, to name just a few. These vine species are often "difficult" because of their inconsistent yields, but may be interesting from an aromatic point of view.

In future, the fledgeling DOC Castelli Romani – with its Bianco, Rosato and Rosso – will provide wines of a simpler and more immediate style, while the classic denominations will promote wines of greater charisma, with Frascati aspiring to the rank of DOCG. Although this may be a realistic target in some DOCs – the likes of Montecompatri Colonna and Marino – the case of others is more complicated: Colli Lanuvini or Colli Albani spring to mind. The potential is certainly there, but so is the risk of creating anonymous variations of the same recipe. Other wines, such as Zagarolo and Velletri Bianco, will only improve if yields are lowered drastically and the percentages of Trebbiano and Malvasia di Candia substantially reduced in the must.

Wines that result from research, or depart from the region's usual methods, have been incredibly successful: among them the sweet wines Frascati Cannellino and Vendemmia Tardiva, and reds from international varieties matured in barrels, such as Vigna del Vassallo by Di Mauro and Quattro Mori from Castel de Paolis. In any case, the potential of the region is far from exhausted.

Notable producers

Casale Marchese, Frascati (RM) With the fine oenologist Sandro Facca now on board, this cantina offers one of the best whites in Frascati – grown from fine, low, thick vines in a prime location. Owner Salvatore Carletti is also committed to the Malvasia del Lazio grape, from which he has made Cortesia – a wine of pleasing purity. Finally, the Rosso Casale Marchese is interesting, made from Montepulciano, Merlot and Cesanese.

Castel de Paolis, Grottaferrata (RM) With the expert help of Professor Attilio Scienza from the University of Milan, Giulio Santarelli radically restructured the property's 11 hectares of vineyards in the late 1980s. New varieties of grapes were used and modern technology applied. Today, the property is among the best in Castelli Romani, with the whites leading the way. The best is the Frascati Campo Vecchio, but the Vigna Adriana selection is more complex and structured. The outstanding red is the Quattro Mori, a blend of Syrah, Cabernet, Merlot and Petit Verdot.

Paola di Mauro-Colle Picchioni, Marino (RM) Paola Di Mauro and her son Armando, with the invaluable advice of oenologist Riccardo Cotarella, produce some of the best wines of Latium at this small estate. Finest is Vigna del Vassallo, a red made from Merlot and Cabernet, with a well developed bouquet and a soft, well-balanced flavour. The Collo Picchioni Rosso – a blend of Montepulciano, Merlot, Cabernet Sauvignon and Cesanese – is lighter but equally balanced. The best white is Vignole, from Malvasia del Lazio, Trebbiano and Sauvignon Blanc, and matured in wood. The two Marino DOCs are Selezione Oro, with more body and a decidedly complex bouquet, and Etichetta Verde, light and attractive.

left *Marino in the Colli Albano, southeast of Rome, has an annual wine festival, the Festa del Vino, when wine rather than water pours from the fountains.*

Gotto d'Oro, Marino (RM) It was 50 years ago that Gotto D'Oro started its first enterprise in Marino. Today, several million bottles of Frascati and Marino emerge each year from its modern wineries at Frattocchie, which represent the production standard of Castelli Romani. Also produces a decent Malvasia del Lazio.

Tenuta Le Quinte, Montecompatri (RM) Francesco Papi's beautiful estate straddles the communes of Montecompatri and Colonna, producing enviable wines from 10 hectares of the best clones of local vines. These account for the bouquet and softness of its splendid Montecompatri Colonna Superiore Virtù Romane.

Fontana Candida, Monteporzio Catone (RM) The first establishment to bottle and commercialise Frascati, now exporting seven-and-a-half-million bottles annually worldwide. Its home-grown vines are behind the Frascati Superiore Santa Teresa, one of the finest wines in the Castelli Romani, an aromatic lesson in gentle seduction – and very reasonably priced. The Malvasia del Lazio della Linea Terre dei Grifi – from the local Puntinata grape – is also interesting.

Villa Simone, Monteporzio Catone (RM) Piero Costantini acquired this estate in the early 1980s, and it is now his country retreat. Modernity and tradition is evident in tasty white wines of medium structure and body, with a slightly fruity bouquet. The style of Frascati Superiore infuses the annata (vintage) version – simple and direct; Vigna dei Preti, with a well-balanced bouquet; and Vigneto Filonardi – clean, with great freshness. Finally, Frascati Superiore Cannellino is a very enjoyable sweet wine.

Conte Zandotti, Roma One of Frascati's most traditional estates, with 30 hectares devoted to Malvasia del Lazio, Trebbiano and Bellone. Produces one of the most convincing Frascatis, and an elegant Frascati Superiore Cannellino, a soft, concentrated wine. Marco Ciarla, the new oenologist, may spring a few surprises.

below *Official approval of bumper grape yields has led many Frascati producers to settle for fair but unspectacular wines.*

Ciociaria and Southern Latium

This sub-region is home to three Cesanese DOCs: Cesanese di Olevano Romano and Cesanese di Affile are in the province of Rome, while the most notable is the Cesanese del Piglio, in the province of Frosinone. In an area crying out for red wines, these regions – situated between the Prenestini and Affilani mountains on the one side, and Ciociaria on the other – carry a weight of expectation that is yet to be satisfied: little from the first two DOCs is bottled, even though Cesanese di Olevano

Dolce is one of the most popular wines in Rome, and Piglio is a difficult grape to tame – it is rich in fruit and sugars, as well as tannins, but very unstable once bottled. This is a red for roasts and grills, but has still to really make its mark independently.

Ciociaria contains the region of Atina, which only recently obtained DOC status, although it has been cultivating French varieties such as Cabernet, Merlot and Sauvignon for over a century. Atina is a small centre near Cassino and it was here in the 19th century that an Italian agronomist, Pasquale Visocchi, planted the varieties which had caught his eye while he was travelling in France. Today, there is only one producer of substance in the region, Giovanni Palombo, but his success is encouraging others – if a little belatedly. His oak-aged Colle della Torre and Rosso delle Chiaie (Merlot and Cabernet, the latter with Syrah, too) and Bianco delle Chiaie (Sauvignon-Sémillon) vindicate his tenacity. These are attractive wines with a clean, modern style, good examples of Latium's campaign for better quality.

Circeo, a new DOC, has been created along the southern hinterland of Latium, within the communes of San Felice Circeo, Terracina, Latina and Sabaudia. This provides for various wines of simple style, ranging from Bianco through variations on the Malvasia-Trebbiano theme to Trebbiano, Rosso, Rosé and Sangiovese.

A final mention should go to the wines of Latina, the region that perhaps more than any other has sought to experiment and establish its own identity. The estate at the centre of all this activity is Casale del Giglio di Borgo Montello. Founded in 1968, this property of Antonio Santarelli has been an experimental centre since the early 1980s. A team of highly qualified scientific advisers – including Attilio Scienza – have given Santarelli and Paolo Tiefenthaler – the estate's oenologist – scope to create wines of notable depth. Once devoted exclusively to Trebbiano, Sangiovese and Merlot varieties of the Aprilia DOC, these vineyards' recent experiments embody the best viticultural research of the Old and the New World. It is an invaluable undertaking: the estate has abandoned the "awning" method of training and today harvests its grapes from densely planted, low-yielding vines not far from the sea, turning out outstanding red and white wines in the international style.

While appreciating a glass of Syrah or Madreselva, or Mater Matuta from Casale del Giglio, one should bear in mind that the future began here some time ago.

Notable producers

Colacicchi, Anagni (FR) At their small but gorgeous estate the Trimani family, originally from Rome, grow the local Cesanese grape alongside Cabernet Sauvignon and Merlot. The latter two are increasingly dominant in the Rosso Torre Ercolana, an important wine which is suitable for long ageing in new oak.

Giovanni Palombo, Atina (FR) A new name in Latium winemaking, whose wines combine a clean, stylistic maturity. Outstanding are Colle della Torre, with Bordeaux-style great elegance and concentration, and Bianco delle Chiaie, from Sauvignon Blanc and Sémillon.

Casale del Giglio, Borgo Montello (LT) The region of Aprilia is not ideal for producing great wines. But after more than ten years of investment and careful experimentation, owner Antonio Santarelli and oenologist Paolo Tiefenthaler have made a wide range of wines, led by the Madreselva, a blend of Bordelais grapes; Mater Matuta, from Syrah and Petit Verdot; Antinoo, from Chardonnay and Viognier grapes; and an excellent Shiraz.

Massimi Berucci, Piglio (FR) Manfredi Massimi Berucci is the standard bearer of the small Ciociaria DOC. His Cesanese del Piglio is tannic and exuberant, with fresh vinous notes. In the best years it is labelled with the name of the *cru* Casale Cervino.

below *Ahead of the pack: Manfredi Berucci is the driving force behind the wines of Ciociaria.*

The Southern Peninsula

The southern part of the Italian peninsula was extolled as the greatest wine region in antiquity in Virgil's *Georgics*, and in poems by Horace, Pliny the elder, Pliny the younger, Columella and many others. It was in Campania, in the district of Falerno, that the most prized wines of antiquity were produced, but Sicily, Calabria, Basilicata and Puglia also produced excellent wines, again toasted in classical literature. Even the Arabs were so fascinated by the amazing harmony which existed between the vines and the soil of these regions that they encouraged winegrowing, and perfected systems for training vines. On paying a tax, wine continued to be produced by the local population, despite the rigours of Muslim rule during centuries of invasion.

Today, the south is in many respects the nation's new wine frontier, despite the fact that renewal and modernisation have been much slower here. The often archaic systems of production, the profusion of low-grade cooperatives and the custom of selling wine in bulk were all factors militating against improvements in Puglia, Campania, Calabria and Basilicata. This is not to say that the wines of these four sub-regions were of low quality: for decades, fleets of wine tankers were sent north to revive the anaemic cuvées of wine merchants in northern Italy and abroad.

But it was in the 1960s, with the creation of the DOC system, that winegrowers finally decided to give a name and a face to wines which, in many cases, had been locally famous for thousands of years: the likes of Asprinio di Aversa, Cirò, Fiano di Avellino, the wines of the Sorrento peninsula, and Primitivo di Manduria to name but a few. Furthermore, the wonderful sun and the many sweet wines made from *appassite* (dried) grapes make it easy to forget that despite their southern latitude, parts of these wine regions are situated at very high altitudes where the climate is often harsh: Irpinia in Campania, Vulture in Basilicata, and the Apennine zones of Calabria spring to mind. In the hottest climes, the vineyards are usually situated in hilly regions which are ideal for quality viticulture.

Since the 1970s, visionaries such as Antonio Mastroberardino in Irpinia and Leone de Castris in Puglia had led from the front, and by the 1980s a new generation of protagonists was persuading producers to launch an assault on the new, quality-driven markets. This second wave of skilled and innovative winegrowers included the likes of Cosimo Taurino and Severino Garofano, Librandi and Calò, Paternoster and D'Angelo, the Feudi di San Gregorio and the Villa Matilde.

However, with the exception of these pioneers, the standard of wines produced in the south still fell below their true potential, at least at the higher end of the scale, and there remains much to do. The south is responsible for over 21 per cent of Italy's total wine production, but the percentage of DOC wines as a proportion of regional production is the lowest in the country: only 2.85% in Campania, barely 3.76% in Puglia, 2.41% in Basilicata and 4.84% for Calabria (the figures are those of the 1997 vintage). The south is still paying for decades of short-sighted agricultural policy on the part of the Italian government and the European Community. In the past, winegrowers were encouraged to plant high-yielding varieties and too many subsidies were handed out, especially to the areas less suited to viticulture: perversely, this attempt to pull the plug on Europe's "wine lake" denied those regions that were less productive yet more likely to produce high-quality wines. Prime wine sites and the historic alberello vineyards were abandoned in favour of more open systems, or to make room for building developments.

But the south has bounced back, driven by a band of celebrated wine-growers keen to re-energise their historic vines and vineyards – this time with a modern slant. Perhaps the south will prove the future as well as the past of Italian winemaking.

right *The Villa Rufolo at Ravello, on the Amalfi Coast. The south's modernists look to their hot and hilly terroir for quality wines.*

Campania

Few regions have cultivated their wine history with as much passion and dedication as Campania. Vineyards in this sun-baked land produced some of the greatest wines of antiquity and are now enjoying a revival, with exquisite whites and reds from vines that have thrived for thousands of years.

Falerno, Greco, Faustiniano and Caleno, the great *crus* of ancient Rome, were produced here under sophisticated techniques replicated throughout the empire. Fermented in *dolia* – waterproofed earthenware vats – the wine was despatched in large amphorae across the continent. This pan-European influence lives on: the aversa rows of vines common to Campania are evident in the Vinho Verde in Portugal, while there are pergolas in Valle D'Aosta similar to those of the terraced vineyards on the Amalfi coast.

Wines and wine styles

Campania is one of Italy's most innovative and successful regions. Its soils and climates produce a myriad styles and characteristics, even in wines made from the same variety. The grapes (almost all native, and direct descendants of the *Vitis hellenica*, Aminea Gemina, Apiana and Alopecis mentioned by Latin authors) provide some uniformity among the score of *denominazioni* in the region.

White grapes such as Greco, Fiano, Biancolella and Falanghina, and reds such as Piedirosso and Aglianico are the core of DOC wines, which represent only four or five per cent of an annual output of over two million hectolitres. Falerno del Massico Bianco and Sant'Agata dei Goti Bianco are the tip of the Falanghina iceberg; Greco di Tufo and Capri Bianco use Greco, while the elegant, complex Fiano di Avellino and Cilento Bianco are based on Fiano. Aglianico is the top red, notably in Taurasi (the region's only DOCG wine), Cilento Rosso, Aglianico del Taburno, Campi Flegrei Rosso, Capri Rosso and Ischia Rosso.

This avalanche of different wines, denominations and zones falls across a wide area: there are vineyards on the coast and inland. In Irpinia, the climate in September and October mirrors that in Piedmont, while that on the Amalfi coast is reminiscent of Sicily. Wines made from Falanghina are mellow near the sea, but fragrant and rather harsh inland. Similarly, Aglianico always makes great reds for ageing, but there is a marked difference between the fiercely tannic Taurasi from Avellino, and the reliable mellow velvet of Falerno del Massico Rosso, made from grapes grown near the sea.

Piedirosso grapes are typical of the coastal zones, where they make delicate, supple wine; they are also used for semi-sparkling reds, such as Gragnano and Lettere della Penisola Sorrentina. Among the most unusual wines is Asprinio di Aversa, a light, acidic white wine, sometimes semi-sparkling and produced in Casertano from vines trained *ad alberata* (up trees) up to five metres high.

Soil, viticulture and climate

With over 460 kilometres of coastline, from Latium to Calabria, as well as hill and mountain regions, Campania has myriad climates and soils. The region can be divided into two strips running parallel with the coast: inland are the Campano and Lucano Apennines, while on the coast lie the Massico mountains, the extinct Roccamonfina volcano, the volcanic Campi Flegrei with Mount Vesuvius, the Lattari, Picentini and Alburni mountains and the rocky hills of Cilento. These ranges are divided by valleys.

The coastal climate is continental – hot and rather dry – while on the high plains and slopes of the Apennines rainfall is more frequent, especially in autumn. The climate reverts to continental in the mountainous regions of Sannio and Avellinese, which are ideal for high-quality wines, providing yields are controlled.

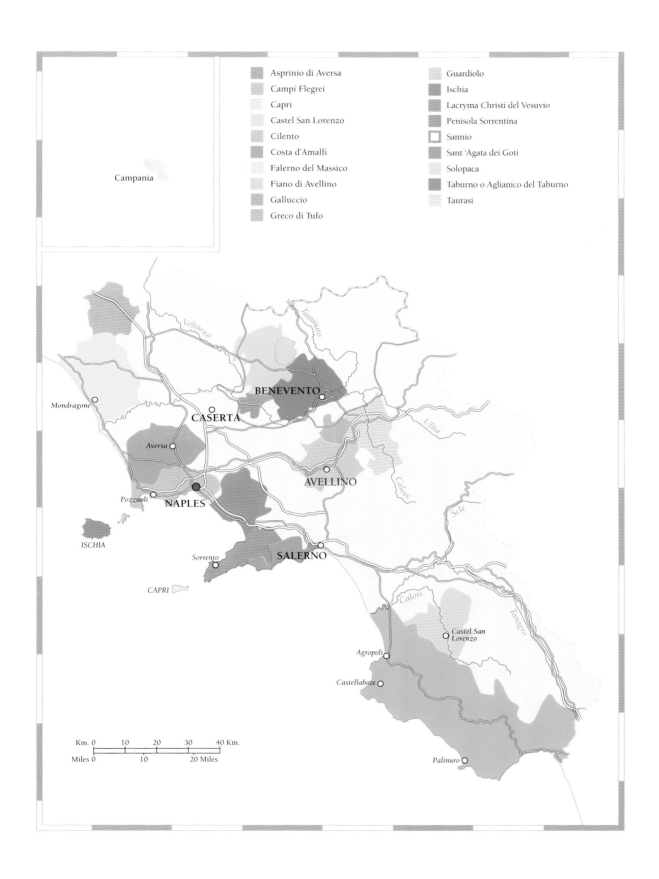

Campania

Asprinio di Aversa

Campi Flegrei

Capri

Castel San Lorenzo

Cilento

Costa d'Amalfi

Falerno del Massico

Fiano di Avellino

Galluccio

Greco di Tufo

Guardiolo

Ischia

Lacryma Christi del Vesuvio

Penisola Sorrentina

Sannio

Sant 'Agata dei Goti

Solopaca

Taburno o Aglianico del Taburno

Taurasi

Mondragone

CASERTA

BENEVENTO

Aversa

Pozzuoli

NAPLES

AVELLINO

ISCHIA

Sorrento

SALERNO

CAPRI

Castel San Lorenzo

Agropoli

Castellabate

Palinuro

Volturno

Tammaro

Volturno

Ufita

Calore

Sele

Calore

Tanagro

Km. 0   10   20   30   40 Km.

Miles 0   10   20 Miles

Irpinia and Sannio

Since the 1970s, when winemaking in Irpinia was revolutionised by Antonio Mastroberardino, this sub-region has set a scorching pace. Mastroberardino created breathtaking whites and reds, and proved that innovative methods and techniques could deliver stylish wines. The great Campania grape varieties and suitability of the land have done the rest and today there are many other famous names in the district. Now, in a lively and constantly evolving environment, the old vines are being replaced by the new, and Irpinia looks set to improve upon an already impressive wine portfolio.

This sense of enterprise has spread to the surrounding DOC zones of Sannio and Taburno, Sant'Agata dei Goti and Solopaca, as well as Guardia Sanframondi – the home of Guardiolo. While many regulations continue to protect the mainstream Italian varieties, the smarter producers have given justifiable preference to the likes of Greco, Fiano, Falanghina, Piedirosso and Aglianico.

They have also changed production tactics, with surprising results. Taurasi, for instance, is a spectacular wine: the only DOCG wine of Campania, it is produced in a hilly part of Irpinia from Aglianico (at least 85 per cent). The ordinary version must be aged for at least three years, one of which is in barrel, before being sold, but the Taurasi Riserva must have an alcohol content of at least 12.5 per cent and be aged for four years, with eighteen months in barrel. This is a concentrated, complex red wine of great refinement: smooth, with rich overtones of red fruit and high levels of tannins, it deserves a place in that powerful front row of Italian reds.

below *Vineyards near Avellino. Fiano is the south's finest white grape, but producers are keen to revitalise other local varieties.*

right *Antonio Mastroberardino and son, in their cellars at Atripalda. Antonio roused Irpinia from its slumber in the early 1970s.*

Notable producers

Antonio, Carlo e Pietro Mastroberardino, Atripalda (AV) The trailblazers of Irpinia, with their Greco di Tufo, Fiano di Avellino and Taurasi. Of the two million bottles produced each year, half are Greco di Tufo – also produced as *cru* Vignadangelo – and Nuova Serra. The *cru* Radici and Vignadora Fiano wines are excellent, and Taurasi, also produced as a Riserva and *cru* Radici – both from Aglianico grapes – is one of the best reds in southern Italy.

De Lucia, Guardia Sanframondi (BN) One of the best wineries in Sannio and the region: managed by the De Lucia cousins – Enrico, Cosimo and Enrico again –with oenologist Riccardo Cotarella on board. Aglianico del Sannio is rich in red fruit aromas, elegant tannins and spicy overtones. Falanghina del Sannio has attractive freshness and fruity aromas, while the Sannio Greco is fragrant and fruity.

Terredora di Paolo, Montefusco (AV) Owned by Walter Mastroberardino and his sons, who recently split from the rest of the family, taking with them some of the best vineyards in Irpinia. Their cellar is likewise an enviable asset. The *cru* Fiano di Avellino Terre di Dora, Greco di Tufo Loggia della Serra and the elegant, complex Taurasi Fatica Contadina are all superb.

Ocone, Ponte (BN) A winery that's big on research and experimentation, and blessed with splendid vineyards at the foot of Mount Taburno. Here, Domenico Ocone grows traditional Campania varieties – Greco, Aglianico, Piedirosso and Falanghina – for a range of Sannio and Taburno DOC wines. The Taburno Diomede is one of the most interesting Aglianicos in the region.

Mustilli, Sant'Agata dei Goti (BN) An important producer in Campania, having started the Falanghina revival in the early 1980s. An excellent range of traditional-style DOC wines includes the Sant'Agata dei Goti Greco di Primicerio; Falanghina; and Rosso Conte Artus, from Aglianico and Piedirosso.

Feudi di San Gregorio, Sorbo Serpico (AV) One of the best Italian producers, due to a shrewd purchase of select vineyards and careful clonal selection. Oenologist Riccardo Cotarella produces exceptional wines: the Taurasi, with incredible concentration and finesse, is probably the best ever produced; Campanaro is a white Fiano matured in new wood; and Serpico, from Aglianico, Piedirosso and Sangiovese, is full-bodied, plump and rich.

Antonio Caggiano, Taurasi (AV) Recently launched some of Campania's most interesting modern wines. The Taurasi Vigna Macchia dei Goti is seductive, as is the white Fiagrè, from Fiano and Greco grapes. Taurì is rich in spicy overtones, produced from Aglianico and Piedirosso.

The Campi Flegrei, Sorrentina Peninsula and Cilento

above *The bay of Naples, looking across to Vesuvius. This southern corner offers some of the most dramatic scenery in Italy.*

Not so long ago, Irpinia, Massico and Sannio stole the limelight from the coastal regions, with the exception of Ischia, while Asprinio di Aversa looked decidedly old-fashioned, with its tall poles and the acidic Vinho Verde. Meanwhile, Lettere and Gragnano were at the mercy of building developers, and Trebbiano and Barbera were still holding court in Cilento. It was hardly surprising that most of these wines were destined for home consumption, or sold as bulk wine. But it was a crime.

The whole of the Tyrrhenian coastal strip – from Tuscany to Calabria – is perfect for winemaking. The sun ripens grapes to perfection and rain is rarely a problem, making this a paradise for great red wines (as Bolgheri has shown!). Although winemakers have traditionally bowed to commercial demands for white varieties, a handful of producers have recovered a heritage of grape varieties and wines that were first appreciated by the Greeks, who settled in Ischia c.770BC. And in the last few years, as the epicentre of Italian winemaking itself has moved south, so too has Campania's – with the southern regions being rediscovered and revitalised.

Campi Flegrei is a place of rare beauty, with natural riches, panoramic views and volcanic eruptions laying down a complex of extinct craters. The region includes seven communes, including Pozzuoli, near Naples, where the grape-friendly soil is rich in tufa, volcanic ash, lapilli and pumice. It is also unaffected by phylloxera, allowing vines to be grown on their own rootstocks. Besides the Bianco – made from Falanghina, Biancolella and Coda di Volpe (known to the ancient Greeks as Alopecis) – there is a Rosso made from Piedirosso, Aglianico and Olivella grapes, and two varietals, Falanghina and Piedirosso.

Campi Flegrei also includes the islands of Procida and Ischia. Biancolella is Ischia's main grape variety, where it is capable of producing meaty, fragrant and fruity whites (especially from vineyards on the steep slopes of Mount Epomeo, where growers harvest the grapes by moving from one terrace to another on a rack-and-pinion trolley running on a monorail). Forastera is a well-structured wine which matures beautifully in the bottle for several years, and Piedirosso is a deliciously fruity red with slight tannic overtones – this is excellent cold, with seafood dishes. Ischia Bianco and Rosso enhance a range which also includes delicious *vini da tavola* such as Verdolino, a fragrant and supple wine.

Capri has honest Rosso, made mainly from Piedirosso, and a Bianco from Falanghina, Greco and Biancolella, which has a pleasing style and is rich in Mediterranean fragrances. One of the most beautiful places on the mainland is the Peni sola Sorrentina (Sorrento Peninsula), which offers Bianco from Falanghina, Biancolella and Greco, and Rosso, a semi-sparkling blend of Piedirosso, Aglianico, Olivella and Sciascinoso (there is no concession to international varieties in this region!). The Rosso takes the name Lettere or Gragnano when produced from either of these two famous communes: both are wonderful with the strongly seasoned Neapolitan cuisine.

The same grapes are the backbone of the Bianco and

Rosso of Costa d'Amalfi (Amalfi Coast), and may bear the name of the outstanding sub-zones of Furore, Ravello or Tramonti. This region forms a link between the provinces of Naples and Salerno, to which it belongs, and its recent wines have improved dramatically.

The rising star of the region is Cilento, an area still unknown to most wine drinkers. Situated in the southern part of the province of Salerno, it boasts a spectacular coastline and extends inland as far as the border with Basilicata. The region has remained almost untouched: the remains of the ancient Greek towns of Paestum and Elea Velia can still be admired, and most of the magnificent mountainous landscape inland has been turned into a national park. The local wine is usually set aside for home consumption, being fairly rustic in character. However, the Cilento DOC was created in 1989 and offers several styles: Rosso, from Aglianico, Piedirosso and – rather strangely – Barbera; Rosato, from Sangiovese and the Rosso ingredients; an Aglianico varietal; and Bianco, from Fiano, Trebbiano and Greco.

The terroir is ideal for great white wines from Fiano, which in many cases is richer and more seductive than its cousins in Irpinia. But it is even better disposed towards great reds, whether from Aglianico, Piedirosso, Cabernet Sauvignon or Merlot. Regulations which provide for Barbera and Trebbiano are mystifying, especially as they produce only modest results.

The same is true in the small DOC of Castel San

Lorenzo, which is also in Salerno province – although it is home to an interesting sweet Moscato, which can also be sparkling, and a Bianco from Trebbiano and Malvasia, reminiscent of the wines of Tuscany and Latium. There is also Castel San Lorenzo Barbera and a rather improbable Rosso, made from Barbera and Sangiovese. Fortunately, this is rarely found outside its production area.

below *Spectacular landscapes, modest wines. Capri offers good soils, but few winemakers produce anything out of the ordinary.*

Notable producers

San Giovanni, Castellabate (SA) From splendid vineyards overlooking the sea, this young estate produces a Fiano under the Paestum IGT category. Its considerable body and elegance confirms the fantastic potential of the Cilento terroir.

D'Ambra Vini d'Ischia, Forio (NA) Corrado and Andrea d'Ambra have fought off the property developers on Ischia and still grow excellent grapes for wines such as the Biancolella Tenuta Frassitelli, Biancolella Vigne di Piellero, Forastera Vigna Cimentorosso and Per'e Palummo della Tenuta Montecorvo. These are among southern Italy's best wines.

Cuomo, Furore (SA) Andrea Ferraioli and his wife Marisa Cuomo produce a complete range of Costa d'Amalfi wines, from hand-picked vines and a state-of-the-art winery. Their Rosso Riserva – Piedirosso and Aglianico from the Furore or Ravello sub-zone – combines great fruit concentration with a remarkably clean, long aftertaste. The Furore and Ravello whites have intriguing aromas.

De Conciliis e Figli, Prignano Cilento (SA) Qualified consultant oenologists, informed use of winery technology and the precise selection of grapes allow Bruno De Conciliis and his siblings to produce excellent wines. Temparubra is an Aglianico and Sangiovese blend, rich in berry fruit and reasonably

priced. The Vigna Perella, from Fiano grapes, is one of the best Cilento wines: fragrant and honeyed, with a good finish.

Cantine Grotta del Sole, Quarto (NA) Gennaro Martusciello is one of Campania's most famous winemakers and has preserved some of its most ancient grape varieties and wines. This "oenological archeology" is seen in beautiful whites and reds, from Lettere and Gragnano in the Penisola Sorrentina (Sorrento Peninsula) to the Piedirosso dei Campi Flegrei.

Montevetrano, San Cipriano Picentino (SA) Montevetrano arrived from nowhere in 1995 and is now regarded as one of the best red wines ever to come out of southern

Italy. Made from Aglianico, Merlot and Cabernet Sauvignon, this elegant wine is produced by Silvia Imparato in collaboration with Riccardo Cotarella. Despite limited production, its "stock" is constantly rising, and is even commanding prices more in keeping with fine Bordeaux.

Luigi Maffini, San Marco di Castellabate (SA) Luigi Maffini is an ambitious producer, whose careful selection of top grapes leaves no room for compromise. His Cenito is a red wine of incredible power and concentration, made from Aglianico and Piedirosso, while Kràtos and Klèos, a white from Fiano grapes and a red from Aglianico and Piedirosso respectively, are enchanting, supple and fragrant wines.

Caserta and Il Massico

Falerno was the most celebrated wine in ancient Rome and its origins are steeped in legend. Legend has it that Bacchus, in disguise, was given shelter by an old man called Falerno. Sufficiently moved by his generosity, Bacchus created the most beautiful vineyards on the slopes of Mount Massico in the province of Caserta, prompting Pliny the elder, Martial, Horace and Cicero to sing its praises. And in the *Satyricon*, Petronius Arbiter describes the famous meal of Trimalchio, where the *haustores* (wine waiters) served a Falernian wine that was over a century old. Ancient wines had an extremely high alcohol content, so they were often diluted: but because of its amazing quality, connoisseurs would drink Falerno undiluted. Pliny wrote that a good Falerno was the only wine that would catch fire if placed close to a naked flame.

Within the region there were at least three distinct styles: the lighter, less valued version from grapes grown in low-lying vineyards; the sweeter, harmonious wine made halfway up the slopes of Mount Massico – in the estate of a certain Faustino and called Faustinianum – and Caucinum, the drier, more austere wine produced from vineyards at the highest altitude. While ancient wine was predominantly white, produced from the Aminea Gemina grape variety – today's Greco variety – the modern Falerno del Massico may be either Bianco or Rosso, but is invariably made from the Falanghina variety.

Two thousand years after seducing some of the greatest names in Italian history, this region is still producing outstanding wines. The well-drained, tufa-rich soils of the volcanic hills are blessed by their proximity to the sea and by the thermal currents of the hills, which contribute to healthy grapes that mature perfectly. The terroir is well-suited to white wines and Falanghina, the grape variety legally stipulated for the Falerno DOC, has produced concentrated, mellow styles in recent years.

However, it's the red wines that take the breath away, with the Aglianico grape in its element. Its name is derived from *Vitis hellenica*, a grape variety introduced by Greek settlers. In Taurasi the red wines are more austere, but in the warmer coastal climate this variety produces red wines which are fragrant with plum and red fruit. These are concentrated and mellow, yet rich in tannins and with a refreshing acidity that helps them to age brilliantly. More recent, sophisticated versions matured in barriques of new oak have been impressive, with their elegance and rich, subtle nuances.

Regulations for producing Falerno permit the use of other red grapes: Piedirosso (also known as Per'e Palummo in other parts of Campania) adds fruit and freshness to the blend, while Primitivo – rarely seen outside Puglia – is a mellow and powerful component. The latter can also provide varietal wines, such as Falerno del Massico Primitivo.

Galluccio is a new DOC covering – not surprisingly –

the zone of Galluccio, which is situated in the hills around the extinct volcano of Roccamonfina. Here, lava deposits rich in trace elements and potassium combine with temperate weather to produce wines with an intense bouquet and remarkable finesse.

Inspired by the regulations of neighbouring Falerno, the laws in Galluccio provide for Rosso and Rosato – produced mainly from Aglianico – and a Falanghina Bianco. That this is a region ideal for winemaking is clearly evident in the outstanding Terra di Lavoro: a red blend of Aglianico, Piedirosso, Cabernet and Merlot.

left *Sessa Arunca is the town in the heart of the Falerno del Massico DOC and home to the Gelardi family (below left). This building is the* duomo.

left *The Galardi family owns the exciting Fontana, and has brought Riccardo Cotarella into the fold.*

Notable producers

Villa Matilde, Cellole (CE) An emerging winery, with beautiful vineyards in Capua. Maria Ida and Salvatore Avallone uphold the ancient tradition of Falerno with the *cru* Vigna Caracci – an excellent white from Falanghina – and a fantastic red from Aglianico and Piedirosso grapes called Vigna Camarato. Also recommended is the Falanghina di Roccamonfina.

Fontana Galardi, Sessa Aurunca (CE) A new establishment whose spectacular Terra di Lavoro attests to the incredible potential of northern Campania. Cousins

Roberto and Maria Luisa Selvaggi, Arturo and Dora Celentano and Francesco Catello own land famous in Roman times, and have acquired the services of Riccardo Cotarella. Their Piedirosso, Aglianico, Cabernet and Merlot blend is very much in tune with the great southern reds, with great power and depth.

Villa San Michele, Vitulazio (CE) Giulio Iannini roduces excellent wines from carefully tended vineyards in Terre del Volturno, all bearing an IGT classification. Some are among the best labels in the region: the Greco is distinctive and spicy; the Falanghina is floral, fruity and dry; while the Aglianico has bags of jammy fruit. Also produces Piedirosso reds and a spumante *metodo classico* in the Don Carlos range, which is bready, with a lasting flavour.

Puglia

Puglia forms a long shelf projecting from continental Italy into the eastern Mediterranean, towards the east and Greece. It has proved a perfect meeting point for the most varied cultures ever since the dawn of history and the Palaeolithic period. The Apulians were Indo-European peoples of Illyrian stock, and divided into the Dauni and Peucezi tribes – who lived in the centre-north of the region – and the Messapi and Salentini, who lived further south.

Winegrowing was a familiar activity throughout Puglia as early as 2000BC. The region was subsequently peacefully colonised by several waves of Greek settlers, who founded Taranto, Gallipoli and Otranto and introduced more advanced systems of viticulture and vinification – ensuring the fame of Puglia's wines in antiquity.

Taranto became the most important city in Magna Graecia, although the Italic tribes of the hinterland would resist invaders and retain their traditions and language. The process of unifying and assimilating the local tribes – which the Greeks failed to achieve – was accomplished by the more martial Romans, who subdued the region after the Pyrrhic wars. At this stage Brindisi was the most important port for trade with the East, and was linked to Rome by one of the most important consular roads, the via Appia. The Roman conquest was followed by the arrival of the Goths, Byzantines, Arabs and Lombards. From the year AD1000, however, the region enjoyed relative peace under the Normans, who brought a period of prosperity and culture to the region which reached its peak with the reign of Friedrich II, in the first half of the 13th century.

Four centuries later Puglia became prosperous again under the Bourbons and exported its wine and oil all over Europe. Since the risorgimento, the process of growth has continued unchanged until the present day. Unfortunately, the phylloxera epidemic of the late 19th century savaged the region, and the subsequent replanting of vineyards was carried out with all eyes fixed on quantity. This trend has only recently been reversed, with winegrowers now pressing for quality yields. After the Second World War, new roads and aqueducts – together with the reclamation and development of new lands – have set Puglia among the most productive agricultural and wine regions in Italy.

Soil, viticulture and climate

Puglia is bordered by Molise, Campania and Basilicata, and the Adriatic and Ionian seas. It is the only southern Italian region not crossed by the Apennines. Less than two per cent of the region is covered by the mountains of the Campania-Molise sub-Apennines; the rest of Puglia consists of hills (40 per cent) and fertile plains (50 per cent).

Gargano, Tavoliere, Murge and Salento proceed from north to south without geographical variation. Gargano is a promontory formed by calcareous and eruptive rocks, and is covered by a magnificent Mediterranean forest with olive trees and Aleppo pines, curiously named the Foresta Umbra. Puglia has no important rivers and lack of water is one of the region's oldest problems. The Fortore and Ofanto – located at the two extremities of Tavoliere – have their source in the Campania Apennines and flow into the Adriatic, but they are not especially impressive rivers, while the other waterways are little more than torrents. The Sele aqueduct brings drinking water from Campania to the region and the land is cultivated as far as the Occhitto dam and the Fortore basin.

Puglia's climate is influenced by the proximity of the Adriatic and Ionian seas, and the resulting winds. There is

below *Vineyards and* trulli *(stone dwellings) near Martina Franca. Puglia is one of Italy's flattest regions, and can suffer from chronic water shortages.*

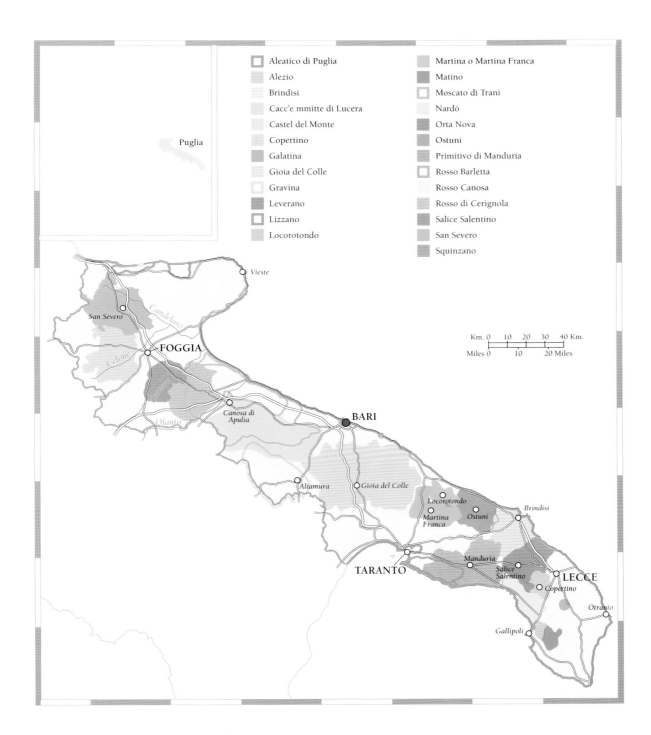

Puglia

□ Aleatico di Puglia		Martina o Martina Franca	
Alezio		Matino	
Brindisi		Moscato di Trani	
Cacc'e mmitte di Lucera		Nardò	
Castel del Monte		Orta Nova	
Copertino		Ostuni	
Galatina		Primitivo di Manduria	
Gioia del Colle		Rosso Barletta	
Gravina		Rosso Canosa	
Leverano		Rosso di Cerignola	
Lizzano		Salice Salentino	
Locorotondo		San Severo	
		Squinzano	

Vieste

San Severo

Candelaro

FOGGIA

Celone

Ofanto

Canosa di Apulia

BARI

Altamura

Gioia del Colle

Locorotondo

Martina Franca

Ostuni

Brindisi

Manduria

TARANTO

Salice Salentino

LECCE

Copertino

Gallipoli

Otranto

Km. 0   10   20   30   40 Km.
Miles 0   10   20 Miles

very little rain, especially in the coastal regions, and most of it falls in the winter months. The temperature range is rather small, but the temperatures can be extreme in summer, often reaching 45°C (113°F) on the plains.

The most common vine training systems are *tendone* (fortunately less popular), Guyot and *cordone speronato* ("spurred cordon"), the latter especially common in the more northern provinces. Moving southwards, the alberello system still produces excellent grapes.

There are numerous grape varieties in Puglia: the main grapes in the northern parts are Montepulciano, Uva di Troia, Tuscan Trebbiano, Bombino Bianco and Bombino Nero. In the valley of Itria, the predominant varieties are Verdeca and Bianco d'Alessano, while further south Negroamaro, Primitivo (also known as Zinfandel) and Malvasia Nera proliferate. Eighty per cent of the vineyards are planted with red grape varieties, and Puglia produces more dessert grapes than any other Italian region.

Castel del Monte

right *The iconic Castel del Monte near Andria, built by Friedrich II of Hohenstaufen in the 13th century.*

The zone of Castel del Monte is named after the magnificent octagonal castle built by Friedrich II near Andria, which is a jewel of Puglian art in the same way as the mosaic in the cathedral in Otranto and the baroque churches of Lecce. This is the centre of the region, in the province of Bari; from the high plateau of the Murge it slowly slopes down to the plain of Bari and the sea. Conditions inland are favourable for winegrowing: the climate is relatively temperate and the good temperature range develops wines with an elegant bouquet.

The Rosso Barletta and Rosso Canosa are made from Uva di Troia on its own, or with varying proportions of Malbec, Sangiovese and Montepulciano in the former, and Sangiovese and Montepulciano in the latter. Minute quantities are produced, and it is pretty forgettable stuff.

The situation is different in the Castel del Monte DOC, an acclaimed territory with excellent vineyards and winemakers, which recently emerged as a first class wine region. Castel del Monte obtained a DOC in 1971 and has produced wines such as Bianco, from Pampanuto, Rosso and Rosato, a best-seller whose blend includes Uva di Troia with Sangiovese and Montepulciano in the northern denominations, Aglianico and even Pinot Nero.

Enthusiastic experimentation with new grape varieties in red soils on top of calcareous strata are producing excellent varietal wines. Aglianico is probably the most promising but Cabernet, Chardonnay, Sauvignon, Pinot Nero and Pinot Bianco are also excellent, as are the many outstanding sparkling wines produced in the region.

Also within the province of Bari is the production zone of Moscato di Trani, a delicious sweet white, which is one of the most interesting dessert wines in southern Italy. Gravina, a delicate white wine made from Malvasia Bianca and Greco grapes, is produced in the hilly region of the Murge, while straddling this zone and a small part of the territory of the province of Taranto is a district which grows at least nine grape varieties used to produce Gioia del Colle. Here, Primitivo makes its first appearance, a fundamentally important grape in Puglia. It is the basic ingredient of Rosso and – obviously – the Primitivo varietal, which is by far the most interesting wine in the zone.

The wine laws also provide for a sweet Aleatico, which can also be fortified up to 18.5 per cent alcohol – at which point it becomes a Liquoroso.

Notable producers

Rivera, Andria (BA) The Rivera winery in Andria is the best producer of the wines of the Castel del Monte DOC. It is also an historic name in Puglian winemaking and one of the most successful on international markets. The family de Corato produces an excellent Castel del Monte Rosso Riserva: Il Falcone is a striking blend of Montepulciano and Uva di Troia, which stands out in every vintage for the richness of its bouquet, its concentration and its sophisticated taste. It matures in barriques of French oak and has a remarkably long-lasting aftertaste. Every wine produced by this winery, from the Moscato di Trani Piani di Tufara to the Castel del Monte Rosé, is well-made and interesting, while progress is afoot with Chardonnay and Aglianico.

Santa Lucia, Corato (BA) The estate owned by the Perrone Capano family is in the hands of Neapolitan father and son Giuseppe and Roberto. It boasts a long tradition and produces a well-made range of Castel del Monte DOC wines. The Rosso, and especially the Rosso Riserva, are excellent choices.

Torrevento, Corato (BA) Torrevento is expanding fast. The Liantonios currently own 25 hectares of "active" vineyards, with another 10 hectares of recently planted vineyards soon to come into production. These will quickly be followed by another 25 hectares. This gives an idea of the dynamism of a winery which has just added state-of-the-art apparatus and is committed to pursuing high-quality wines. Oenologist Lino Carparelli produces an excellent

selection, including the outstanding Moscato di Trani Dulcis in Fundo, and the red Torre del Falco.

Botromagno, Gravina di Puglia (BA)

The Botromagno winery in Gravina produces a well-made Gravina Bianco, which is considered among the best of the region, and perhaps the best Pugliese white wine from native grapes. It also produces Silvium – an interesting Rosato – and in good years the Pier delle Vigne, a full-bodied red wine.

Cantina del Locorotondo, Locorotondo
(BA) Although this winery is more famous for its Locorotondo DOC wines, in recent years it has proven capable of producing good red wines such as Casale San Giorgio, made from Negroamaro and Primitivo, and Primitivo di Manduria. An expanding winery.

Vigneti del Sud, Rutigliano (BA)
The Puglian outpost of the giant Antinori group, which has recognised the enormous potential of the climate and terroir of Puglia. At present the Florence-based company owns two wine estates in this part of Italy, one of 100 hectares in Minervino Murge, in the Castel del Monte, and the other of over 500 hectares at San Pietro Vernotico, in the heart of the Salento region. Vigneti del Sud produces two excellent wines in Minervino: Tormaresca Bianco is produced from Chardonnay grapes, and Tormaresca Rosso is a blended wine. Both offer remarkable value for money.

D'Alfonso del Sordo, San Severo (FG)
In a zone which is not reputed for well-structured, modern wines, the D'Alfonso del Sordo winery produces some excellent red wines with great personality, such as the Montero (a rosso) and Casteldrione selections. The Gianfelice d'Alfonso del Sordo is a new star at the winery, a blend of Sangiovese, Montepulciano and Uva di Troia aged in oak barrels.

Nugnes, Trani (BA) Probably the best "interpreter" of the precious and rather rare Moscato di Trani, which it produces in a worthy traditional version.

right This new installation at Cantina Sociale Locorotondo gives some idea of the size of modern winery equipment.

Salento

The greatest Puglian developments of recent years have taken place in the southernmost part of the region, where the plateau slopes down into the Tarantine Murge, the Salentine Murge and the plains of Tavoliere and Terra d'Otranto. Many factors contribute to the excellent wines of this area. The land is arid, but excellent air currents are provided by warm winds from the Ionian sea and colder winds from the Adriatic. Vines thrive in red soil on top of calcareous rock and a good temperature range between night and day gives wines an aromatic finesse. Primitivo, Negroamaro and Malvasia Nera are alberello-trained and their extremely low yields deliver outstanding results. Newly planted vines are trained on low espaliers which are cultivated partly mechanically, unlike the traditional hand-worked system.

Salento is chiefly the land of Negroamaro, a grape variety with amazing potential and the backbone of almost all the red and rosé wines of Brindisino and Leccese Salento – Alezio, Salice Salentino Rosso, Lizzano, Brindisi, Squinzano, Copertino, Nardò, Leverano and Matino, and Galatina – with the exception of the excellent Primitivo di Manduria. Optional small additions of Malvasia Nera or occasionally Montepulciano, Sangiovese or Bombino Nero produce red wines famous for an explosive power and an intense colour that almost stains the glass. The rosés are undoubtedly among the best in Italy, with firm body, power and plenty of fruit, freshness and longevity.

Some acclaimed innovative wines have recently been developed in Salice Salentino, including a Bianco from Chardonnay, and a Pinot Bianco – both are full-bodied, mellow wines. Numerous red and white varietal wines have also been introduced, providing an opportunity for traditional varieties such as Negroamaro, Malvasia Nera and Aleatico to reassert their credentials.

below *The Chiostro San Niccolò e Cataldo, at Lecce. The region's superb architecture is a legacy of its polyglot history and culture.*

Notable producers

Rosa del Golfo, Alezio (LE) One of the best known wineries in Puglia. Mino Calò, who died recently, developed new-style wines, smooth and elegant with an intense fruity fragrance, and his son Damiano has stepped into the breach. A new version of the traditional Salentino rosé, Rosa del Golfo, is one of the best Italian rosés ever made. The red Portulano is also excellent, as are the white wines.

Sinfarosa, Avetrana (TA) A perfect example of the revival of Primitivo di Manduria. Gregory Perrucci and the team from the Accademia dei Racemi, a headline-making company, produce Primitivo di Manduria "Zinfandel", one of the best red wines in Puglia and indeed Italy, which has been highly acclaimed on the American market. Gregory's secret is modern, quality-led vinification techniques, but his prize asset is a vineyard of Primitivo, alberello-trained and over 40 years old. His wine is classy, elegant and complex, with incredible concentration and plenty of spicy notes.

Cantina Sociale Copertino, Copertino (LE) A reference point of Salento oenology. Run with great skill by oenologist Severino Garofano, this winery produces well-made versions of Copertino, structured and powerful, and an excellent Chardonnay with plenty of aromatic notes.

Masseria Monaci, Copertino (LE) Famous for years for the excellent quality of its reds, such as the Copertino Eloquenzia, Primitivo I Censi and the red Simposia. Severino Garofano, the estate's oenologist, also produces some good white wines and an interesting rosé, Santa Brigida.

Cosimo Taurino, Guagnano (LE) A huge presence in recent Pugliese winemaking, though Cosimo Taurino – its driving force – has passed away. In the 1970s, Cosimo introduced low yields, over-ripe grapes and the vinification of individual vineyards, which established him and his oenologist Severino Garofano (who works for some of the best wineries in the region) as true pioneers.

Patriglione, a Negroamaro varietal with a monumental personality, is a cult wine in the US and the red Notarpanaro is one of the best in the region. All the wines from this estate deserve attention, from the Chardonnay del Salento to the best rosé.

Agricole Vallone, Lecce The Vallone sisters produce excellent wines, whose star is the red Graticciaia, a kind of Amarone del Sud. This is a great red wine made from Negroamaro grapes which have been lightly dried on reed mats before pressing. It is generous, friendly, concentrated and complex, and can be kept for a very long time. The rest of their excellent range, looked after by – you've guessed it – Severino Garofano, includes elegant reds such as Brindisi Vigna Flaminio and the excellent Salice Salentino Vereto, and a fascinating southern version of Sauvignon Blanc, Corte Valesio.

Conti Zecca, Leverano (LE) One of the most impressive estates in Puglia, this family business has over 800 hectares of land, of which 300 are vineyards, with an annual production of approximately one million bottles. Antonio Romano, oenologist and director of the winery, and consultant Giorgio Marone have made solid changes to the estate in recent years and now produce excellent wines such as Nero – a blend of Negroamaro, Malvasia Nera and Cabernet – Leverano Malvasia Vigna del Saraceno, and Salentino Cantalupi, which are outstanding and surprisingly reasonably priced.

Felline, Manduria (TA) Played a leading part in Puglia's revival. The Perrucci family works in collaboration with the famous consultant Roberto Cipresso. Their 33ha of vines are all alberello-trained and include Primitivo, Negroamaro, Cabernet Sauvignon and Merlot. These produce one of the best Pugliese red wines of recent years, Vigna del Feudo. They also make one of the best Primitivo di Manduria, and Alberello, a

right Severino Garofano (left), the late Cosimo Taurino and Francesco Taurino view plans for their new winery at Guagnano.

magnificent blend of Negroamaro and Primitivo which has also been incredibly successful, commercially.

Pervini, Manduria (TA) The Perrucci brothers are the force behind the Accademia dei Racemi, an association of small wineries saved from neglect and ruin and which now produce well-made, modern wines with the help of well-known oenologists (besides Fabrizio Perruccio, the in-house oenologist). Their range includes excellent wines such as the Primitivo di Manduria Archidamo, the red Salento Bizantino, and Primo Amore, a sweet Primitivo of the Manduria DOC.

Masseria Pepe, Maruggio (TA) Masseria Pepe, owned by Alberto Pagano, is another member of the Accademia dei Racemi. He has some beautiful vineyards in the coastal zone of the Manduria DOC, and produces several Primitivo di Manduria wines such as Dunico, a meaty wine with fascinating Mediterranean fragrances.

Leone de Castris, Salice Salentino (LE) One of Puglia's best-known wineries overseas. The flagship wine is the elegant, full-bodied Salentino rosé Five Roses, but a vast range includes several famous labels, such as the powerful and complex Salice Salentino Riserva Donna Lisa.

Francesco Candido, Sandonaci (BR) One of the best estates in Puglia, producing a large range of wines. Reds include Duca d'Aragona, made from Negroamaro and Montepulciano; Cappello di Prete (Negroamaro and Malvasia Nera); and some well-made white and rosé wines.

Castel di Salve, Tricase (LE) Francesco Marra and Francesco Winspeare's excellent winery is up there with the other Puglia stars. The estate's 36ha of vineyards produce Sangiovese Volo di Alessandro, Negroamaro Armecolo and Priante, which have all proved successful – and deservedly so.

Basilicata

Basilicata is an ancient land. One of the most important Palaeolithic settlements in Italy was discovered here, at Venosa – the birthplace of Horace – and around 1200BC the region was invaded by the Lyki people from Anatolia, from whom the name Lucania derived. They were a highly advanced civilisation who became involved in the Samnite wars, firstly as an ally of Rome but subsequently siding with Pyrrhus and Hannibal. The Romans were unforgiving of this treachery and razed every city in Lucania to the ground. Later, the Lucanians sided with Spartacus, provoking strong repression and isolation by Rome, which retaliated by annexing Lucania as well as Calabria.

In the 11th century the Normans realised that part of the region's value lay in its access to the Tyrrhenian sea and the Gulf of Taranto. The town of Menfi then became its capital and hosted the Councils of the Church in 1059 and 1089. Under Urban II the region went through a terrible recession and was turned into a justiciary called Basilicata; governed by an official of the Basileus. From then on, Basilicata shared the fate of all the border countries.

Soil, viticulture and climate

Basilicata covers about 10,000 square kilometres and is bordered to the north by Campania and Puglia, and to the south by Calabria. It is one of the most mountainous regions in Italy: only 8 per cent of the total surface area is flat, while the hilly region where most of the vineyards are located is in the north of Basilicata. Here, the Aglianico del Vulture is the predominant grape variety.

Most of the other vineyards are situated near Matera, in river valleys and maritime plains around Metaponto. The soil consists mostly of calcareous and sandy rocks with very little vegetation.

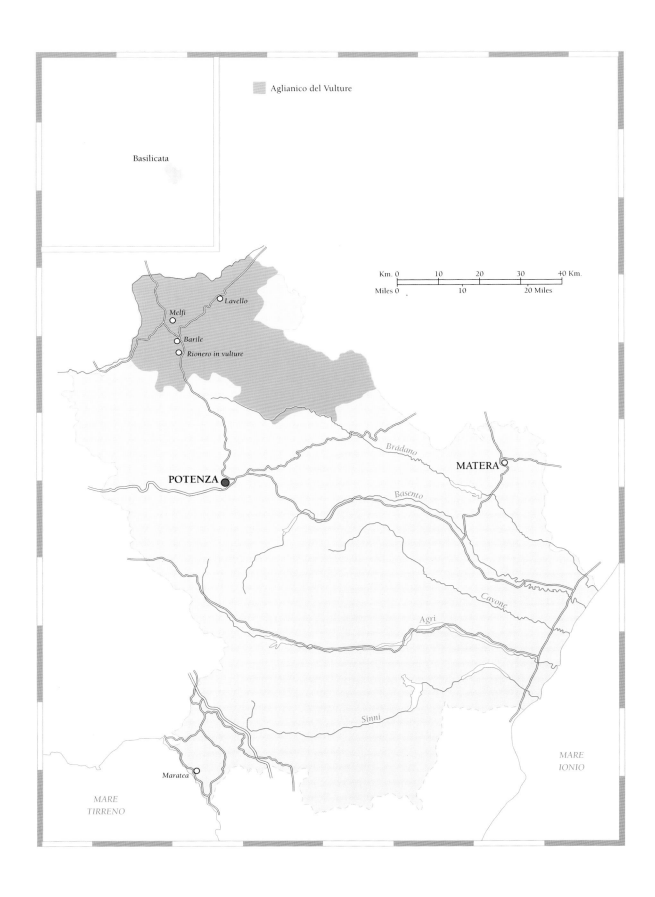

Aglianico del Vulture

Basilicata

Km. 0   10   20   30   40 Km.

Miles 0   10   20 Miles

Lavello

Melfi

Barile

Rionero in vulture

Bradano

MATERA

POTENZA

Basento

Cavone

Agri

Sinni

MARE IONIO

Maratea

MARE TIRRENO

Basilicata's most important mountain ranges are Monte Pollino (2,248 metres) and Monte Sirino (2,005 metres), and to the north is an imposing volcanic mountain chain dominated by Monte Vulture (1,326 metres). On the smaller hills the soil is predominantly clay and sand, while the bottom of the valleys consists of alluvial and maritime deposits, which explains the fertility of these districts.

Winegrowing in Basilicata was introduced by the Greeks and dates back to the 6th century BC. Since then the primary grape variety has been the "ellinico" ("Greek"), today known as Aglianico. The most widespread training system was traditionally *alberello speronato*, but today the vines are trained vertically, using variations on the Guyot system. In antiquity, the hillside caves served as maturation cellars: today, the wines are matured in large barrels of Slovenian oak.

The viticultural heart of Basilicata is situated in the fertile area around the Vulture massif, but the region has great climatic variation. The Apennine mountains block the mild air currents from the Tyrrhenian sea to the west, and the climate is further cooled by cold winds blowing from the Balkans, across the Adriatic and Puglia. Potenza, which is 800 metres above sea level, is almost always the

below *Vineyards at d'Angelo. Basilicata grows a huge range of obscure grape varieties, and only the Vulture sub-region has a DOC.*

coldest town in Italy. Rainfall is abundant and there is snow from December to March, though the area around Matera has a milder, drier climate. The Ionic coast – which is exposed to the warm winds blowing from North Africa – is dry and rather hot, and consequently suitable for the cultivation of citrus fruits.

Wines and winemaking

Very little wine is made in Basilicata. Production is under 500,000 hectolitres and less than three per cent is DOC – represented solely by Aglianico del Vulture, the only denomination. The reasons are obvious: the land is harsh and mountainous, and little suited to winegrowing. Even the unusually cool climate would seem to be unfavourable. This is somewhat paradoxical in view of the fact that southern Italy is usually considered a semi-tropical region where the sun always shines, and where it is warm in winter. Basilicata also has one of the lowest yields per hectare of all Italian regions.

The district of Vulture is situated in the northernmost part of the region, extending from Irpinia to Capitanata, and between Campania and Puglia, just beyond the Ofanto river. Monte Vulture is an ancient extinct volcano, and gives its name to Aglianico's production region, which embraces Melfi, Rionero, Lavello, Venosa and ten other small communes. Aglianico del Vulture is a powerful, full-bodied red wine that needs a few years' ageing before it can be drunk. The basic style must be matured for at least one year by the producer, while the riserva has to be kept for a minimum of five years, at least two years in barrel, before being sold.

The Aglianico grape variety has traditionally been considered Greek (Hellenic) in origin, hence its evolved name. However, a more recent theory suggests that the grape was introduced into Italy when the region was under Aragonese rule, and that its name is perhaps an Italianisation of "vino de llanos", wine of the plains. Besides Aglianico, Basilicata has an amazing range of grape varieties, but they are seldom put to use. It is not widely known, for instance, that Basilicata produces very pleasant Moscato and excellent Malvasia, as well as Primitivo, Sangiovese and Montepulciano, not to mention remarkable reds made from Bombino. While Basilicata tends to be thought of for the time being as the land of Aglianico, the recently created IGT could well be the springboard towards bigger and better things.

Notable producers

Basilium, Acerenza (PZ) Located towards the southern reaches of Basilicata is one of the most important cooperative wineries in the region, which has made a name for itself with a range of remarkable red wines. Its flagship is undoubtedly the Aglianico del Vulture Valle del Trono, which is matured in oak barrels of five hectolitres. It has a beautiful dark ruby colour, is elegant on the nose and voluptuous on the palate.

Equally outstanding is the Aglianico del Vulture I Portali, a velvety red wine with well-judged tannins and impeccable style. Finally, the Pipoli is also worth a mention, a wine that reproduces the fruity notes of the other two Aglianicos, whilst adding body and a mellow quality.

Consorzio Viticoltori Associati del Vulture, Barile (PZ) Founded in the late 1970s, this consortium is a group of five cooperative wineries who own a huge amount of land, plus contributing members. Within a potential annual production of 20,000 hectolitres, a quarter of which is matured in oak barrels, the consortium offers an excellent selected Aglianico, Carpe Diem, named in honour of the 2000th anniversary of the death of the poet, Horace. Also worth trying is the Aglianico del Vulture, which has a fine ruby colour and pleasant aromatic notes of cherry and ripe plum. There are also a brace of sparkling wines, the Ellenico and Moscato.

Paternoster, Barile (PZ) The Paternoster brothers, Vito, Sergio and Anselmo, have created one of the foremost wineries in the Vulture region. From their seven hectares of vineyards – situated between 450-600 metres' altitude – they produce modern, clean wines, well-structured and above all very typical.

The best is the varietal Aglianico del Vulture Don Anselmo: it has attractive ruby colour and aromas of ripe red fruit and spices, and is pleasantly tannic on the palate. The straight Aglianico del Vulture has plenty of ripe red cherries on the nose, balanced by delicate vegetal notes. It is quite astringent on the palate because of its tannins, but is still a well-balanced, fleshy and harmonious wine. After ageing for 18-20 months in oak barrels, the wine is aged in bottle for at least seven months.

D'Angelo, Rionero in Vulture (PZ) Year after year, the d'Angelo wine estate confirms its reputation as one of the best wineries in southern Italy. This progressive company believes in the importance of modern techniques, experimenting with both production processes and the cultivation of its 12 hectares of vines, and yet it manages to preserve regional typicity.

For the past eight years the winery has been working with innovative white grape varieties, as well as producing a small amount of Aglianico spumante for local consumption. Most of all, though, it has concentrated on the vinification of great red wines. The most important label is Canneto, which is made from pure Aglianico grapes from the vineyards of the Rionero district, harvested late and matured for 15 months in small oak barrels. Dark ruby in colour, it opens up on the nose with a bouquet of black fruit, tobacco, toast and spices. It is a wine with remarkable ageing potential, perhaps 15 years.

Finally, Aglianico del Vulture is a full-bodied red with wonderful structure, even if it lacks the finesse of the Canneto.

below *Donato d'Angelo tests his most important wine, Canneto. This is a red made from Aglianico grapes, whose origins may be ancient Greek or Aragonese.*

Calabria

Calabria was a splendid wine region under the Ancient Greeks, and a series of rich settlements ranged along its coast played a fundamental part in the Magna Graecia civilisation. After siding with Rome's enemies in the Punic wars, Calabria was subdued by the Romans and then suffered a procession of invasions. After a period of stability under the Bourbons, the Calabresi campaigned for national unification, fuelled by the ideas of Mazzini and the Carboneria (a secret political society.)

Soil, viticulture and climate

Calabria is the southern extremity of the Italian peninsula, and is separated from Sicily by a narrow stretch of water. It's bordered to the north by Basilicata and the rest of the region is surrounded by the Tyrrhenian and Ionian seas.

Calabria is almost entirely covered by mountains and hills: only nine per cent of its area is flat and forty-two per cent mountainous, mostly along the coastline. The rivers are rather short (the longest are the Crati and the Neto, which flow into the Ionian sea) and very often flow like torrents, while the hot, Mediterranean climate along the coast gives way to a continental climate with very cold winters in Sila. Rainfall is usually good, especially at higher altitudes, but less so along the coasts. Because of

below *Spring flowers outside Verbicaro. Calabria is a patchwork of mountains and hills, and has one of Italy's greatest wine legacies.*

the climate, vineyards in much of ancient Calabria were cultivated at higher altitudes than in Sicily and Puglia.

Vineyards have always thrived in Calabria: by the 6th century BC Greek settlers had located the most suitable areas and were turning out excellent wines. Winners in the ancient Olympic Games were offered red wine from Krimisa, produced from grapes grown along the Ionian coast, and wines were distributed throughout the ancient world via an efficient commercial network.

Calabrian wines have been famous since the Middle Ages, but they were seriously affected by phylloxera at the start of the 20th century and production levels have never recovered. The best vineyards favour the *alberello basso* and *cordone speronato* training systems: 80 per cent are planted with red grape varieties, predominantly Gaglioppo, with Greco the prevalent white variety.

Wines and winemaking

Only four per cent of Calabria's annual output of a million hectolitres boasts a DOC. Despite the region's potential, only a minority of producers and cooperative wineries market bottled wine – the rest makes up the usual lake of red and white wine, sold in bulk. Poor profits have led to a slow but inexorable decline in winegrowing, a problem mirrored in all the southern wine regions.

The major production zones and almost all the DOC areas are situated in central-north Calabria. All the reds are based on the Gaglioppo grape, and almost all white wines on Greco. The most famous and characteristic wine is Cirò, in the Rosso version, which can be produced as a Superiore if it exceeds 13.5 per cent alcohol, as a Riserva if matured for at least two years, and as a Classico when it is produced from vineyards situated in the oldest traditional zone. There is also Rosato, made from Gaglioppo, and Bianco, from Greco. Cirò is a powerful wine with a high alcohol content, perhaps a little old-fashioned in style, but with considerable potential.

Many other DOC wines are produced from identical grapes in different regions, including Pollino, Sant'Anna di Isola Capo Rizzuto, Melissa, Savuto and Donnici. San Vito di Luzzi and Scavigna are only produced in a red version, while Lamezia bucks the white rule with a Bianco made from Greco, Trebbiano and Malvasia. The Rosso is made from Nerello Mascalese, Greco Nero and Gaglioppo.

Finally, Greco di Bianco is a rare but delicious sweet white wine, produced in the coastal region of Locride.

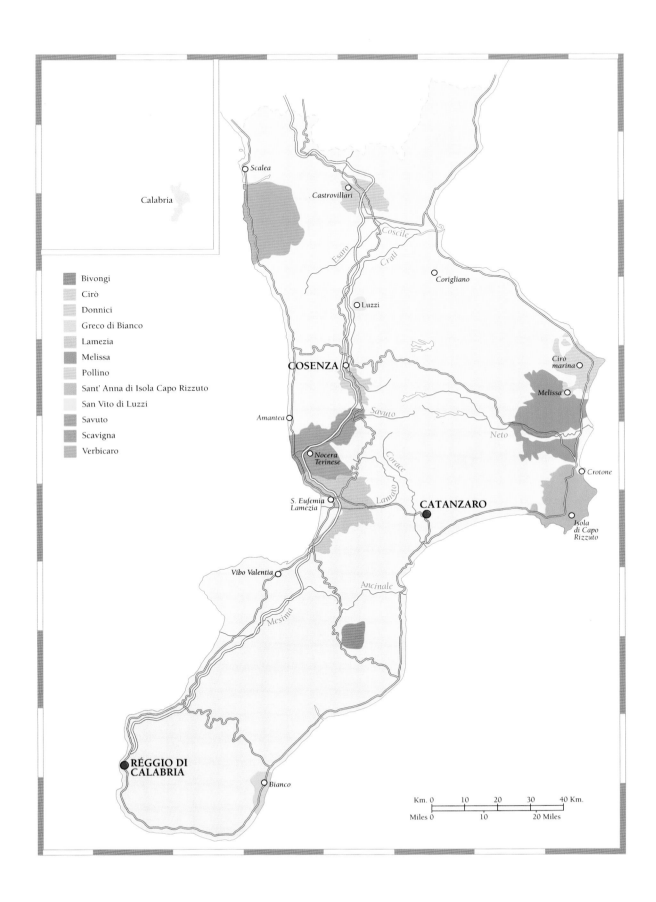

Calabria

Bivongi
Cirò
Donnici
Greco di Bianco
Lamezia
Melissa
Pollino
Sant' Anna di Isola Capo Rizzuto
San Vito di Luzzi
Savuto
Scavigna
Verbicaro

Scalea

Castrovillari

Coscile

Esaro

Crati

Corigliano

Luzzi

Cirò
marina

COSENZA

Melissa

Savuto

Neto

Amantea

Nocera
Terinese

Crotone

S. Eufemia
Lamezia

Lamato

Corace

CATANZARO

Isola
di Capo
Rizzuto

Vibo Valentia

Ancinale

Mesima

RÉGGIO DI
CALABRIA

Bianco

Km. 0   10   20   30   40 Km.

Miles 0   10   20 Miles

Cirò

right *The Sila region stretches from the coast to the Apennines. Winegrowing here is labour-intensive and often archaic.*

Cirò is the one wine big enough to assume the mantle of international ambassador for Calabria. It has been made in the region of Cirò for thousands of years and its area of production includes the communes of Cirò, the beachy Cirò Marina – which combine to form the sub-zone of the Cirò Classico – and part of the Melissa and Crucoli regions, in the province of Crotone. This is the site of the ancient Greek city of Krimisa, which once built an impressive temple in honour of Dionysus.

Cirò is situated to the east of Sila, amid coastal hills, valleys and ravines created by the erosion of the marl soil, which is rich in clay and sand and typical of this region. The winters are never too cold, because of the maritime influence, and rainfall is good. Summers, on the other hand, are extremely hot, with scarcely a drop of rain.

Red Cirò is made predominantly from Gaglioppo and the white version is mostly Greco. Gaglioppo is widely thought to be of Greek origin, and until recently had been confused with Arvino, Magliocco, Lacrima Nera and Mantonico Nero. Besides its starring role in Cirò, it is also the basic variety in almost all Calabrese red wines.

However, Cirò and Gaglioppo have benefited very little from Italy's recent oenological revival. Apart from a few of the more inspired selections, Cirò remains a small, closed world where tradition persists – often for the worse – but where innovations are only sometimes for the best.

The finest vineyards employ the alberello training system, which admittedly produces high-quality grapes, but all the work has to be done by hand. In recent years the alberello-trained vines have gradually been replaced by more practical systems – such as tall espalier training (the shoots are trained on wires), and in some cases tendone or palmetta training (the vines are trained high) – but at the expense of quality. The wineries, on the other hand, are several decades behind the rest of Italy in respect of equipment: concrete and fibreglass tanks, large, old wooden vats and an almost complete lack of instruments for temperature control explain the lingering limitations of Cirò, and of many other wines in Calabria.

The few wineries that have mobilised to join the rest of Italy in its revival have been rewarded with success on the international markets. Despite that, Cirò – like much of Calabria – is still trying to shake off that often euphemistic tag of "enormous potential".

Notable producers

Librandi, Cirò Marina (Crotone) Twenty years ago, Nicodemo Librandi was the first producer in the region to sense that the world of wine was changing, and that Cirò could become a great red. He was also one of the first to employ an oenologist as consultant, a role held until recently – and with distinction – by Severino Garofano. Today, Librandi is assisted by oenologist Donato Lanati and produces some of the best wines in southern Italy. His flagship wine is the award-winning Gravello, a magnificent red blend of Gaglioppo and Cabernet Sauvignon, matured in barriques. It is full-bodied and mellow, with the amazing complexity that only a great wine can call upon.

The Cirò Rosso Classico Riserva Duca di Sanfelice is warm, tannic and firm, while the young Cirò Classico is more direct, with stylistic purity, firmness and good balance. Librandi also produces Critone, one of the best Calabrian white wines – made from a blend of Chardonnay and Sauvignon – and a sweet Le Passule.

Fattoria San Francesco, Cirò (Crotone) Francesco Siciliani has decided to turn his winery in the Cirò district into a model estate, by replanting his vines and modernising the equipment. He was joined by Fabrizio Ciufoli, an expert oenologist from Tuscany. This revamp has propelled the wines of the Fattoria San Francesco into the region's top flight.

The Cirò Rosso Classico Superiore Ronco dei Quattroventi musters incredible concentration and a mellow style, along with very fruity tones and spicy notes. A deep ruby colour adds to the allure. The Cirò Rosé is simply one of the best Italian rosé wines, while the rest of the range is excellent. A truly flourishing winery.

Odoardi, Nocera Terinese (Cosenza) Gregorio Odoardi's wine estate is one of the few outside the Cirò district that merits consideration, and continues a fine family history. It's situated on the Tyrrhenian mountain slopes, in the territory of the Savuto and Scavigna DOC. Not unexpectedly, the finest wine is a Scavigna: the *cru* Vigna Garrone is produced in collaboration with the famous oenologist Luca D'Attoma, and is a blend of Aglianico, Merlot, Cabernet Franc and Cabernet Sauvignon, matured in barriques of French oak. It's wonderfully fruity, with delicious fragrances of ripe red and black fruit, enhanced by complex, spicy tones. It's also powerfully rich on the palate, with elegant, fine tannins. The rest of the range is also stunning and includes a superb Savuto Superiore Vigna Mortilla.

left *Francesco Siciliani has proved one of the more progressive and successful producers in Cirò.*

left *Critics deride the antiquated equipment and introverted attitude in Cirò, yet local winemakers remain fiercely loyal to tradition.*

The Islands

Sicily and Sardinia are the two largest islands in the Mediterranean, and both have a wine culture that dates back thousands of years – long before the Greek settlers founded their magnificent cities in Sicily, and when the Sardinian inhabitants of *nuraghe* (truncated cone-shaped towers) still ruled their island. However, in terms of quality the islands' wines were lagging behind the rest of Italy as recently as ten years ago. Despite the profusion of native grape varieties and a spread of production zones, this was bulk wine territory: Sicily and Sardinia seemed to have accepted their lot as suppliers of fair, honest wine for supermarkets. The great traditional fortified wines, such as the Sicilian Marsala and Sardinian Vernaccia di Oristano, have long fought an uphill battle.

Sicily competes with Puglia for the title of Italy's most productive wine region. In 1997 its eight million hectolitres accounted for nearly 16 per cent of the national output, though barely two per cent of this ocean of wine can claim a DOC. This problem will not be resolved overnight: for decades, Sicily's competitively priced wines were extremely successful abroad, notably the Corvo wines of Duca di Salaparuta – Sicily's largest and best-known winery – and those of the Settesoli di Menfi cooperative. In the past, many vineyards and wineries have been modernised, but not always with quality in mind, while the emphasis on white grape varieties, such as the honest but bland Catarratto, led to unexciting wines. In many vineyards, growers appeared to be drifting away from the traditional alberello training system, which was employed by the ancient Greeks, towards the easier espalier and the notorious tendone.

Since the mid-1980s, Sicily and Sardinia have begun to rise to the challenges of the 21st century, urged on at first by just a few wineries and then by a rising number of growers. Today, with a few producers concentrating on high-quality wines, Sicily has shown its mettle with a range of great new reds. Traditional varieties including Nero d'Avola (thought to be a close relative of Syrah), Frappato and Nerello Mascalese are being revitalised. A number of wine enterprises from other regions and other countries are now investing in Sicily, where it is still possible to buy, at reasonable prices, old vineyards with red grape varieties trained on the alberello system. These vineyards can produce wonderful wines when treated with care, while the excellent climate enables growers to harvest fairly late and to pick grapes when they are perfectly ripe, even in vineyards with very high yields per hectare.

With its great diversity of climates and grape varieties, Sardinia has developed along the same lines as Sicily. It also once had a quantity bias, and growers were more inclined to sell their grapes rather than vinify and market them under their own label. In recent years most Sardinian wines have been produced by cooperatives, but thanks to a few wineries – such as Sella & Mosca – Vermentino has become one of the most successful Italian white wines. Vermentino di Gallura, from the north of the island, has also won rave reviews and the same revival has energised red grapes such as Cannonau and Carignano.

Sardinia, with its vast mountainous regions and dry plains, produces only two per cent of Italy's wine and less than six per cent of this has DOC status. While output is unlikely to increase, there are signs of an upturn in quality. Several of the best Italian oenologists have been tempted to the island by its impressive native grape varieties and a climate that is ideally suited to winemaking. They are now busy redesigning Sardinia's burgeoning quality wines, while privately owned wineries and a few avant-garde cooperatives have created several internationally successful styles in just a few years. Finally, international varieties such as Cabernet Sauvignon have also shown themselves perfectly at home among the Sardinian hills and plains.

left *The Costa Paradiso, Sardinia. This is one of Italy's more remote and enigmatic regions – friendly yet fiercely non-conformist.*

Sardinia

Sardinia has been inhabited for over 150,000 years, with the native people engaged in an eternal tussle with the Greeks, Phoenicians and Carthaginians. Next came the Romans, who ruled the whole of Sardinia for 700 years, stamping an indelible mark on the island's language and customs, before the Aragonese brought the Spanish language and viniculture. The Piedmontese conquered Sardinia in 1720 and remained in control until unification. Despite these intrusions, the Sardinians remain fiercely independent yet friendly people.

above *A domed roof at Alghero. Sardinia has been shaped and scarred by centuries of war, and the island is a more rugged state than its northern compatriots.*

Soil, viticulture and climate

The Sardinia zone includes a number of small surrounding islands, from Asinara to Caprera, San Pietro to Sant'Antioco. Mountains account for over 13 per cent of the main island, mostly in the north and east, and plains occupy over 18 per cent. The western side is more hilly and the island is bisected diagonally by the plain of Campidano.

Sardinia has few rivers – the most important is the Tirso – and most turn into torrents in the rainy winter months, and dry out in summer. Large-scale deforestation over the past 300 years has seriously affected the climate and water supply, and in the last 50 years several reservoirs have been built to enable farmers to irrigate their fields in summer. The climate is insular and Mediterranean, with high rainfall during the short, mild winter and virtual drought during the long, hot summer.

Sardinia's patchwork of grape varieties was ravaged by phylloxera in the late 19th century and vineyards were replanted with very little attention to quality, until recently. White grape varieties were preferred for table wines and more prolific training systems appeared. The alberello system – a traditional symbol – survived in only a few DOC areas, such as Gallura, but has only recently become popular again, as have the great traditional white and red grape varieties. Sadly, the island's important fortified and *meditazione* wines are now less popular with consumers, who tend to prefer lower-alcohol wines. But we have not heard the last of Vernaccia di Oristano and Malvasia di Bosa.

Wines and winemaking

Sardinia produces less wine than might be expected – barely a million hectolitres, around 15 per cent DOC. However, it is also progressing faster with quality mid-range wines than any other part of southern Italy, with the award of a DOCG to Vermentino di Gallura and the success of some first-class private and cooperative wineries.

The island's extensive range of wines reflects the wide variations of climate, terrain and grape varieties, and there are numerous DOCs, which sometimes cover the entire regional territory. In this case the name of the region will be mentioned alongside the grape variety. So, Cannonau (the best comes from Jerzu, or from the district around Nuoro, or from the sub-zones of Capo Ferrato in Cagliari), Monica, Moscato and Vermentino bear the di Sardegna suffix, while Sardegna Semidano is produced as far and wide as Cagliari to Sassari, from Olbia to Carbonia. The first two are red, the rest are white.

The province of Cagliari is home to Monica, Nasco, Moscato, Malvasia and Girò (now with the Cagliari suffix): the first is a dry red, the others medium-sweet or sweet wines, often in fortified or dry fortified versions. Finally, there is Nuragus di Cagliari, a widespread and popular dry white. It lacks character, as a result of the "generous" wine regulations that permit a maximum yield of 20,000 kilograms per hectare. In bumper harvests that may be increased by 20 per cent, to 24,000 kilograms per hectare. These wines form the backbone of Sardinian wine; they are the most widespread and best known, and account for almost the entire DOC production.

There are other wines from smaller districts, real traditionalists produced in the various sub-zones into which Sardinia has historically been divided. Two very special white wines are produced in the western-central zone of the island: the first is Vernaccia di Oristano, a dry white wine with a high alcohol content, and the other is Malvasia di Bosa, a very rare white wine which is similar in many respects to non-fortified sherry.

Also in the province of Oristano are Campidano di Terralba – a red wine from Bovale grapes – Trebbiano, and Sangiovese di Arborea. Further south, in Sulcis, is the local hero Carignano del Sulcis, a delicious mellow red wine, interesting but obscure. The production area of another red wine, Mandrolisai – a blend of Bovale and Cannonau grapes – is in the heart of the island, around the provinces of Nuoro, near Sorgono, in Barbagia and in the massif of Gennargentu. This is also the area where most Cannonau di Sardegna is produced, especially in the zone which slopes down from the Gennargentu towards the east coast of the island. But these wines clearly suffer from the technological tardiness of the wineries and, apart from a few exceptions, do scant justice to the potential of

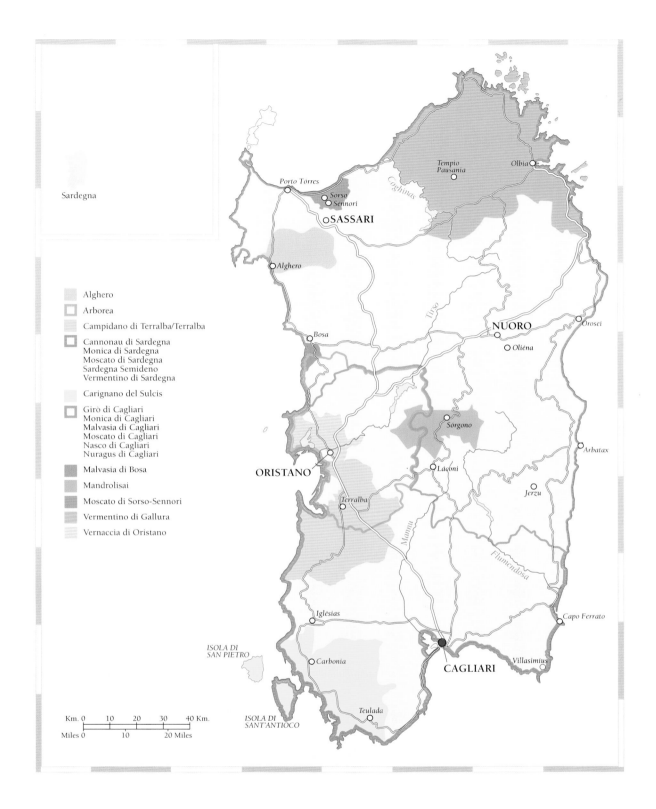

Sardegna

- Alghero
- Arborea
- Campidano di Terralba/Terralba
- Cannonau di Sardegna
  Monica di Sardegna
  Moscato di Sardegna
  Sardegna Semideno
  Vermentino di Sardegna
- Carignano del Sulcis
- Girò di Cagliari
  Monica di Cagliari
  Malvasia di Cagliari
  Moscato di Cagliari
  Nasco di Cagliari
  Nuragus di Cagliari
- Malvasia di Bosa
- Mandrolisai
- Moscato di Sorso-Sennori
- Vermentino di Gallura
- Vernaccia di Oristano

Km. 0   10   20   30   40 Km.

Miles 0   10   20 Miles

the Cannonau grape. However, here too we are seeing a process of innovation which should soon bear fruit.

To the north of Sassari is the zone of Moscato di Sorso-Sennori, producing a sweet and pleasantly aromatic white wine, while the relatively new DOC Alghero deserves a mention. It is practically the monopoly of Sella & Mosca and of the Santa Maria La Palma winery, and is home to the rare Torbato di Alghero, an excellent white wine. Also on show are a more familiar quartet of Sauvignon Blanc, Chardonnay, Cabernet and Sangiovese.

Alghero and Gallura

The Alghero DOC was only created in 1995, yet wines from the plain of Alghero have represented Sardinia for several decades. After the huge drainage operation that took place from the end of the 19th century through to the 1950s, the vast expanse of the Piani – north of the city, and extending as far west as the Nurra hills and due east to Sassari and Logudoro – became a reservoir of wine, with a host of small-scale cantinas lining up alongside the more influential and larger wineries.

Alghero is also home to one of the most famous Italian wineries, Sella & Mosca, which has been operating here for over a century. Its vineyards have been responsible for the highly successful Vermentino di Sardegna, a lightly sparkling white wine which delights tourists to the Costa Smeralda in summer. It also makes Torbato (the French Malvoisie du Roussillon), rosé wines made predominantly

below *Alghero, on the northwest tip of Sardinia, is responsible for more wine than any other zone on the island.*

from Cabernet, and excellent reds from Cannonau. This large outfit also specialises in an interesting fortified red, Anghelu Ruju (or Angelo Rosso), named after a prehistoric necropolis that was discovered in the grounds of the estate. Anghelu is produced in the same way as port, but Cannonau grapes from the estate's vineyards are left out to dry before pressing – and some of the best vintages are memorable. Sella & Mosca's progressive approach to innovation and experimentation has led to some excellent table wines, notably the Tanca Farrà, a powerful red blend of Cannonau and Cabernet. In the late 1970s this blend inspired many other Sardinian producers to concentrate on full-bodied reds. The company has also researched and developed a top-of-the-range list, culminating in a superb Cabernet Sauvignon and intensely aromatic and fresh white wines based on Sauvignon Blanc.

Today, the Alghero DOC represents all of the grape varieties grown in the zone, from the traditional Torbato (also in sparkling form) and Cagnulari (a variety used in eponymous reds), to Cabernet Sauvignon, Chardonnay, Sauvignon Blanc and Sangiovese.

Gallura

This northern region's rocky granite soil is suited to high-quality wines. Vineyards cultivated in these hills are situated at altitudes of 300-500 metres, and low rainfall restricts the yield of the alberello-trained vines.

The award of the DOCG to Vermentino di Gallura in 1996 was a milestone in Sardinian wine and the wine laws covering this excellent white wine can only improve its pedigree. Grape production must not exceed 10,000 kilograms per hectare and no plant may produce more than three kilos. There must be a minimum of 3,250 vine plants per hectare and even during drought, irrigation is allowed only twice. These rules have enabled producers of Vermentino di Gallura – almost all of them associated with cooperatives – to develop some good wines: powerful, aromatic, fruity and well-balanced, with excellent ageing potential and an alcohol content that can exceed 13 per cent.

Vermentino di Gallura makes an excellent partner for the local cuisine and is far removed from the Vermentino di Sardegna, the light, easy-drinking and popular white wine. Other varieties cultivated include the Nebbiolo, introduced by the Piedmontese in the 19th century and used in powerful, concentrated wines in the Colli del Limbara, and Moscato, notable here for sparkling wines.

Notable producers

Cantina Sociale Santa Maria La Palma, Alghero (Sassari) This winery is still associated with the drainage of the area after the Second World War. The vineyards are protected from the *mistral* by rows of eucalyptus trees, or interplanted with olive trees in the lee of the Mediterranean *maquis*. The winery is famous for good, easy-drinking wines, but has recently developed more complex styles. Cannonau di Sardegna Le Bombarde and Vermentino di Sardegna Aragosta are interesting.

Sella & Mosca, Alghero (Sassari)
A winery whose history dates back over a century and which in recent years has shown an incredible improvement in quality. Its director is the oenologist Mario Consorte, who produces some outstanding wines of international repute, as well as the classic best-sellers such as Vermentino di Sardegna, Vermentino di Sardegna La Cala and Alghero Rosé Oleandro. His Alghero Cabernet Marchese di Villamarina is superb, and in the top rank of Italian reds. The fresh Sauvignon Le Arenarie is also very good. Last but not least come the red Raim, which is made largely from Carignano grapes, and the vintage Anghelu Ruju Riserva, a great *meditazione* wine.

Tenute Capichera, Arzachena (Sassari)
The Ragnedda brothers were the first to realise the latent quality of the traditional Vermentino di Gallura variety. They produce some excellent versions, well-structured, mature, complex and full-bodied wines. Besides Capichera, the brothers also make a rich and elegant Vendemmia Tardiva.

Cantina Sociale del Vermentino, Monti (Sassari) This winery, with over 350 associated winegrowers, is a specialist in the production of Vermentino di Gallura. It offers a wide range of wines, including three outstanding versions of Vermentino: Funtanaliras has plenty of rich and fruity fragrances; Superiore Aghiloia is a warm, full-bodied and harmonious wine with delicate aromatic notes; and S'Eleme is well-structured, with interesting complexity.

Piero Mancini, Olbia (Sassari) One of the most important private wineries on the island. Piero Mancini and his sons make a skilful team, and produce an excellent range of modern wines offering great purity, but are careful not to ignore traditional values. Their best selections are the aromatic and dry Cannonau di Sardegna – an alcoholic yet fruity and balanced wine – and the fragrant, exotic Vermentino di Gallura Cucaione. These wines also represent very good value for money.

Cantina Sociale Gallura, Tempio Pausania (Sassari) One of the best cooperative wineries in Sardinia, thanks to the efforts of oenologist Dino Addis. Every wine in the range is excellent, but the starting point has to be the Vermentino di Gallura Superiore Canayli, considered one of the authoritative pillars of the DOCG, and arguably one of the top Italian white wines made from a native grape variety. It's a lesson in rich, fruity, powerful intensity. Other irresistible candidates include the white Balajana, an elegant and complex wine produced from Vermentino and matured in barriques. The red Dolmen made from Nebbiolo, also matured in new wood, has elegant tannins and rich fruitiness, while the Karana, made from Nebbiolo grown in the hills of Limbara, is fresh and fragrant. Finally, the Vermentino di Sardegna Piras has a superb bouquet.

left *The green giant – Sella & Mosca is one of Sardinia's twin peaks, a vinous centurion that combines quality with volume.*

below *Dino Addis, of Cantina Sociale Gallura, produces one of Italy's finest "native" white wines.*

Oristano and Vernaccia

The Catalan-speaking city of Oristano is situated south of Alghero, amid a sea of vineyards that produce some of Sardinia's most characteristic wines. To the north and along the coast are the hills of Planargia, near the commune of Bosa, home of the rare Malvasia di Bosa, one of the most attractive Italian *meditazione* wines. Here, Malvasia grapes are grown on alberello-trained vines; they are harvested over-ripe and the wine is allowed to age for a few years in

barrels, exposed to light and air and sudden changes in temperature. The most traditional style has a Madeira-like bouquet, resulting from ageing in barrels that are not completely full, on top of which a form of yeast – or *flor* – often develops. This adds complexity to an aroma that is reminiscent of the sherries of Jérez de la Frontera. Besides the natural dolce (sweet) and secco (dry) styles with their 15 per cent alcohol, there are two versions lightly fortified

below *These vines belonging to Contini, in the Oristano province, help produce classic examples of Vernaccia, for which the family has been famous for decades.*

with wine distillate to 16 per cent abv.

The other great wine of Oristano is Vernaccia, which is produced from alberello-trained vines planted in the sandy, gravelly, alluvial soils of the vast Tirso basin. Vernaccia is made from over-ripe Vernaccia grapes and was famous across the Mediterranean until the Renaissance. This is a great apéritif and *meditazione* wine, a dry wine rarely fortified with wine distillate and even less common as a sweet style. The wine has an alcohol content of 15 per cent and is aged for years in small chestnut barrels – exposed to light and air – and then stored in *magazzini*, or depots. Like Malvasia di Bosa and sherry, the barrels are filled to only 90 per cent of their capacity, so that *flor* can develop on top, contributing to its unique character.

The Riserva is dated and aged for a long time in the barrel, but unlike sherry Vernaccia does not go through the solera system.

Outside the Bosa DOC area there are some interesting dry Malvasia della Planargia wines, with similar features to the one from Bosa, but still awaiting a DOC. Campidano di Terralba, also produced in the province of Cagliari, is a good red only marketed locally, while the Trebbiano and Sangiovese wines of the Arborea DOC seldom rise above the ordinary.

Finally, Sardegna Semidano is a typical white wine produced from native grapes grown in the sub-zone of Mogoro, located to the south of Oristano. It is well-structured and full-bodied, but remains the preserve of local winemakers.

Notable producers

Contini, Cabras (Oristano) Vernaccia di Oristano may be famous and traditional but in recent years it has not proven very successful commercially. Contini di Cabras has been one of the most successful and prestigious labels, and has recently been producing more complex and fascinating Vernaccia. The vintage Riserva and Antico Gregori selezione are excellent, but the whole range is interesting, from the white Karmis to the Elibaria, matured in new wood. The Niederra and Cannonau di Sardegna reds are worthy cohorts.

Naitana, Magomadas (Nuoro) Although Malvasia di Bosa is a local legend, there are some producers who are trying to obtain the DOC for a larger area – not least because it is very difficult to find any bottles outside its zone of production. One of these pioneers is Gianvittorio Naitana, a young producer who concentrates on the semi-sweet and sweet versions of the local Malvasia. This younger style is fast gaining support, though official regulations have yet to bend to its needs. Naitana's pleasant Malvasia della Planargia Murapiscados is a delicate wine, boasting stylish peachy aromas and a superbly balanced sweetness of sugar and glycerine.

Giuseppe Gabbas (Nuoro) Giuseppe Gabbas is increasingly synonymous with

Cannonau and a worthy choice to represent the Cannonau producers of the Nuoro. His red wines are rated among the very best of this variety and his lead over rival producers in the region is clear. Hopefully they will follow his example of carefully tended vineyards, low yields and

a modern, well-equipped winery. These assets explain the excellence both of Gabbas's Cannonau di Sardegna Lillovè and his Dule, a successful blend of Cannonau, Cabernet Sauvignon, Sangiovese and Montepulciano, which is matured in new wood.

above *The alberello vine-training system rewards Sardinians with some fine wines, including a sherry-style Malvasia di Bosa.*

Cagliari and Sulcis

above *The natural attractions and terroir of the Mediterranean islands tempted Giacomo Tachis south from Tuscany.*

If there was ever a region devoted to high yields and dominated by large cooperative wineries geared up to quantity rather than quality, it was the Cagliari province. Yet in this zone, too, a dire situation which appeared to be irreversible in the 1970s has been transformed, thanks to two excellent wineries – Santadi and Argiolas di Serdiana.

Change has come at a price, as many cooperatives and wine cellars have closed down, and private wineries have had to rethink their strategy. But after the launch of two great red wines in the late 1980s (discussed in this section) the situation rapidly evolved: quality became the buzzword and most wineries have retained this dynamic approach.

The 1980s marked the beginning of a new era in Sulcis. It was the time of the "wine war" with France and most of the Carignano grapes grown in the province were heading for the front line. Slowly but inexorably, growers in the region – led by Santadi, the large cooperative winery – recognised the need to market their own wine in bottles. The old alberello-trained vines, often grown near the sea,

used to provide the raw material for bulk wines, but they were about to be given special treatment.

The driving force behind this overhaul was Giacomo Tachis, Italy's most famous winemaker and the creator of three of the nation's greatest reds: Antinori's Tignanello and Solaia, and Sassicaia degli Incisa della Rocchetta. Tachis firmly believed in the great potential for winemaking in the warm Mediterranean regions, and duly accepted the challenge of producing quality wines at Santadi. Under his guidance, Santadi developed an impressive range of wines. The Terre Brune, made from Carignano grapes (cousins of French Carignan or Spanish Cariñena) with a sprinkling of Bovaleddu, came to symbolise the revival in Sulcis. Aged in barriques of new oak, Terre Brune offers incredible elegance, concentration and international class.

To the north of the province – between Trexenta and Parteolla – is Argiolas of Serdiana, a privately owned and quality-driven winery. Antonio Argiolas is over 90 years old and has spent more than 70 years producing excellent wines, and delicious olive oil. Today, he has entrusted the running of his business to his sons Franco and Peppeto, who have achieved amazing results under the tutelage of Tachis. Their best red wine is Turriga, produced from a careful blend of Cannonau (70 per cent) with additions of Carignano, Malvasia Nera and Bovale. This outstanding wine is powerful, concentrated and mellow, with excellent ageing potential. You'll find it cropping up on wine lists in top restaurants around the world.

Besides these magnificent wines, Santadi and Argiolas have developed two enviable selections – the Monica di Sardegna, a red wine with mellow fruity tones, and several versions of Carignano del Sulcis DOC. Between them they also account for a fabulous Chardonnay matured in barrel, a good Nuragus, and Latinia, a promising version of the region's *meditazione* wine from Nasco grapes. Argiolas has also developed a white Argiolas wine, which is rich in fruit and has a delicious aromatic fragrance – a fascinating choice. There is also an excellent Vermentino di Sardegna, some very good Cannonau, a captivating modern red wine – Kore – and Angialis, a sweet wine made from Nasco.

Following the lead of these two wineries, others – both cooperatives and independents – have planned their wines for the future, with high but not unrealistic hopes. Perhaps even the old traditional sweet wines, such as Moscato di Cagliari and the red Girò di Cagliari, will return to their former glory. After all, one cannot live on Nuragus alone!

Notable producers

Cantine di Dolianova, Dolianova (Cagliari) One of the largest cooperative wineries in the province of Cagliari, and in recent years its wines have enjoyed more and more success. Most of the production consists of simple, fragrant white wines, but we particularly enjoyed the red Falconaro – a blend of Cannonau, Carignano, Pascale, Barbera and other red grapes – and the excellent Moscato di Cagliari.

Cantina Sociale Santadi, Santadi (Cagliari) One would probably have to travel as far north as Alto Adige to discover cooperative wineries capable of competing with Santadi. In the course of ten years it has reached the top of regional winemaking with a series of incredible wines, produced in collaboration with the peerless oenologist

Giacomo Tachis. Besides the famous Terre Brune, Santadi also produces a wide range of reds made predominantly from Carignano grapes – such as Carignano del Sulcis Rocca Rubia Riserva and Baie Rosse – and sophisticated white wines like the Chardonnay Villa di Chiesa. Also worth keeping an eye on are the Vermentino di Sardegna Cala Silente and the Nuragus di Cagliari Pedraia.

Meloni, Selargius (Cagliari) Meloni is a very successful commercial label, both in Sardinia and abroad. Besides the simpler but commercially viable wines, Meloni also specialises in the traditional sweet wines and *meditazione* wines of the Cagliari region. We liked the fascinating Nasco di Cagliari, Malvasia di Cagliari, Moscato di Cagliari and Girò di Cagliari in the Donna Jolanda range.

Argiolas, Serdiana (Cagliari) Antonio Argiolas's winery is a family-run business, and produces very prestigious wines. The Argiolas family played a major part in the revival of Sardinian oenology and their wines were the first to join those of the giant Sella & Mosca in top wine cellars around the world.

This family empire has not yet exhausted the great potential of its vineyards and winery. It has few equals and brothers Franco and Pepetto are well placed to deliver more fascinating wines in the next few years. The following selections are particularly recommended: the signature Turriga, the Monica di Sardegna Perdera, and Cannonau di Sardegna Costera, and, among the whites, there is the Vermentino di Sardegna Costamolino, the Argiolas and the fascinating Angialis – a sweet wine made from Nasco grapes.

Sicily

Sicily has been inhabited since the end of the Palaeolithic period, and it was the earliest inhabitants – first the Sicani, then the Siculi – who gave the island its name. Sicily is situated in the middle of the Mediterranean and has been an important crossroads for trade and the migrating peoples of the Mediterranean since the dawn of civilisation. After the various migratory waves of the Siculi, Ausoni and Morgeti in the late Bronze Age, it was the turn of the Greeks, who founded numerous cities along the coast – including Messina, Naxos, Catania and Syracuse – in the 8th century BC.

below *The Pretoria Fountain in Palermo. The capital was founded by the Carthaginians, but Sicily became Rome's first province.*

Then came the Punic Phoenicians – better known as the Carthaginians – who founded important colonies such as Mozia, Palermo and Solunto, thus entering into conflict with the Greek cities. Their wars with the Greeks and later the Romans lasted over 500 years, but once Rome had defeated Carthage, Sicily became Rome's first province. The foundations for winegrowing had been laid by the Greeks and then the Romans, while the Byzantines later created large ecclesiastical estates including vineyards.

Between AD827 and 1061, Sicily was invaded by the Arabs, who restructured the land registry system, created an irrigation network and introduced numerous new varieties of vegetables and fruit. The production of wine did not increase but it was tolerated, and land set aside for vineyards greatly increased – especially for grape varieties used for drying, such as Zibibbo (a kind of Muscatel).

The Normans then conquered Sicily, returning it to Christianity and reinstituting the feudal system. Viticulture prospered under the Hohenstaufen rulers – Frederick II in particular – while under the houses of Anjou and Aragon the island was exploited economically and abandoned to the feudal lords. The Spanish remained in Sicily until 1713.

After a brief spell of Piedmontese and Austrian occupation, Sicily was claimed by the House of Bourbon, which created the Kingdom of the Two Sicilies in the early 18th century. The Bourbons then promoted agriculture and viticulture until 1860, when Garibaldi conquered the island and handed it over to the king of Italy.

Soil, viticulture and climate

Sicily is the largest island in the Mediterranean and includes the Egadi, Lipari and Pelagian islands, and the islands of Ustica and Pantelleria. It has over 1,400 kilometres of coastline: almost a quarter of the territory is mountainous, some 60 per cent is hilly and the remaining 14 per cent is flat. The mountain ranges are concentrated in the northeastern part of the island, with the highest peak in the Etna massif. The Sicilian Apennines are the continuation of the Calabrese and consist of three mountain ranges: the Peloritani, the Nebrodi and the Madonie. Wide plains are situated to the south of Etna, around Catania and along the coast.

Sicily has a Mediterranean climate, hot and quite dry in the coastal regions, and temperate and moist inland, especially at higher altitude. The massive deforestation of the past and the strong warm winds from the south result

Km. 0   10   20   30   40 Km.

Miles 0   10   20 Miles

Sicilia

ISOLE LIPARI

MESSINA

Cefalù

PALERMO

TRAPANI

Alcamo

Giarre

Belice

San Leonardo

Vallelunga Pratameno

Marsala

Castelvetrano

CATANIA

Platani

ENNA

Menfi

CALTANISSETTA

Sciacca

PANTELLERIA

AGRIGENTO

SIRACUSA

Irminio

Vittoria

Noto

RAGUSA

▮ Bianco Alcamo	
▮ Cerasuolo di Vittoria	
▮ Contea di Sclafani	▯ Marsala
▮ Contessa Entellina	▮ Menfi
▮ Delia Nivolelli	▮ Moscato di Noto
▯ Eloro	▮ Moscato di Pantelleria
▮ Etna	▮ Moscato di Siracusa
▮ Faro	▯ Sambuca di Sicilia
▮ Malvasia delle Lipari	▮ Santa Margherita di Belice
	▮ Sciacca

in a rather arid climate, which is exacerbated by very low rainfall, except around Etna.

It is well documented that viticulture in Sicily dates back around 4,000 years, but while ancient Sicilian wines earned prestige around the world, modern winegrowing has focused on high production and on dessert grapes. In recent years, however, there has been a gradual conversion towards quality. Fortunately, over 40 per cent of the vineyards are still planted with old alberello-trained vines which ensure the best quality grapes. Expanded systems and irrigated vineyards created for blending wines are now in decline.

Wines and winemaking

In his Italian journey, Goethe sang the praises of Sicily as the land which produced everything. He was referring not only to the ancient civilisations of the island, but also to the oenological tradition.

Sicily is a cradle of Italian wine and its annual output of 10 million hectolitres puts it top of Italy's production league. Much of the wine of southern Italy is anonymous, sold in bulk or in tanks, and to some extent this is true of Sicily – only two per cent of its output is DOC . And yet certain labels that have not used the DOC for years have

above *Fishing boats moored in the harbour at Siracusa, one of a succession of port towns settled by the Greeks 3,000 years ago.*

made a name for themselves. Duca di Salaparuta, responsible for the Corvo brand, is a good example, making wines from grapes bought from anywhere and vinified to standard methods. If viticulture and vinification techniques were better suited to the production of quality wines (lower yields per hectare, low alberello-trained vines, and more modern vinification procedures), this island could produce real vinous treasures. Then, comparison with the wine industries of California and Australia would not be far-fetched.

The Sicilian sun does not stress the vines, it promotes perfect ripening, and great wines can only be made from ripe grapes. That may sound obvious, but unfortunately the average Sicilian wine is still far from realising its

potential. But things are changing. Small and medium-sized wineries are being created, and winegrowers from other Italian regions (and even from other countries) are buying large areas of vineyard and introducing new expertise. There may still be a future for high-quality wines on this wonderful island.

The main DOCs

The province of Messina, in the east of the the island, is home to a red wine called Faro, made from Nerello Mascalese and Nerello Cappuccio grapes. Sadly, only a few wineries now produce this, and in very small quantities. It is made from grapes grown in vineyards on the eastern slopes of the Peloritani range, in the area between Messina and Taormina.

Malvasia delle Lipari is produced on the island of Salina, one of the largest of the Aeolian or Lipari islands. There is at present only a tiny production of this delicious sweet aromatic white wine, some in naturale and some in passita form, and they are distinguished by an unmistakable fragrance of dried apricots.

The vast wine region of Etna is situated in the province of Catania, where vineyards reach up to 1,000 metres above sea-level, planted in a soil rich in volcanic ash and potassium. Etna Bianco is made here, from Carricante and Catarratto grapes, and Etna Rosso chiefly from Nerello Mascalese. The former can be labelled Superiore if its alcohol level is at least 12 per cent, while the Rosso is complex, elegant and rich in unusual floral fragrances.

Still further south are the zones of Siracusa and Ragusa, which produce the rare Moscato di Siracusa and Moscato di Noto – sweet white wines almost unobtainable outside the zone – as well as Eloro, in its different versions. One such is the legendary Eloro Pachino, an explosive, dense and full-bodied red made from Nero d'Avola grapes, cultivated in alberello-trained vineyards in the district of Pachino, south of Noto. This is a very important zone for the future of Sicilian wine, as many great wines will undoubtedly be produced here in the near future.

Currently the most representative DOC wine in the southeastern part of Sicily is Cerasuolo di Vittoria, which is made from Frappato grapes with a dash of Nero d'Avola, known here as Calabrese. A mellow, rounded and often highly alcoholic wine, it is a perfect accompaniment to the region's meat dishes.

There are many vineyards along the southern coast, but no DOC wines. The only DOC zones to be found beyond Agrigento are Menfi, Sambuca di Sicilia and Santa Margherita di Belice, where the vineyards are dominated by white varieties such as Catarratto and Inzolia, with Nero d'Avola and Perricone leading the reds. But these are areas where a less traditional approach to winegrowing is stimulating exciting results with newly introduced grape varieties such as Chardonnay, Cabernet Sauvignon, Merlot and Syrah. The driving force behind this new initiative is Settesoli, a large cooperative that produces as much wine as the entire region of Basilicata, yet manages to maintain its excellent quality.

Between these zones and the province of Palermo are two new and interesting DOCs, Contessa Entellina and

Contea di Sclafani, which were created to provide a regulated legal framework for the wines of two important producers – Tenuta di Donnafugata and the wine estate of the counts of Tasca d'Almerita, universally known as Regaleali. In both cases, besides traditional varieties such as Ansonica/Inzolia and Grecanico, they also produce highly innovative wines from international grapes such as Cabernet, Merlot, Syrah, Pinot Nero and Chardonnay. These wines have brought great financial reward and international credit to their producers.

Some way off the coast, between the provinces of Agrigento and Trapani, is the island of Pantelleria, which is home to Moscato di Pantelleria – one of the best Italian sweet white wines. This is produced from low-growing Zibibbo grapes, which are very difficult to grow. The passito version has highly concentrated aromatic sweetness, and is delicious with almond-based desserts.

The Alcamo or Bianco d'Alcamo DOC, which harvests almost exclusively Catarratto grapes, straddles the provinces of Palermo and Trapani; while Marsala, a wine that has been rather ill-treated in recent years, remains an oenological reference point and a legend on the island.

above *Citrus groves on Monti Iblei, Siracusa. Optimists are now looking to Syracuse province for signs of a revival in quality wines.*

Etna and the Northeast

At the beginning of the 20th century Messina and Etna were responsible for a significant percentage of total Sicilian wine production. Then the arrival of phylloxera plunged the area into a deep crisis from which it never recovered, and which gradually led to the abandonment of many vineyards. The DOCs in these territories, Faro and Etna, are more a homage to the past than a reflection of the present-day industry. Fortunately there are encouraging signs of a revival: there are already several talented winegrowers in both zones who are fuelling a renaissance, producing wines of great elegance that would have been unthinkable a decade ago.

Faro is Italian for "lighthouse" and takes its name from the lighthouse on Capo Peltro, which indicated to sailors the entrance to the strait leading to Messina's harbour. The Faro production region extends between the lighthouse itself and the other end of the strait, at the foothills of Monte Poverello. Here Mycenaeans and Phoenicians cultivated low-growing alberello-trained vines. The Romans named the resulting red wine Mamertino, and Julius Caesar drank it at the celebrations of his third consulate. At the end of the 19th century there were 40,000 hectares in the Messina region, but phylloxera battered these vineyards, and by 1985 there were hardly 5,400 hectares in the whole province. In the last few years, though, Faro has been rediscovered. A wine of great refinement and depth, it is made from Nerello Mascalese, Nocera and Nerello Cappuccio with additions of Calabrese (Nero d'Avola) and Gaglioppo.

Further south, in the province of Catania, the Etna wine district tells a similar story. The heyday of these vineyards was in the late 19th century, when France – itself ravaged by phylloxera – was forced to import wine from Italy. The Etna region was transformed into one enormous vineyard and the local railway was built to carry grapes to the wineries at top speed. Meanwhile, one of the ports north of Catania, now abandoned, was used exclusively for the worldwide export of wine. Then, from an annual output of over 800,000 hectolitres in the early 20th century, production fell here to a pitiful level. Volcanic eruptions don't help, but even today there are decent vineyards on Etna's slopes at up to 800 metres lying semi-abandoned.

Thanks to the well-drained volcanic soil and widely fluctuating day and night temperatures, the wines produced here are excellent, and some of the vines are up to 80 years old. Etna Rosso and Rosato are made from Nerello Mascalese (at least 80 per cent) and Nerello Cappuccio, while Etna Bianco is made from the native Carricante grape, blended with Catarratto and small additions of other grape varieties. The Bianco is a well-structured wine with pronounced acidity and good ageing potential, especially the Superiore, which is almost all Carricante. Experiments blending local grapes with Chardonnay and Cabernet Sauvignon have also produced some excellent results.

The Aeolian – or Lipari – islands north of Messina are home to the ancient Malvasia delle Lipari, one of the most attractive sweet wines of the Mediterranean. This elegant, intense passito is made from Malvasia delle Lipari and a little Corinto Nero. The over-ripe grapes are dried for two weeks in the sun, then pressed and fermented for months in small casks. The wine matures for about a year before being bottled. (A fortified liquoroso version is allowed for in the regulations, but has been practically abandoned.) Malvasia delle Lipari has incredible concentration and a delicious fragrance combining apricot jam, dried figs and other Mediterranean aromas. It is an extremely sweet wine, and a perfect match for the ripe and pungent local cheeses, as well as the Sicilian pastries.

below *The remains of a Greco-Roman theatre, with Mount Etna providing the backdrop.*

Notable producers

Colosi, Messina This is one of the historic estates of Malvasia delle Lipari, which makes both a Naturale and a Passita version from seven hectares of vineyards it owns in Malfa, on the island of Salina. The Passito di Pantelleria produced by Pietro Colosi is also an extremely interesting wine.

Palari, Messina Salvatore Geraci has driven the Faro *denominazione* back into the front rank of Italian wines. This estate is situated in Palari, between Messina and Taormina, and produces what is surely the benchmark Faro, albeit in very limited quantities. It is a powerful, heady and

concentrated red wine, rich in mellow tannins and boasting an impressively long-lasting finish.

Hauner, Salina (ME) Carlo Hauner, a native of Milan, was largely responsible for the great success of Malvasia delle Lipari over the last 20 years. He recently passed away, but his children – Gjona, Ida, Alda and Carlo junior – are continuing his work with the same passion and enthusiasm that he himself devoted to this classic wine. They produce two versions of Malvasia delle Lipari, a Naturale and a Passita, the latter distinguished for its irresistibly concentrated and aromatic notes, unctuous sweetness and balance.

Benanti, Viagrande (CT) Salvatore Benanti has devoted himself to salvaging some of the magnificent vineyards that had been neglected for far too long on the slopes of Mount Etna. He is regarded as one of the best winemakers in southern Italy and his sense of initiative has paid off handsomely, in the form of some great wines: Etna Rosso Rovitello, Etna Bianco Superiore, Pietramarina and a handful of blended wines made from both traditional and international grape varieties. These include Lamoremio (a mixture of Cabernet Sauvignon, Nero d'Avola and Nerello Mascalese) which offers a good bouquet and firm tannins, and Edelmio (which blends Chardonnay and Carricante).

above *The volcanic soils on the slopes of Etna are a sound base for some excellent wines, many produced from local varieties.*

Marsala

right *The salt pans at Trapani. This western zone is the source of Marsala, a dessert wine with surprisingly English origins.*

Had it not been for the War of Spanish Succession in the early 18th century, Marsala would probably not exist today, and nor would port or sherry. All three famous wines are the result of the Anglo-French rivalry and in particular the disputes linked to their respective roles in Europe during that period.

Until then, the market for French wines – and above all the famous clarets of Bordeaux – monopolised the interest of English wine merchants. But when the relationship between the two countries began to deteriorate during the War of Spanish Succession, the import of French products into Britain was forbidden and the subjects of Queen Anne were forced to make do with Scotch whisky or gin, the latter proving very fashionable in more elegant circles.

The problem was resolved by the development of certain wine regions outside France. First came port from Portugal, then sherry from Andalucía and finally, in the mid-18th century, Marsala from Sicily. At that time Marsala was a rustic wine of high alcohol content, made mainly from three typical indigenous grapes – Grillo, Catarratto and Inzolia. Its flavour was strong and slightly salty, reminiscent of the very driest styles of sherry. But there was one outstanding problem; that of transporting the wines from their country of origin to the English ports. For Marsala, the journey was especially arduous, and could take as long as two months. Contemporary vinification techniques could not guarantee the stability needed to prevent spoilage during transportation.

This problem was solved in the way it was with Spanish and Portuguese wines: a small percentage of spirit was added to the wine. Two English merchants, Woodhouse and Ingham, built their fortune on this wine and created a classic drink. The development of the English market acted as a slow fuse, lighting the way for other producers such as Florio and Pellegrino, who made Marsala one of the world's classic wines. Today, Marsala is perhaps not as revered as it was a generation ago, when it was almost synonymous with dessert wine.

Production in recent years has fallen, but quality is distinctly better, with some Marsalas now better than ever. The wine received its DOC in 1969, stipulating specific types and regulations, which were consolidated in 1986. The main styles are Fine and Superiore, both produced using the ancient method of adding spirit. The most highly esteemed version is the unsweetened Vergine, which can bear the *stravecchio* (very old) label after ten years' solera ageing. This amber wine is strong and dry; well-suited to sweet desserts like *marrons glacés* and Sicilian marzipan, and delicious in combinations that are beyond the scope of other wines, such as chocolate tortes and pastries.

Notable producers

Alvis-Rallo, Marsala (TP) This ancient, traditional winery produces many good wines, both table wines and *vini de meditazione* (meditation wines). Best in the range are the Passito di Pantelleria Mare d'Ambra, the Nero d'Avola and the Marsala Superiore Ambra Semisecco.

Marco De Bartoli, Marsala (TP) Marco De Bartoli is one of the leading figures on the Sicilian winemaking scene and a pioneer in its renaissance. His Marsala Vergine and especially the Vecchio Samperi were important landmarks; both meditation wines made from Marsala, aged using the solera system and unfortified. Equally fascinating

are the powerful Moscato Passito di Pantelleria Bukkuram and the Moscato Secco Pietranera, but there are other distinguished offerings.

Tenuta di Donnafugata, Marsala (TP) The Rallo family produces some outstanding wines. Among the numerous labels marketed by this impressive winery are some superb offerings, among which we recommend Chiarandà del Merlo, an elegant, aristocratic Chardonnay that is matured in small barriques, and the poetically named Milleunanotte ("a thousand and one nights"), a fascinating red wine made predominantly from Nero d'Avola grapes, and shaping up to be one of the island's greatest wines of recent times.

Vinicola Italiana Florio, Marsala (TP) If Marsala has survived the decline that has affected most other liqueur wines in recent years, it is probably largely due to this historic winery, which has successfully maintained the highest quality. Thanks to ancient reserves and excellent vinification, its Marsala Superiore Vecchioflorio Riserva Millesimato, Marsala Vergine Soleras Oro and Marsala Superiore Targa Riserva are among the best interpretations of this wine.

Carlo Pellegrino, Marsala (TP) This ancient Marsala-based winery has diversified from the famous liqueur wine (its Marsala Vergine Vintage is superb) to include many other wines in the Etna, Delia Nivolelli and Passito di Pantelleria DOC.

right *Vines growing in the shadow of Monte Inici, near Castellammare del Golfo. Marsala is produced from Cataratto, Grillo and Inzolia grapes.*

Western Sicily

above *The citadel at Erice, in the far west of Sicily. The hot climate favours concentrated wines from lesser-known grape varieties.*

There is more to Western Sicily than just Marsala. The majority of wine produced on the island comes from the provinces of Trapani and Palermo and the few prestige wineries situated outside these zones, such as Tasca d'Almerita, come under its influence. Western Sicily represent 80 per cent of the island's quality output, with Trapani, Contessa Entellina and the west-central part of Palermo by far the most productive in the region.

Gruppo Italiano Vini (GIV) is a major presence here, having bought up part of Rapitalà, the most important winery in the region. GIV is now its distributor and has facilitated considerable improvements in quality. Principal white grapes in this area are Catarratto, Inzolia and Grillo around Marsala, plus Damaschino, while the leading reds are Pignatello and Nero d'Avola.

Many wineries in this part of the island produce *vini da tavola*; indeed, only recently has a system of DOCs been set up, and it is still ignored by many producers. The Contea di Sclafani DOC, for instance, covers a vast

territory in the region, across Palermo, Agrigento and Caltanissetta, and is home to Tasca d'Almerita. Besides wines like the Rosso (made from Nero d'Avola and Perricone) a Nerello Mascalese rosé and a Bianco (from Catarratto, Inzolia and Grecanico) the DOC includes a range of varietal wines, from Chardonnay to Sauvignon, Cabernet to Pinot Nero, Syrah to Merlot. There are also more traditional wines, such as unblended Nerello Mascalese and Nero d'Avola.

In the south of Palermo, the Contessa Entellina DOC includes 12 wines, among them a red blend of Calabrese and Syrah, Sauvignon Blanc and Chardonnay, Cabernet, Merlot and Pinot Nero – varietals which feature at another important winery, the Tenuta di Donnafugata. The Delia Nivolelli DOC covers a vast area of Trapani and specialises in varietal wines, but the DOC has a small role. The Menfi DOC straddles Trapani and Agrigento, and its 15 wines encompass delicate Inzolia, Chardonnay and Catarratto whites, to important reds such as Nero d'Avola, Cabernet Sauvignon, Syrah and Bonera – in which Cabernet and Merlot meet Nero d'Avola, Syrah and Sangiovese. The cooperative winery Settesoli di Menfi makes a fine late-harvested wine here.

Among other good DOCs is Sambuca di Sicilia in Palermo and Agrigento, which is the home of Planeta – a rising star of Sicilian oenology, famed for its Chardonnay and Cabernet varietals. Sciacca and Santa Margherita di Belice, also in Agrigento, complete the complex network of regional DOCs.

Last but not least are the famous wines of Pantelleria, an enchanting island to the south of Sicily that the Arabs renamed Ben Ryè, "daughter of the wind". Winegrowing on these volcanic rocks, scorched by hot African winds, is tricky. The vines stick close to the ground to survive, sheltering in hollows or behind dry stone walls to avoid being scorched by salt deposits. But they produce unique wines. Once again, the star is a Moscato, made from Zibibbo or Moscatellone grapes grown on alberello-trained vines. Dried grapes are transformed into a golden blend of sun, sweet and concentrated aromas of fruit, and wild Mediterranean herbs. Only a few hundred hectolitres are produced, but this is one of Italy's finest wines.

Finally, Moscato di Pantelleria Naturale is topped up with lightly dried grapes, while the rarer fortified version has added grape spirit, which increases its strength to 21.5 per cent abv. Passito di Pantelleria is the most aristocratic version, and is made exclusively (or almost exclusively) from dried grapes.

Notable producers

Melia, Alcamo (TP) The brothers Antonino, Giuseppe and Vincenzo Melia are behind an excellent, promising red wine from the district of Alcamo. Ceuso – a blend of Nero d'Avola, Merlot and Cabernet Sauvignon matured in barrels of new oak – is generous, with great depth and complexity.

Abbazia Sant'Anastasia, Castelbuono (PA) Until this winery was founded, the zone of Cefalù was practically unknown to wine-lovers. In collaboration with the oenologist Giacomo Tachis, this winery produces one of the best red wines of southern Italy, the Litra, made from Cabernet Sauvignon (90 per cent) and Nero d'Avola. All their wines are extremely good.

Duca di Salaparuta - Vini Corvo, Casteldaccia (Palermo) This is the giant of Sicilian oenology and probably one of the most famous Italian wine labels in the world. The vast range of wines at this enterprise is centred on the excellent Corvo Bianco and Corvo Rosso, which are both fruity, well-made and offering an outstanding price/quality ratio. At the top of the house range are a great Nero d'Avola red called Duca Enrico, and Bianco di Valguarnera.

Fazio Wines, Erice (TP) The Fazio brothers have put the name of the Trapani province back on the map, with some remarkable wines that have garnered international acclaim. From 600 hectares of vineyards, the brothers produce an excellent range of reds and whites, of which the finest is their Cabernet Sauvignon.

Settesoli, Menfi (Agrigento) This very large wine estate with 9,000 hectares of vineyards produces a range of wines that has few rivals in Sicily, as far as quality and quantity are concerned. Among its best are a Nero d'Avola of great character and a very successful Nero d'Avola/Cabernet blend.

Firriato Paceco (TP) In a region of no great oenological tradition, the Di Gaetano brothers and the Australian winemaker and Master of Wine Kym Milne have created one of the most dynamic wineries in Sicily. From the establishment's vast range of wines with an incredible price/quality ratio, the two Santagostino wines stand out: a Catarratto/Chardonnay Bianco, and a Rosso made from Nero d'Avola and Syrah.

Aziende Vinicole Miceli, Palermo Ignazio Miceli, who died recently, was a key figure in Sicilian winemaking and played an important part in its international success. The winery continues to produce interesting wines under his label, such as Zibibbo Vivace Garighe, Nero d'Avola, Passito di Pantelleria Janir and the aromatic Zibibbo Secco Yrnm.

Spadafora, Palermo Franco Spadafora and consultant oenologist Luca D'Attoma have created one of the most interesting estates in western Sicily. The wines are made from grapes grown in the estate's own vineyards (100 hectares), which are planted with traditional and international varieties. Their Don Pietro Rosso and Vigna Virzì Rosso are highly impressive.

Salvatore Murana, Pantelleria (TP) Salvatore Murana, a fireman and winegrower, is unanimously acclaimed as one of the best producers of Pantelleria wines. His Moscato Passito from the Martingana, Khamma and Mueggen districts have the irresistible fascination of the great traditional sweet wines of the Mediterranean.

D'Ancona, Pantelleria (TP) Giacomo D'Ancona has recently come into the limelight with his excellent Passito di Pantelleria, Solidea, which is manna to the traditionalists' cause. He also makes a fascinating Moscato di Pantelleria and a very fragrant dry Zibibbo.

Planeta, Sambuca di Sicilia (AG) This winery is one of the most striking phenomena on the Italian wine scene and in a mere four years it has achieved an outstanding reputation. With the help of oenologist Carlo Corino, the cousins Alessio, Francesca and Santi Planeta have produced some internationally acclaimed wines. Their Chardonnay is among the best ever produced in Italy, and Santa Cecilia, a successful blend of Nero d'Avola, Cabernet Sauvignon and Merlot, is also outstanding. The Alastro, a blend of Cataratto and Grecanico, is worth watching too.

Cantina Sociale di Trapani, (TP) This cooperative winery has 120 members and first-class management. The beautiful vineyards scattered between Trapani, Erice, Kinisia, Rocca del Giglio and Val d'Erice are planted with traditional varieties, alongside international favourites Chardonnay and Sauvignon Blanc. The results are the magnificent Forti Terre di Sicilia Cabernet Sauvignon and the remarkable Forti Terre di Sicilia Rosso; the range is completed by Forti Terre di Sicilia Bianco.

above *The late Count Giuseppe Tasca d'Almerita has left a fine legacy at this superb estate, but is a tough act to follow.*

Tasca d'Almerita, Vallelunga Pratameno (CL) The Tasca d'Almerita family has built one of the most important Italian wineries on their magnificent estate, which is situated in the centre of Sicily. The death of the founder, Giuseppe, has been a body blow, but his son Lucio is an admirable successor. Thanks to the climatic conditions of the zone and the very modern approach to winegrowing and vinification, Tasca d'Almerita has long succeeded in producing a range of magnificent wines. Besides its core Regaleali range, the winery also produces a number of internationally acclaimed varietals, such as Cabernet Sauvignon and Chardonnay.

Southeastern Sicily

One of the most promising wine regions in Sicily is in the southeast of the island, extending across parts of the provinces of Siracusa, Ragusa and Caltanissetta, though the range of DOCs is not particularly complex. Siracusa is famous for its Moscato, which has become popular again as the interest in sweet wines has revived. The zone of Moscato di Siracusa is adjacent to that of Moscato di Noto, and has the same low, alberello-trained vines which are cultivated all around the city of Noto. The wine laws also permit a sparkling and a fortified version, but production remains on the drawing-board.

The most important DOC of the region is without doubt the Cerasuolo di Vittoria, which is named after the cherry colour of this fruity wine when young. Its principal grape variety is Frappato – with its characteristic ripe cherry fragrance – which is blended with Calabrese (aka Nero d'Avola). This traditional wine is easy to drink, with midweight structure, but it is not intended for ageing. However, more progressive wineries use grapes grown in low-yielding vineyards, and are producing more aristocratic versions with greater depth and concentration, and consequently ageing potential.

The southernmost tip of the island has always been an important region for viticulture, with a terroir particularly

below *The steep-sited town of Ragusa is found in the southeast of Sicily, in an area dominated by blending wines.*

suited to winegrowing and to red varieties, especially Nero d'Avola. Wines made from grapes grown on the alberello system likewise prosper, and are usually blessed with great elegance and concentration.

Many wineries in the region have made substantial investment in research and development. The Eloro DOC, which straddles the provinces of Siracusa and Ragusa, stipulates a blended red wine, a

rosé and three varietals – namely Nero d'Avola, Frappato and Pignatello. This trio is producing exciting results, especially in the district of Pachino – a sub-zone recognised within the Eloro DOC – from where a Riserva may also be produced.

Perhaps more than in any other region, the future of Sicilian oenology is being determined in these vineyards.

left *Not to be trifled with: the impressive double act at Cos, Giambattista Cilia (left) and Giusto Occhipinti.*

Notable producers

Cantine Torrevecchia, Acate (RG)
This winery, owned by the Favuzza family, is one of the most successful labels in Sicilian winemaking. Its flagship wine is Rosso Casale dei Biscari, made from Nero d'Avola grapes. The Bianco Biscari, from Inzolia and Chardonnay, is also excellent, and the Syrah looks extremely promising too.

Valle dell'Acate, Acate (RG) Gaetana Jacono is a young, passionate winegrower who has worked very hard to relaunch the wines of Vittoria. Her Cerasuolo DOC is excellent, as is her Frappato – made exclusively from the grape of that name. The rest of the range is also interesting.

Vitivinicola Avide, Comiso (RG) This winery produces some excellent versions of Cerasuolo di Vittoria, such as Barocco and

Selezione Etichetta Nera. Besides these selections there are good white wines such as Vigne d'Oro, made from Inzolia grapes. An improving outfit.

Cooperativa Interprovinciale Elorina, Rosolini (SR) This is a young winery producing Eloro DOC wines, comprising a range of well-made, reliable reds. The Rosso Pachino in particular is a very promising wine, and with sustained

attention to detail could rival the top Syrah of the Rhône or Barossa Valley.

COS, Vittoria (Ragusa) This winery has recently produced some of the most interesting wines in southeastern Sicily. The Cerasuolo di Vittoria Sciri and Vigne di Bastonaca selections, Rosso Le Vigne di Cos, Bianco Ramingallo (made from Inzolia grapes) and Moscato Dolce Aestas Siciliae are all excellent.

Glossary

ABBOCCATO: A slightly sweet wine, containing a small amount of residual sugar.

ACERBO [unripe]: A wine that is not yet mature, and distinguished by unpleasant excess acidity.

ACIDITY, FIXED: The level of non-volatile acids.

ACIDITY, TOTAL: A fundamental element of a wine, this is the sum of the various fixed and volatile acids present – malic, tartaric, citric and acetic, expressed in grams per litre. The health and the good keeping qualities of a wine depend on this, as does its attractiveness.

ACIDITY, VOLATILE: Type of acidity determined by the presence and precise condition of acetic acid in the wine. In small quantities it is positive and necessary to the development of a wine's perfume. In excessive quantity it can give a prickly, vinegary quality on the nose.

ACIDULO [acidulous]: Slightly acidic.

ACINO [grape]: The grape on the vine.

ALBERELLO: Typical system of training vines in the Mediterranean regions. It is derived from ancient Greek techniques; the vines have no wires or supports and grow low and densely in the vineyard.

ALCOHOL, ETHYL: The most important product of the fermentation of sugars contained in the must.

ALCOHOL, METHYL: Alcohol made by fermentation of cellulose and the solid parts of the grape. Minute traces are formed during the alcoholic fermentation of the grape must. In stronger concentrations it is a powerful poison.

ALLAPPANTE: A wine that is hard, rough and astringent through excessive tannin.

AMABILE: Semi-sweet wine.

AMBRATO [amber-coloured]: Colour of many passito and/or liquoroso wines (Passito of Pantelleria, Marsala Superiore etc.) and of oxidised, decrepit whites.

AMPELOGRAPHY: The discipline of describing and classifying vines.

AMPIO [ample]: Description given to particularly rich, complex wines with a generous bouquet.

ANNATA [year]: The year of a wine's harvest. Synonymous with millesimo, vintage, colheita, vendange and vendemmia.

ANTHOCYANINS: Polyphenolic substances responsible for the colour of red wines.

ARISTOCRATIC: Fine and elegant, but also a description that can mean unique, of rare quality or superior to its peers. These are the greatest wines, both for their historic traditions and tasting characteristics.

AROMA: Olfactory sensation perceived before and after swallowing wine, through the nasal cavity. Also refers to fragrances created by aromatic substances (mainly terpenes) found in certain grape varieties – notably Muscat, Traminer, Brachetto, some Malvasias, Rhine Riesling and Müller-Thurgau.

AROMATICO: Wine rich in aromatic substances that are present in the keynote grape.

ASTRINGENT: Wine with an excess of tannin and acidity, tasting rough-textured and drying the mouth.

AUSTERE: Imposing or mature, with a fully formed bouquet and a long finish, often tasting slightly bitter.

BARREL: Container made from oak or chestnut staves, used for the maturation and ageing of wines. The capacity is usually from 500-20,000 litres.

BARRIQUE: Small barrel of French oak (usually cut from timber in Allier, Tronçais, Limousin or Vosges) with a capacity of 225-228 litres, such as those used in Bordeaux. These are usually made from staves exposed to direct flame, so that the inside is charred to varying degrees, depending on the length of contact with the flames.

BEVA: This can mean "easy" or "ready", and indicates when the wine is most suitable for drinking.

BEVERINO: Light and easy to drink

BLANC DE BLANCS: White wine, usually sparkling, made from white grapes.

BLANC DE NOIRS: White wine, usually sparkling, made from red grapes.

BODY: The sum of the elements that make up a wine, and which give it "fullness".

BOTRITIZZATO [botrytised]: Wine made from grapes affected by noble rot (botrytis cinerea).

BOUQUET: The fragrance that a wine acquires through ageing, the so-called "tertiary fragrances".

BRUT: Sparkling dry wine, with only a small addition of liqueur d'expédition (sweetening liquor).

CALDO [hot]: Feeling of heat given by a wine rich in alcohol and glycerine.

CAPPUCCINA or CAPOVOLTO [turned upside-down]: Form of Guyot pruning, with the shoots bent downward. It is widespread in Tuscany and the northeast of Italy, particularly in Friuli.

CARATELLO: Small barrel, generally of chestnut wood and with a capacity of less than 200 litres, used in Tuscany for the maturation of Vin Santo.

CARATO: Italian name for the barrique.

CASARSA: System of training vines on high wires, very widespread on the level plains of northeast Italy.

CHARACTERISTIC: Wine whose vine/grape of origin is obvious and/or true.

CLONES: Group of plants created by multiplication from a single selected plant.

CORDONE SPERONATO [spurred cordon]: Pruning technique for vines trained on wires, typical of many zones of central-northern Italy.

CORTO [short]: Denotes a wine lacking persistence, that leaves hardly any aftertaste in the mouth.

CRU: A French term for a specific vineyard, or even a

above *Pruning Trebbiano grapes. This is one of the most widespread varieties in Italy, but its status varies from one region to the next.*

small, precisely defined part of a vineyard in one particular zone. Grapes from *crus* are highly regarded.

CULTIVAR: Sub-species of a vine variety.

CUVEE: The result of blending wines of different origins and perhaps years, usually but not invariably as the basis of the traditional method of making sparkling wine.

DECREPIT: Excessively old wine that has completely lost its defining characteristics.

DELICATO [delicate]: A wine that has characteristics of harmony, refinement and lightness.

DISCORDANT: Wine in which the lack or excess of one element creates a severe imbalance.

DOC: *Denominazione di Origine Controllata* [Denomination of Controlled Origin]. The second-highest wine category in Italy, currently applicable to more than 300 wines.

DOCG: *Denominazione di Origine Controllata e Garantita,* [Denomination of Controlled and Guaranteed Origin]. The highest of the four-tier hierarchy of Italian wines.

DORATO [gilded]: Typical colour of white wines that have body and structure, especially if matured in wood.

DRY: English term to describe a wine, usually sparkling, with a higher sugar content than a Brut.

ELEGANTE [elegant]: A balanced wine, aristocratic and thoroughbred.

ENOTRIA: Ancient Greek name for Italy, meaning "the land of wine".

EQUILIBRATO [balanced]: A wine whose main components are in harmony with each other.

ESTERS: Fragrant, volatile substances formed by the synthesis of acids and alcohols during fermentation.

ETHEREAL: A flavour typical of aged wines, somewhat pungent and alcoholic, created by the presence of ethers.

FECCIOSO [dreggy]: A wine full of dregs or sediment and therefore not clear.

FERMENTATION, ALCOHOLIC: Process by which yeast turns the sugars contained in the grape juice into alcohol and carbon dioxide.

FERMENTATION, MALOLACTIC: Secondary fermentation that takes place after primary or alcoholic fermentation. Lactic bacteria transforms malic acid into lactic acid: this results in a loss of overall acidity in the wine. It is especially encouraged in red wines and full-bodied whites matured in wood.

FILARE: System of training vines which is widespread in many zones of central-northern Italy.

FILTRATO DOLCE [sweet filtrate]: Partially fermented must, whereby complete alcoholic fermentation is prevented through sterile filtration that eliminates the yeasts. The sweet filtrates made from Muscat grapes form the basis of Asti wines.

FINE: Elegantly fragrant and harmonious in taste.

FRAGRANT: An intense, fine bouquet.

FRESCO [fresh]: In a bouquet it indicates fruity or lemony flavours, and, on the palate, pleasant and youthful acidity.

FRUTTATO [fruity]: Characteristic of young wines that have fresh fruit perfumes and tastes.

GENEROSO [generous]: Denotes a high level of alcohol.

GLYCERINE: Substance produced in small quantities during the alcoholic fermentation of the grape must.

GOUDRON: Akin to "tar". A typical feature of the bouquet of great red wines when aged.

GRANATO: Colour of great red wines when aged.

GRAPPA: Typical Italian spirit made from the distillation of the grape residue after pressing. Widespread, especially in the northern regions.

GRASSO [fat]: A wine rich in essential substances. This sensation is also tactile, indicating density in a wine.

GRASSY: Characteristic often found in wines made from Cabernet or Merlot, also in young or not-quite-ripe wines.

GUYOT: Method of pruning and training, named after its French inventor.

HARMONIOUS: A wine is defined as harmonious or balanced when its components are in pleasant proportion to each other, a state reached through proper maturation.

IGT: *Indicazione Geografica Tipica* [Typical Geographical Indication]. A sort of "sub-DOC", the third strata in the quality hierarchy and currently covering just over 100 wines in Italy.

INNESTO [graft]: The practice of joining a piece of one vine variety onto the rootstock or shoot of another.

INTENSO [intense]: In colour it refers to the tone; in bouquet to the breadth of sensation; and in taste to persistence on the palate.

INVAIATURA [change of colour]: The moment when red grapes begin to take on colour. This generally happens about two months before the harvest.

LEGGERO [light]: Wine of low alcoholic content, but balanced and pleasant.

LIQUOROSO [liqueur-like]: Wine resembling a liqueur in alcoholic strength, structure and sweetness. Wine with added alcohol, always stronger than 15 per cent.

MADERIZZATO [maderised]: A wine that is clearly oxidised; sometimes this is not a defect but a defining characteristic (Madeira, Marsala).

MAGRO [thin]: A weak wine with little body, and short of essential substances.

MARSALATO: *Maderizzato*/maderised.

MATTONATO [brick]: Colour of a very old red wine, on the verge of maderisation.

MATURE: A wine that has reached its peak of maturity, whether young or old.

METODO CHARMAT [Charmat method]: Also known as "cuve close", this is a method of making sparkling wine in special steel tanks which are capable of supporting the pressure of carbon dioxide. Since it cannot disperse in the air, the gas dissolves in the wine as bubbles.

METODO CLASSICO [traditional method]: Method of making sparkling wine, similar to that used for making Champagne in France.

above *The vineyards of Chianti have been the setting for much of the spirited progress made by modern Italian winemakers.*

MORBIDO [soft]: Balanced wine with a certain roundness, created by abundant alcohol and glycerine.

MOLLE [soak]: Excessively soft, without backbone or character.

MUST: The juice produced by pressing fresh grapes, and which is capable of producing an alcohol strength of not less than eight per cent.

NERBO [backbone]: Characteristic of a wine that has acidity, body and structure.

NETTO [clean]: A clean perfume or taste; frank and without defects.

OXIDISED: A wine that through contact with the air has lost its freshness, become a darker colour than normal, and is tending towards maderisation.

PAGLIERINO [straw-coloured]: Yellow in colour, reminiscent of straw.

PAMPINI: Vine leaves.

PASSITO: Wine made from grapes dried in the open or under cover, and with a high level of alcohol and sugar.

PASTOSO [doughy]: Wine rich in sugars, extracts and glycerine.

PENETRANTE [penetrating odour]: Acute and sometimes unpleasant odour caused by volatile substances (ethyl acetate) or by gases (hydrogen sulphide).

PERLAGE: The name for the "fountain" of little bubbles of carbon dioxide that form in a glass filled with sparkling wine, otherwise known as the "mousse". The smaller and more continuous the bubbles, the better the quality of the wine.

PERSISTENZA [persistence]: The last of the taste sensations produced by a wine, sometimes referred to as the "finish". The greater the persistence/longer the finish, the better the wine.

PESANTE [heavy]: Too rich in alcohol, difficult to drink.

PIENO [full]: Wine with body and structure, well-balanced.

POLYPHENOLS: The whole gamut of colouring substances in a wine (anthocyanins, tannins, flavonoids, etc), that determines the depth of its taste and also its potential longevity.

PORPORA [purple]: Colour of young, light-bodied red wines, particularly of new ("nouveau") wine.

PORTAINNESTO [rootstock]: The root system of American vinestock, to which the upper part of European vines are grafted.

PERFUMED: A wine that has very pleasant aromatic, fragrant sensations.

PRONTO [ready]: Wine that is ready to be drunk without further ageing.

RASPO [grape stalk]: The woody part of a cluster of grapes.

RETROGUSTO [aftertaste]: The sensations experienced after swallowing the wine.

RIDOTTO [reduced]: Bouquet typical of wines aged for a long time in an environment that is poor in oxygen (such

below *Lake Iseo in Lombardy. Italy's stunning lakes contribute to favourable microclimates in many of its wine regions.*

as in the bottle).This bouquet tends to diminish rapidly on contact with the air.

ROBUSTO [strong]: Wine that is rich in alcohol, or built with a solid structure.

ROTONDO [round]: Wine softened by its sugar content; of moderate acidity and full-bodied.

RUBINO [ruby]: Colour typical of young red wine.

SACCHAROMYCES: Micro-organisms that carry out the alcoholic fermentation of grape must. See also *yeasts*.

SAPIDO [savoury]: Wine rich in mineral salts.

SBOCCATURA [dégorgement]: Operation by which the deposits of secondary fermentation are removed during the traditional method of making sparkling wine. If the disgorgement date is declared on the label, it indicates the age of non-vintage wine.

SPALLIERA [espalier]: Method of training vines at a medium-to-high aspect. Widespread in certain zones of northwestern Italy.

SPUNTO [sourness]: Excess of unpleasant volatile components, such as acetic aldehyde.

STOFFA [material]: Summary of a wine's taste. Typical descriptions include "light", "silky", "velvety", or "heavy".

STRUTTURA [structure]: The overall sum of the components of a wine.

STRUTTURATO [structured]: Wine rich in alcohol and polyphenols.

SVANITO [vanished]: A flat-tasting wine, enervated by excessive exposure to the air.

TAGLIO [blend]: The blending of wines of different grape varieties or vintages.

TANNICO [tannic]: Astringent, excessively rich in tannin.

TANNINO [tannin]: Substance given to the wine by grape skins, stalks and pips, especially in reds. Tannins play an important part in preserving the wine and its colour. They give an astringent, rough sensation to the taste, but this becomes milder with ageing.

TENDONE [awning]: Form of pergola training which is widespread in some zones of central-southern Italy, particularly in Abruzzo.

TENUE [SLIGHT]: Light and evanescent colour or bouquet.

TERROIR: Combination of soil, vine type and growing conditions that determines the unique character of a wine.

TIPICO [typical]: A wine that is fully characteristic of its category. Recognisable as coming from or referring to a particular region or grape variety.

TRALCIO [shoot]: The part of the vine on which the clusters of grapes grow.

TRANQUILLO [still]: A wine that has completed its fermentation without gathering traces of carbon dioxide.

UVAGGIO [blend]: Blend of different grapes that are mixed together to give a single wine.

VARIETAL: Wine made entirely from, or overwhelmingly dominated by, one grape variety.

VELATO [veiled]: A wine that is not quite clear.

VELLUTATO [velvety]: A harmonious, soft and usually endearing wine.

VERDOLINO [pale green]: A slightly greenish colour, which is a sign of the presence of chlorophyll in the grapes. Characteristic colour of the wines of the north, and further north in Europe, particularly Rhine Riesling or Sauvignon Blanc.

VERTICALE [vertical]: Wine in which the tannic and acid components prevail over the softness of alcohol and glycerine.

VINACCE [marc]: The solid residue of alcoholic fermentation. This is made up of *raspo*/grape stalks and grape skins. Grappa is made by distilling this residue.

VINAGGIO: Neologism for *taglio*/blend.

VINOSO [vinous]: Young wine whose aroma is reminiscent of fermenting must.

VITE MARITATA [married vines]: Ancient form of training, where the vine is supported by a tree (maple, olive or mulberry). It is still possible to find examples in some parts of the Marches, Lazio and Molise.

VITIGNO [grape variety]: The grape variety from which a particular wine is made.

VITIS VINIFERA: The vine species suitable for producing wine grapes.

VIVACE [lively]: Young wine showing the presence of carbon dioxide.

YEASTS: Micro-organisms causing alcoholic fermentation.

above *Cabernet Sauvignon is most prevalent in the northeast, but its influence has spread now that Italy is a global player.*

Index

Acknowledgements

Front cover top Cephas Picture Library
Front cover bottom Cephas Picture Library/Andy Christodolo
Back cover top Octopus Publishing Group Ltd./Jason Lowe
Back cover bottom Octopus Publishing Group/Jason Lowe

1 Cephas Picture Library/Mick Rock; 3 top Scope/Bernard Galeron; 3 bottom Cephas Picture Library/Mick Rock; 4 Cephas Picture Library/Andy Christodolo; 6-7 Andrea Pistolesi; 8-9 AKG; London/ © DACS 2000; 10 Ancient Art and Architecture Collection; 11 AKG; London; 12 Patrick Eagar/Mike Newton; 13 Cephas Picture Library; 14 Cephas Picture Library/Mick Rock; 15 Cephas Picture Library/Mick Rock; 18 Cephas Picture Library/Mick Rock; 19 Cephas Picture Library/Mick Rock; 20 Laura Ronchi/Innehofer & Partner; 21 Cephas Picture Library/Mick Rock; 22 left Cephas Picture Library/Mick Rock; 22 right Cephas Picture Library/Mick Rock; 23 Cephas Picture Library/Mick Rock; 24 top Vivai Cooperativi Rauscedo/Negro Amaro; 24 bottom Cephas Picture Library/Mick Rock; 25 Cephas Picture Library/Mick Rock; 26 Vivai Cooperativi Rauscedo; 27 left Cephas Picture Library/Mick Rock; 27 right Cephas Picture Library/Mick Rock; 28 Cephas Picture Library/Mick Rock; 29 Cephas Picture Library/Mick Rock; 30-31 Anthony Blake Photo Library/John Sims; 32 Scope/Jacques Guillard; 34 Cephas Picture Library/Mick Rock; 36 Cephas Picture Library/Andy Christodolo; 37 top Franca Speranza Agenzia Fotografica, Milan/Walter Leonardi; 37 bottom Claes Lofgren; 38 Scope/Jacques Guillard; 39 Cephas Picture Library/Mick Rock; 40 Cephas Picture Library/Andy Christodolo; 41 Cephas Picture Library/Andy Christolodo; 42 Scope/Jacques Guillard; 43 Ikona; 44 Patrick Eagar; 45 Cephas Picture Library/Mick Rock; 46 Cephas Picture Library/Mick Rock; 47 Guiseppe Carfagna/Ikona; 49 Cephas Picture Library/Mick Rock; 50 Guiseppe Carfagna/Ikona; 51 Ikona; 52 top Cephas Picture Library/Mick Rock; 52 bottom Jean Charles Gesquire/Scope; 54 left Guiseppe Carfagna/Ikona; 54 right Cephas Picture Library/Mick Rock; 55 Guiseppe Carfagna/Ikona; 56 Cephas Picture Library/Mick Rock; 57 left Mategani/Laura Ronchi; 57 right Ikona; 58 Cephas Picture Library/Mick Rock; 59 left Cephas Picture, Library/Mick Rock; 59 right Guglielmo de 'Micheli/Grazia Neri; 60 Claes Lofgren; 61 Cephas Picture Library/Mick Rock; 62 Paulo Negri/Laura Ronchi; 63 Ikona/Paulo Della Corte; 64 Cephas Picture Library/Mick Rock; 66 Cephas Picture Library/Mick Rock; 67 Cephas Picture Library/Mick Rock; 68 Cephas Picture Library/Mick Rock; 70 John Heseltine; 71 Foto Mairani; 72-73 Cephas Picture Library/Mick Rock; 74 Scope/Bernard Galeron; 76 Claes Lofgren; 77 The Travel Library/Stuart Black; 78 Cephas Picture Library/Mick Rock; 79 Cephas Picture Library/Mick Rock; 80 Cephas Picture Library/Herbert Lehmann; 81 Patrick Eagar; 82 Art Directors & TRIP Photo Library/J. Moscrop; 83 left Scope/Bernard Galeron; 83 right Scope/Bernard Galeron; 84 Steven Morris; 86 Cephas Picture Library/Mick Rock; 87 Ikona; 88 Cephas Picture Library/Mick Rock; 90 Cephas Picture Library/Andy Christodolo; 91 Fotos der Weinwelt; 92 Cephas Picture Library/Mick Rock; 94 Elio & Stefano Ciol; 95 Scope/Sara Matthews; 96 Octopus Publishing Group Ltd/Alan Williams; 97 Cephas Picture Library/Herbert Lehmann; 98 Tenuta Beltrame; 99 Azienda Agricola Borgo san Daniele; 100-101 Andrea Pistolesi; 102 Cephas Picture Library/Mick Rock; 104 Scope/Jaques Guillard; 105 Cephas Picture Library/R A Beatty; 106 Cephas Picture Library/Mick Rock; 107 Scope/Bernard Galeron; 108 Cephas Picture Library/Mick Rock; 110 Cephas Picture Library/Mick Rock; 111 Cephas Picture Library/Mick Rock; 112 Laura Ronchi/Stefano Stefani; 113 top Azienda Agricola Alessandro Moroder; 113 bottom Azienda Agricola Alessandro Moroder; 114 Cephas Picture Library/Mick Rock; 115 Cephas Picture Library/Mick Rock; 116 Fotos der Weinwelt/Hans-Peter Siffert; 117 Cephas Picture Library/Mick Rock; 118-119 Steven Morris; 120 The Travel Library/Ch. Hermes; 122 Patrick Eagar/Jan Traylen; 124 Axiom Photographic Agency/Chris Coe; 125 Art Directors & TRIP Photo Library /Streano/Havens; 126 Cephas Picture Library/Mick Rock; 127 Cephas Picture Library/Mick Rock; 128 Claes Lofgren; 129 Cephas Picture Library/Mick Rock; 130 Grazia Neri/Fabio Muzzi; 131 Art Directors & TRIP Photo Library/N. & J. Wiseman; 131 Patrick Eagar/Jan Treylen; 132 top Claes Lofgren; 132 botto Claes Lofgren; 133 Anthony Blake Photo Library/John Sims; 134 Scope/Jean-Luc Barde; 135 Claes Lofgren; 136 Steven Morris; 137 top Claes Lofgren; 137 bottom Grazia Neri/Stefano Cellai; 138 Cephas Picture Library/Mick Rock; 139 left Andrea Pistolesi; 139 right Andrea Pistolesi; 140 The Travel Library/Philip Enticknap; 141 Scope/Jean Luc Bardem; 142 Cephas Picture Library/Mick Rock; 143 Cephas Picture Library/Mick Rock; 144 Foto Mairani; 145 Ikona; 146 top left Franca Speranza/Bruno Morandi; 146 bottom The Travel Library/Stuart Black; 147 Anthony Blake Photo Library/John Sims; 148 The Travel Library/Philip Enticknap; 150 Cephas Picture Library/Mick Rock; 151 Claes Lofgren; 152 Cephas Picture Library/Mick Rock; 153 right Cephas Picture Library/Mick Rock; 153 bottom left Claes Lofgren; 154 John Heseltine; 156 Cephas Picture Library/Mick Rock; 157 Cephas Picture Library/Mick Rock; 158 Franca Speranza Agenzia Fotografica, Milan/Sandro Vannini; 159 Foto Mairani; 160 Foto Mairani; 161 Foto Mairani; 162 Corbis UK Ltd; 163 Ikona; 164-165 J Allan Cash Ltd; 166 Scope/Michel Gotin; 168 John Ferro Sims; 169 Ikona/Pasquale Stanzione; 170 Scope/Michel Gotin; 171 Scope/Michel Gotin; 172 Foto Mairani; 173 top Foto Mairani; 173 bottom Fontana Galardi; 174 Cephas Picture Library/Mick Rock; 176 Cephas Picture Library/Mick Rock; 177 Cephas Picture Library/Mick Rock; 178 Franca Speranza Agenzian Fotografica, Milan/Stefano Torrione; 179 Cephas Picture Library/Mick Rock; 180 Franca Speranza Agenzia Fotografica, Milan/Sandro Vannini; 182 Cephas Picture Library/Mick Rock; 183 Cephas Picture Library/Mick Rock; 184 Cephas Picture Library/Mick Rock; 186 Franca Speranza Agenzia Fotografica, Milan/Rosario Elia; 187 Ikona; 187 bottom Franca Speranza Agenzia Fotografica, Milan/G Carfagna; 188-189 Pictures Colour Library Ltd; 190 Pictures Colour Library Ltd; 192 Index/Baldi; 193 top Sella & Mosca; 193 bottom Ikona; 194 Grazia Neri/Giulio Veggi/White Star; 194 Azienda Vinicola Attilio Contini spa Contini; 195 Grazia Neri/Giulio Veggi/White Star; 196 Grazia Neri/Curzio Baraggi; 197 Agriolas; 198 Anthony Blake Photo Library/John Sims; 200 Corbis UK Ltd; 201 Cephas Picture Library/Mick Rock; 202 The Travel Library/Philip Enticknap; 203 Cephas Picture Library/Mick Rock; 204 John Heseltine; 205 Cephas Picture Library/Mick Rock; 206 The Travel Library/Stuart Black; 207 Cephas Picture Library/Mick Rock; 208 Corbis UK Ltd; 209 Ikona/Massimo Siragusa; 211 Cephas Picture Library/Andy Christodolo; 212 Cephas Picture Library/Mick Rock; 213 Cephas Picture Library/Mick Rock; 214 The Travel Library/Stuart Black; 215 Cephas Picture Library/Mick Rock.

Marco Sabellico would like to thank his wife Alessandra Capogna, and Daniele Cernilli would like to thank his wife Marina Thompson for their active support and cooperation throughout the writing of this book. The authors would also like to thank Rebecca Spry, Lucy Bridgers, Adrian Tempany, Tracy Killick and Colin Goody for their hard work in producing this book.